D0886797

GHETTO

GHETTO

THE HISTORY OF A WORD

Daniel B. Schwartz

HARVARD UNIVERSITY PRESS

CAMBRIDGE, MASSACHUSETTS

LONDON, ENGLAND

2019

Library of Congress Cataloging-in-Publication Data
is available from loc.gov
ISBN: 978-0-674-73753-2 (alk. paper)

For Max, Sophie, and Maddie

Those who would codify the meaning of words fight a losing battle, for words, like the ideas and things they are meant to signify, have a history.

—Joan Scott, *Gender and the Politics of History*

CONTENTS

Introduction   1

1 The Early History of the Ghetto   9

2 The Nineteenth-Century
   Transformation of the Ghetto   49

3 The Ghetto Comes to America   86

4 The Nazi Ghettos of the Holocaust   125

5 The Ghetto in Postwar America   163

   Conclusion   195

   NOTES   205

   ACKNOWLEDGMENTS   241

   ILLUSTRATION CREDITS   245

   INDEX   247

GHETTO

INTRODUCTION

On March 29, 1516, the Venetian Republic ordered that the Jews of Venice be restricted to a small island on the northern edge of the city. Christian inhabitants of this area were compelled to vacate their homes; all outward-facing doors, windows, and quays on the island were to be bricked over; and gates were to be erected in two places, to be locked at sunset. The new Venetian enclave was hardly the first example in history of the "Jewish street" or "Jewish quarter," which dated to the origins of the Jewish Diaspora in antiquity. Nor was it the first instance in which the Jews of a European town or city were compelled to live in an enclosed area separately from Christians, although segregation of this kind, especially in Italy, certainly grew more common in its wake. Yet the establishment of an enforced and exclusive residential space for the Jews of Venice was a historical beginning in at least one crucial respect. It marked the start of a fateful link between the idea of segregation and a particular word: "ghetto."

While there are many theories concerning the etymology of *ghetto,* the most widely held traces it to the fact that the Venetian island was already known as the *Ghetto Nuovo* (or New Ghetto) before issuance of the 1516 edict that required Jews to relocate there. *Ghetto* is generally thought to derive from the Venetian verb *gettare,* meaning to throw or to cast, which would evoke the copper foundry that had once occupied the area that was to become an all-Jewish district. From these origins, the word *ghetto* has journeyed a great distance. What started as the name for one specific place where Jews were forced to live became, over the sixteenth century, the principal term for mandatory and exclusive urban Jewish quarters throughout Italy. Later, in the nineteenth century, as Jews throughout the West were emancipated and ghettos in their original form were dismantled, the word *ghetto* transcended its Italian roots and was fashioned into a general metaphor for "traditional" and "premodern" Judaism, even as it also came to designate new Jewish spaces—from the voluntary immigrant neighborhoods of turn-of-the-century London, New York, and Chicago to the hypersegregated holding pens of Nazi-occupied Europe— that were as dissimilar from the pre-emancipation ghettos as they were from each other. Later still, the word *ghetto* broke free of its Jewish origins entirely, emerging in the course of the last seventy years or so as a term more commonly associated with African Americans than with Jews. A noun with a long history of being used as an adjective (from the "ghetto Jew" to "that's so ghetto"); a term that, depending on how it is used and who is using it, can suggest both danger and security, weakness and toughness, social pathology and communal solidarity, a prison and a fortress; a descriptive sociological concept that is hardly value free; and a keyword of both the Jewish and African American imaginaries—the ghetto, historically, has been all of the above. In its very ubiquity and elusiveness, it exemplifies Nietzsche's claim in *On the Genealogy of Morals* that "only that which has no history is definable."[1]

Yet the word *ghetto* does have a history, one of shifting and cascading meanings in both Jewish contexts and beyond. Beginning with an exploration of the prehistory of both the word and the concept, this book chronicles the evolution of the term in early modern Italy through its nineteenth-century transformations, its crossing of the Atlantic, and return to Europe before crossing the Atlantic again with the "blackening" of the ghetto in postwar America. The historical odyssey of this particular term affords new ways of thinking about how we approach the problem of defining the ghetto and discovering its significance in the Jewish experience.

What is a ghetto? The second edition of the *Oxford English Dictionary* (1989) provides two definitions:

> 1. The quarter of a city, chiefly in Italy, to which Jews were restricted.

2. *transf.* and *fig.* A quarter in a city, esp. a thickly populated slum area, inhabited by a minority group or groups, usually as a result of economic or social pressures; an area, etc., occupied by an isolated group; an isolated or segregated group, community, or area.[2]

To the dictionary's descriptive definition of how the term is used in practice can be added numerous prescriptive definitions by those making arguments about how the term *should* be used. The historian Benjamin Ravid, a specialist on the Jews of early modern Venice, claims that the term "ghetto" should be reserved for areas that are legally compulsory, completely segregated, and enclosed.[3] When defining the Nazi ghetto, the editors of the United States Holocaust Memorial Museum's *Encyclopedia of Camps and Ghettos, 1933–1945*, explain that "in essence, a ghetto is a place where Germans concentrated Jews"; that is, where "the German authorities ordered the Jews . . . into a certain area where only Jews were permitted to live."[4] Sociologists who focus on urban neighborhoods today vie over their own definitions. Paul Jargowsky and Mary Jo Bane define contemporary ghettos as areas with an overall poverty rate higher than 40 percent, while William Julius Wilson has used a criterion of at least 40 percent. Loïc Wacquant, who of all sociologists has been the most adamant about theorizing the institution from its origins to the present, argues for a more race- than class-based conception. He reduces the ghetto to "four constituent elements": stigma, constraint, spatial confinement, and institutional parallelism. Mitchell Duneier, whose recent book traces the intellectual history of the black ghetto and examines its relationship to its Jewish prototype, asserts that ghettos can no longer be defined solely by spatial segregation, but must be reinterpreted as places of invasive policing and social control. And there are some sociologists, like Mario Small, who have called for abandoning the ghetto concept altogether. Among other things, Small alleges that the areas typically designated as ghettos are in fact more racially and ethnically heterogeneous than their labeling would suggest and that their composition is more a product of "constrained choice" than "involuntary segregation."[5]

All definitions of "ghetto" tend to draw on some combination of the following attributes: compulsion, homogeneity, spatial segregation, immobility, and socioeconomic deprivation. Yet they do not always incorporate every feature, nor do they agree over how these traits should be ranked in importance or understood. If force is a necessary element, must it be de jure, or can it also include de facto structural and societal impediments to integration? How uniform in its composition does a neighborhood have to be to qualify, and must this sameness be racial or religious, or can it also be based on class or sexual orientation or some other criterion of identity? Is social and economic disadvantage a sine qua non? Can one choose to live in a ghetto?

Definitions are important. It is essential that a site of mandatory segregation like the Venetian or Roman Ghetto be distinguished from the more common social and spatial form of the voluntary Jewish quarter. Historians of the Holocaust must be clear on how the "ghetto" differed from the "labor camp," despite resemblances in some cases. Social scientists who use the ghetto as an analytical concept must be transparent on what, in their view, the term includes and what it excludes. Yet there are certain "keywords" that are not so easily confined within definitions. In the first of many ironies, "ghetto," notwithstanding its linkage with confinement, is one of them. Like a snowball rolling down a hill, the word *ghetto*, in its more than five hundred years, has accumulated multiple layers of meaning. It contains within it recollections of iconic places, diverse histories and images, and ambivalent associations. As the historian Michael Meng writes, "The word 'ghetto' provokes emotions and memories that far outstrip the putatively neutral facts that one may wish to claim the term represents."[6] Efforts to suppress the "folk" notions of the ghetto in the name of analytical rigor and clarity may be necessary for the construction of certain field- and discipline-appropriate typologies. But the idea that one can provide a satisfying answer to the question, "What is a ghetto?" by simply deleting the resonances that deviate from what is held to be the correct use of the word is misguided.

Raymond Williams's concept of keywords as "significant, binding words in certain activities and their interpretation" and "significant, indicative words in certain forms of thought" is a helpful guide here. These are words that become indispensable not only for "discussing but at another level . . . seeing many of our central experiences." What the keyword gains in "general and variable usage," it loses in the clarity of its meaning and the sharpness of its contours: it becomes difficult to pin down, precisely because it is pressed into service so frequently to name and describe an increasingly elastic set of ideas and things.[7] Drawing on Williams's con-

cept of the keyword and mindful of Nietzsche's aforementioned apho-
rism that "only that which has no history is definable," our path toward
understanding the ghetto is one grounded in the quest for a *genealogy*,
rather than a general essence or codification of the term. The aim is to
unravel the different connotations bound up with the word, to reveal
when they emerged and when, in some cases, they faded from recall. In
this way, we come to see the ghetto not as a neat conceptual package,
but as a changing and contested conglomeration of diverse elements,
brought together by the contingencies of history and the projections of
memory. The history of ghettos is, to a substantial degree, a history of
struggle and argument over the meaning, usage, and application of the
label *ghetto* itself. It is only by sifting through, retracing, and sometimes
retrieving the cluster of images and beliefs associated with the term *ghetto*
that its history can be written.

Since the nineteenth century, the ghetto has figured in Jewish historical
consciousness as the ultimate "before" to modernity's "now" or "after."
In this master narrative, which popular writers as well as academic historians did much to foster, premodern Judaism became identified with the
"age of the ghetto" or "ghetto times" (independent of whether a particular Jewry lived in an actual ghetto), and modern Judaism with an exit
from the ghetto as a consequence of both political emancipation and social acculturation and mobility. The title alone of Jacob Katz's 1973 *Out
of the Ghetto: The Social Background of Jewish Emancipation, 1770–
1870*—still, for all its datedness, the most influential study of the project
and process of Jewish emancipation written in the last half century—
speaks to the staying power of this schema.[8] The notion that premodern
Jews by and large lived in ghettos remains, in many ways, the conventional wisdom. It is by no means unusual to encounter a passage like the
following from a recent winner of the National Jewish Book Award in
the area of history: "In the millennium preceding 1897 [the year of the
First Zionist Congress], Jewish survival was guaranteed by the two great
g's: God and ghetto. What enabled Jews to maintain their identity and
their civilization was their closeness to God and their detachment from
the surrounding non-Jewish world."[9] Note the seeming equivalence of
ghetto existence with the full sweep of the pre-emancipatory European

Jewish experience. Nevertheless, in recent decades, scholars working in different areas have whittled away at this equation of the ghetto with pre-modern Judaism writ large. Historians of Italian Jews, for example, have painted a more complex picture of the *cinquecento* institution in its orig-inal context and periodized the ghetto as an early modern rather than premodern phenomenon.[10] At the same time, historians of East European Jews, who rarely lived as urban minorities in walled quarters before the Holocaust, have disputed the universality of the "from ghetto to emanci-pation" emplotment of Jewish modernity.[11]

Revisionist work generates a richer and more nuanced view both of the Jewish ghetto and of modernization in Jewish history. However, it fails to explain how and why the "ghetto" became so seminal to Jewish per-ceptions of the past and expectations of the future. Even while challenging the traditional view of the ghetto as "medieval" or "premodern," those who periodize the ghetto as "early modern" agree that it is primarily of significance to Jewish history before emancipation. Yet, a genealogical ap-proach that traces shifts in the usage of the word *ghetto* over the *longue durée* demonstrates that the ghetto came to have far more of a purchase on Jewish consciousness after emancipation, when its prominence surged in discourse by and about Jews. Arguments from silence are notoriously slippery, yet the relative lack of discussion of the ghetto in early modern Jewish writing suggests that it was not as freighted or as much of a fixa-tion for Jews as it would later become. It was only in the midst and af-termath of emancipation that the word *ghetto* became a Jewish "key-word." Starting in the nineteenth century, it became a root-metaphor of the modern Jewish imagination, a constitutive element of Jewish identity, joining the ranks of terms like "exodus," "exile," and "diaspora" in framing the Jewish experience and especially the experience of moder-nity. It has figured prominently in virtually all the major developments of modern Jewish history, from enlightenment to emancipation, from urban-ization to suburbanization, and from mass migration to mass murder. The "ghetto" has been fundamental to the very definition of Jewish mo-dernity as its informing myth, its chief foil, and its counter-concept.

The question posed by the postcolonial historian Dipesh Chakrabarty— "Can the designation of something or some group as *non-* or *premodern* ever be anything but a gesture of the powerful?"—resonates strongly with the history of the ghetto.[12] And yet, it would be profoundly mistaken to view this history as one in which Jews have been passive and powerless. Jewish thinkers, such as the English novelist Israel Zangwill or the American sociologist Louis Wirth, enlisted and elaborated the ghetto concept not simply to distance themselves from the past (to demonstrate what they *were no longer*) but also to place Jewish history at the very center of European and American history by making Jews paradigmatic of the encounter with modernity.

Considering how crucial the word *ghetto* has been to the Jewish experience, the past several decades have been striking for the extent to which the term has journeyed beyond it. "The word *ghetto* today," writes one American urban historian, "just like everything else these days, has gone global."[13] Throughout Europe, mostly right-wing politicians invoke the specter of the "ghetto" to stoke fears about allegedly unassimilable immigrant (and usually Muslim) enclaves in cities; rap musicians and street artists of widely different backgrounds identify with the term as a badge of authenticity; and social scientists debate its application to marginalized urban spaces around the world. For all this globalization of the term, the word *ghetto* has arguably become central to the collective memory and identity of only one other people beyond Jews: the African American experience is the only other case in which *ghetto* has truly acquired keyword status. Once thought of primarily as a Jewish term, the word *ghetto* is now perceived around the world as a symbol of blackness first and foremost. Mitchell Duneier's recent book traces African Americans' appropriation of the word *ghetto* to represent their own experience of segregation and relates the history of the black ghetto in American social thought from the 1940s to the present. While Duneier has much to say about similarities and differences between the evolving black ghetto and the early modern Jewish ghettos where the term originated, his book contains little commentary on the reverberations of the blackening of the *ghetto* in black–Jewish relations of the twentieth century.[14] There existed a spectrum of Jewish (and black) attitudes about the shared "ownership" of the word *ghetto,* ranging from a sense of commonality and solidarity ("we have both lived in ghettos in our history") to antipathy and conflict ("now that you are out of the ghetto, you have no qualms about keeping us in"). There were Jews who endorsed and even contributed to the application of the word *ghetto* to black neighborhoods—and Jews who rejected it; the same was true, incidentally, for blacks themselves. Much of the discussion of the suitability of the appropriation hinged on the perceived uniqueness of the black and Jewish experiences, the relative prominence in the collective memory of earlier uses of the term (from the immigrant ghetto to the Holocaust ghetto), and the ethics of analogy and comparison.

The degree to which the historical saga of *ghetto* resembles the saga of the word *Jew* is striking.[15] In both cases, a clearly anchored term with a limited range of reference—a mandatory and exclusive Jewish quarter of an Italian city in one instance, a native of the territory of ancient Judea in the other—evolves over time into a more general signifier of a way of life, with particular values and mores. In both cases, moreover, the loosening of the original attachment between word and thing ultimately makes for the possibility of appropriation of the term by other groups, often against the initial "owners" of the label. This may be mere coincidence or simply the way keywords work. Still, the comparison suggests that in tracing the biography of the word *ghetto*, we are following a trail blazed by the word *Jew* itself. Considering that *ghetto* has been code for Jewishness for a substantial part of the word's history, that seems appropriate.

1

THE EARLY HISTORY
OF THE GHETTO

WHAT'S IN A NAME? It is not surprising that a history of the word *ghetto* would begin with one of the most well-known questions in Shakespeare's oeuvre. For Juliet, the answer is perfectly obvious: nothing. It should not matter that her sweetheart Romeo is a Montague and she a Capulet, feuding families in the strife-riven city of medieval Verona. "'Tis but thy name that is my enemy," Juliet assures Romeo. He could cease to be a Montague, he could cease even to be Romeo, and he would remain her beloved. "O! Be some other name: What's in a name? That which we call a rose by any other name would smell as sweet."[1]

Juliet's answer is difficult to square not only with the ultimate fate of the star-crossed lovers in Shakespeare's classic play but also with the controversies that frequently attend the application to someone or something of a highly charged label. True, it is common to hear the accusation "it's just semantics" directed at a person who seems to invest too much significance in words, yet our most pressing cultural arguments often hinge on whether a particular descriptive term is appropriate or misplaced. Indeed, the phrase "one man's terrorist is another's freedom fighter," however clichéd, suggests the very opposite of Juliet's answer to her own question. Names matter. The action being described may be the same, but how it is termed can make all the difference.

The genealogy of the ghetto would seem, similarly, to contradict Juliet. For any attempt to write a history of the ghetto will repeatedly bump up against the problem, What *is* a ghetto? How should the term be used and defined? The meaning of ghetto has been stretched and contracted, appropriated for new groups and contexts, reclaimed by its original "owners," and accepted and rejected. The answer to the "What's in a name?" question becomes, with respect to the word *ghetto*, "quite a lot."

Through the eve of emancipation in the late eighteenth century, however, the word *ghetto* had a more limited bandwidth of meaning and usage. Its origins lay in geographic happenstance, the sheer coincidence that Venice decided to create an all-Jewish mandatory quarter on an island, at the northern edge of the city, already known as the *Ghetto* (or *Geto) Nuovo*—and even later attempts to imbue this arbitrary term with motivation and purpose did not significantly expand its signifying power and reach. For centuries, there is no evidence of debate over the definition of *ghetto*. A ghetto was a compulsory Jewish quarter of an Italian town or city. True to its association with spatial confinement and enclosure, the word *ghetto* itself was more restricted in its semantic range in this early period than it would later become.

Venice is often held up as the site of the world's first ghetto. In the words of Shaul Bassi, a Venetian Jewish scholar and writer and one of the driving forces behind Venice's year-long series of exhibitions and conferences held to commemorate the ghetto's five hundredth anniversary in 2016, "the concept of the ghetto was born here in Venice. . . . And that is why we must never forget the place."[2] Few today dispute the derivation of the term *ghetto* from the Venetian *geto,* or foundry, or that the word's association with segregated Jewish space began in the wake of the 1516 edict confining Jews to an island in the northern part of the lagoon city that was already known as the *Ghetto Nuovo*. The word *ghetto* was almost certainly born in Venice. The origins of the idea itself—the signified as opposed to signifier—are somewhat murkier. On the one hand, it is fair to say that there was no familiar, ready-to-wear concept of a mandatory and homogeneous Jewish enclosure that was available to the Venetians in 1516 and that they simply outfitted with the name "ghetto." On the other, the idea of such an enclosure was already a part (albeit a minor one) of Christian Europe's toolkit for dealing with its "Jewish Question." In fact, there were European ghettos that preceded the Ghetto of Venice.

As the preeminent historian of Jewish Venice, Benjamin Ravid, has written, "to apply the term 'ghetto' to a Jewish area prior to 1516 is anachronistic, while to state that the first ghetto was established in Venice in 1516 is something of a misrepresentation. It would be more precise to say that [the] compulsory, segregated and enclosed Jewish quarter received the name 'ghetto' as a result of developments in Venice in 1516."[3]

The difficulty of pinpointing the beginning of the ghetto is compounded by the elusiveness of the term itself. Where we start will, to some degree, follow from how we define the word *ghetto*. In the early twentieth century, most historians and sociologists tended toward a capacious definition of the ghetto as, at root, a densely populated Jewish quarter; they generally believed that the seeds of the ghetto lay in the traditional inclination of Jews, for religious and cultural reasons or to achieve safety in numbers, to cluster together by choice. On the basis of this definition, the ghetto could be traced to the distant Jewish past, indeed as far back as the Diaspora itself. The German and later American liberal rabbi Joachim Prinz began his 1937 *Life in the Ghetto,* a series of five historical portraits of Jewish urban life, with a long chapter on the Jews of ancient Alexandria, the largest, most prosperous, and cosmopolitan Jewish community of the Hellenistic Diaspora. Alexandrian Jews, who numbered in the hundreds of thousands, lived predominantly in two of the city's five sectors, above all in the fourth or Delta district. Prinz conceded, "It was not an actual ghetto, since many of the well-off lived in the inner parts of the city and in the villa quarters of the rich," but was more of a "foreign colony," of the sort found in nearly all port cities. Still, "the strange and unusual customs of the Jews"—their dietary restrictions, their avoidance of the temples of the city with all their statues, their worship of an imageless God—"made such a quarter necessary."[4] Louis Wirth, the German-born American Jewish sociologist whose 1928 *The Ghetto* sought to trace the history of the Jewish ghetto to his own day, opened his account later than Prinz, in the European Middle Ages, yet endorsed a similarly loose usage of the term. In a section significantly titled "The Voluntary Ghetto," he explained, "The segregation of the Jews into separate local areas in the medieval cities did not originate with any formal edict of church or state. The ghetto was not, as sometimes mistakenly . . . believed, the arbitrary creation of the authorities, designed to deal with an alien people . . . but rather the unwitting crystallization of needs and practices rooted in the customs and heritages, religious and secular, of the Jews themselves."[5] The acclaimed twentieth-century Jewish historian Salo W. Baron's classic "Ghetto and Emancipation" essay of that same year took a more sanguine view of the ghetto and the Jewish Middle Ages than did his contemporary Wirth, yet likewise underscored the originally elective nature of the ghetto system. "It must not be forgotten," Baron wrote, "that the Ghetto grew up voluntarily as a result of Jewish self-government, and it was only in a later development that public law interfered and made it a legal compulsion for *all* Jews to live in a secluded district in which no Christian was allowed to dwell." At its inception, "the Ghetto was an institution that the Jews had found it to their interest to create themselves."[6]

While the institution of the "Jewish quarter" still awaits comprehensive treatment, it does seem to be true that de facto Jewish streets and neighborhoods surfaced in virtually every town or city where Jews settled. Very often their presence in a particular district was represented in the place name. Nearly every European language had a set of native terms, often varying by region and dialect, for the "Jewish street" or "Jewish quarter." To give only a few examples, there was the Latin *Vicus Judeorum, Burgus Judeorum,* or *Judaica;* the French *Rue des Juifs, Carrière des Juifs,* or *Juiverie;* the German *Judengasse, Judenstrasse,* or *Judenviertel;* the English *Jewry;* the Spanish *Judería;* and the Italian *Giudecca* or *Zudecca.* Since Jews tended to be distinguished from the Christian population not only religiously but also economically, as merchants and moneylenders, their geographic concentration was fully in accord with a premodern social order where it was common for members of the same occupational group (shoemakers, bakers, and the like) to live in the same locality. These Jewish quarters tended to be situated near either the main market square or the seat of political power in the city. They were extensively, but not exclusively Jewish; there were Christians who lived within the Jewish sector and Jews who lived on its outskirts. Moreover, the quarters were occasionally, but not always, set apart and surrounded by gates and walls. While these areas typically contained the main Jewish communal institutions—one or several synagogues and houses of study, a ritual bathhouse, a kosher slaughterhouse—it was not unheard of for a church or even diocese to be located either in those quarters or in the immediate vicinity.[7] In the case of medieval Cologne, the city hall *(Bürgerhaus)* actually was in the very heart of the Jewish quarter.[8] By means of the ritual enclosures (or *eruvin*) they created to permit transporting objects in public space on the Sabbath, Jews themselves projected onto these areas boundaries drawn from halakhah, or Jewish law, rendering them not only sociologically but also spiritually and symbolically Jewish.

Wirth and Baron were right to argue that a secluded yet basically open and legally voluntary Jewish quarter was the normative form of Jewish settlement in medieval Europe before the mandatory ghetto. They were wrong, however, to imply that the former was a conceptual precursor of the latter and that both were essentially variations on the idea of the ghetto. An accurate picture of the beginnings of the ghetto must distinguish it sharply from the older, more generic concept of the Jewish quarter. For Benjamin Ravid, the term *ghetto* should be applied solely to Jewish residential areas that—like the Italian Jewish communities beginning in the sixteenth century that were the first to be known as ghettos—were legally mandatory, exclusively Jewish, and physically cordoned off via gates and walls.[9] A Jewish neighborhood with all three characteristics, even if it was never referred to by the name "ghetto" (e.g., the Frankfurt *Judengasse*), could be so labeled (albeit anachronistically); conversely, an area that might popularly have been known as a "ghetto" (e.g., the Jewish immigrant enclaves of the early twentieth century), but lacked these characteristics, should not be. The history of the ghetto, according to Ravid, as distinct from the history of the Jewish quarter more broadly, begins with the creation of or at least the call for Jewish communities that were compulsory, segregated, and enclosed.

Even with this stricter definition, a case can be made that the history of the ghetto begins in Second Temple times. In 38 C.E., the Jews of Alexandria were victims of an unprecedented eruption of urban mob violence. The only two sources on these riots, the ancient Alexandrian Jewish philosopher Philo's *Against Flaccus* and *Embassy to Gaius,* together yield the following account of the role that segregation played in the anti-Jewish violence. After the Roman governor of the city, Flaccus, publicly branded Alexandria's Jews aliens and foreigners, stripping them of their civil and political rights, the largely Greek populace "drove the Jews entirely out of four quarters, and crammed them all into a very small portion of one."[10] This "very narrow space" into which "countless myriads of men, and women, and children" were concentrated "like so many herds of sheep and oxen" was presumably the original Jewish section, located on the eastern side of the city.[11] According to Philo, the conditions in the quarter were atrocious. Having abandoned their homes and businesses in haste, the Jews suffered impoverishment and even starvation, and the terrible overcrowding ("like a pen") corrupted the air and made simple breathing difficult. Eventually, Rome intervened to end Flaccus's reign of terror, and a few years later the rights of the Jews of Alexandria were restored, including, we can assume, their right to live where they chose. Much remains uncertain about this historical episode. Rhetorical exaggeration is part of the DNA of ancient historiography, Philo's *Against Flaccus* and *Embassy to Gaius* being no exception, and it can be difficult to tell where fact ends and embellishment begins. Still, it would appear that what many have called the "first pogrom"[12] also gave rise to the "first known ghetto in the world,"[13] however short its lifespan proved to be.

But even if we apply the term *ghetto* to this first-century Alexandrian case, it was clearly not a landmark in the eventual emergence of the ghetto as an institution. The history of the "ghetto before the *ghetto*" begins later, in medieval Christian Europe, though how much later remains in question. One possibility is to begin with an early written charter from 1084 granting Jews the right to settle in the Rhineland city of Speyer on favorable terms. The local ruler, Bishop Rüdiger Huozmann, asserting that it "would add to the honor of our place by bringing in Jews," boasted of having "located them [the Jews] outside of the community and habitation of the other citizens" and "surrounded them with a wall," so that "they might not readily be disturbed by the insolence of the populace." All this, the bishop claimed, was part of a package of "laws better than the Jewish people has in any city of the German empire."[14] Some have seen this as the first instance of a ghetto in the sense of a separate and enclosed Jewish residential area outside of which Jews were not permitted to settle.[15] Yet, even were we to assume that Jews were required to live in the walled area provided for in the document and that Christians were prohibited from doing so—and there is no evidence in the text of the charter to support (or disprove) either—it would still be far-fetched to label this enclave a "ghetto," for the simple reason that the site bore no official stigma.[16] The bishop described the settling of Jews in Speyer as something that "would add to the honor of our place" (though the encircling of the community with a protective wall was perhaps an acknowledgment that not everyone in the town would have agreed). The walled quarter was a concession meant to induce Jews to settle in Speyer, not an imposition. To speak typologically, the Speyer case seems to fit much better what Carl Nightingale, in his global history of segregation, labels a "foreign merchant district"—a separate, walled-off quarter that medieval merchants themselves negotiated from rulers to guarantee their protection from the surrounding populace—than it does a "scapegoat ghetto."[17]

The origins of ghettoization should not be sought in voluntary Jewish urban clusterings or even in walled streets or enclaves specifically designated or even built for Jewish settlement. Rather, the roots lie in the medieval church's mounting efforts to fortify Christendom by minimizing Christian exposure to the spiritual pollution of Jews and Judaism. In 1267, a provincial synod in the Polish city of Wrocław (Breslau), led by the papal legate Guido, issued several regulations concerning the Jews, one of which stated,

> Since the Polish country is still a young plant in the body of Christendom, the Christian people might be the more easily infected by the superstitious and depraved norms of the Jews living with them. In order that the Christian faith be more easily and quickly implemented in the hearts of the faithful in these regions, we strictly prescribe that the Jews inhabiting this province of Gniezno should not indiscriminately dwell among the Christians, but should possess contiguous or adjoining houses in a segregated location of each city or village. This should be so arranged that the Jewish quarter be separated from the common habitation of the Christians by a fence, a wall, or a ditch.[18]

This is the first legal document, ecclesiastical or otherwise, that calls for a mandatory and exclusive Jewish enclosure in medieval Europe. It must be seen in the context of segregationist measures promoted in previous, more ecumenical church councils. In 1179, the Third Lateran Council had prohibited Christians from working as servants or nurses for Jews and living in their homes while calling for the excommunication of those who did. The Fourth Lateran Council, in 1215, went further by creating the infamous Jewish badge. These as well as other steps aimed at marking, separating, and stigmatizing Jews that had been previously introduced, from the prohibition on the sharing of meals with non-Christians to the segregation of bathhouses, are reiterated in the Breslau resolutions. The demand for strict ghettoization, however, is new. There is little to suggest that this order was a natural evolution of the church's segregationist program. The text itself justifies ghettoization as a pragmatic response to a regional problem, the fact that Polish Christians were relatively new to the faith and thus more at risk at being corrupted by the Jews living among them. Whether this was indeed the principal motivation for creating a ghetto, or more of a pretext for an action whose true impetus lay elsewhere, is unclear.[19] Regardless, the fact is that the embrace of residential segregation in Breslau did not signify a shift in church policy or initiate any kind of trend. The church would only return to advocating ghettoization in the fifteenth century, and even then, it rarely spoke with one voice or took the lead before Pope Paul IV's bull *Cum nimis absurdum* established ghettos in the papal states in 1555. Even in Breslau, the call for a ghetto appears to have gone unheeded. Apparently, the Jewish community—then the second largest in East Central Europe, after Prague—thrived, to the point that the bishop of Breslau in 1287 could write to his Roman contacts that the Jews in the realm of the duke of Breslau lived better than the clergy.[20]

For the next two centuries, even as the situation of Jews in Western and Central Europe grew increasingly precarious, the pursuit of forced segregation was at best haphazard. While city ordinances calling for the creation and walling off of compulsory and exclusive Jewish quarters began to proliferate in France, Spain, and Italy, they rarely achieved total segregation and generally proved abortive, whether as a result of a lack of follow-through or because sterner measures—most notably, expulsion—were eventually adopted.[21] The cases of Frankfurt am Main and the Spanish kingdoms of Castile-Leon and Aragon stand out. Together, they indicate the growing appeal of ghettoization to Christian rulers in the second half of the fifteenth century—and also the limits to this attraction.

The most significant example of a ghetto before the "ghetto," indeed one that puts Venice's pioneering status into some doubt, is the *Judengasse* (Jewish street) of Frankfurt am Main. Traditionally, the Jews had lived primarily in a central part of the city just south of the seat of the church in Frankfurt, St. Bartholomew's Cathedral. Jewish life in Frankfurt had twice been interrupted by devastating pogroms, in 1241 and 1349, although after each the city eventually permitted Jews to return and rebuild their community. Nevertheless, by the fifteenth century, the Jews of Frankfurt were a shell of their former selves, much diminished in both overall number and economic clout. In 1460, the city council ordered the Jews to move to a neighborhood on the eastern edge of Frankfurt, outside yet immediately adjacent to the old city wall, but still within the new city limits. The decree cited the disturbance caused to Christian worship by daily exposure to the sight and in particular the sound of nearby Jews, foreshadowing the word *ghetto*'s later association with Jewish noise. Indeed, local church officials had for decades demanded the removal of Jews from the area of the cathedral for this very reason. Nevertheless, the fact that the desire to purge Frankfurt of a Jewish presence resulted in ghettoization and not, as was the case in most other German municipalities with a Jewish community in the fifteenth and sixteenth centuries, in expulsion was ultimately due to the complex politics of the city. It was principally the intervention of the Holy Roman Emperor Friedrich III, who had originally called for segregating Frankfurt's Jews in 1443, that saved the Jews from expulsion. Friedrich III may have fancied ghettoization because it allowed him to protect his financial interest in the city's Jews while at the same time burnishing his reputation as a defender of Christendom. The city council, which had jurisdiction in this matter, initially balked at the emperor's intervention, but by the time they were ready to evict the Jews from the city center in 1460, they opted for ghettoization over expulsion; perhaps their change of heart was due to their recognition of the emperor's special connection to the Free Imperial City of Frankfurt, the seat of both imperial elections and coronations. The Jews bitterly protested the edict, although, significantly, their objection was not to ghettoization per se—the Jews themselves offered to wall off their traditional neighborhood and brick over their outward-facing doors and windows—but to the requirement that they move to a remote, sparsely populated, and little developed part of Frankfurt. Though it made a few accommodations, the council would not budge from its order, and thus in 1462—some fifty-four years before the Jews of Venice moved into the Ghetto Nuovo—the Jews of Frankfurt moved into their own new ghetto, the relocated Judengasse, a narrow, gated street that from an early point was popularly referred to as "New Egypt."[22]

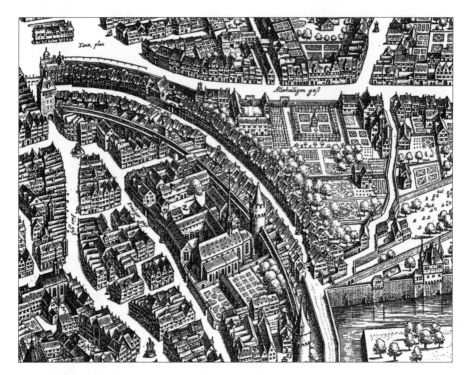

A view of the *Judengasse* from Matthäus Merian's 1628 woodcut aerial map of Frankfurt am Main. The street curves from the upper left to the lower right.

Spain, home to the largest Jewish community in Europe in the medieval period, was also the site of the most ambitious and far-reaching campaign for enforced separation of Jews from Christians before the sixteenth century. Through the late fourteenth century, Spanish Jews, at least those who lived in cities, tended to live in unofficial Jewish quarters (so-called *juderìas*), and these quarters frequently were separated by gates and walls, although typically non-Jews numbered among their inhabitants. Here and there, we find sources that suggest growing interest in making this de facto separation de jure, but nothing that indicates a concerted, statewide push for legal segregation.[23] That changed swiftly in the aftermath of the 1391 massacres that swept across the Iberian peninsula, decimating entire communities and ushering in a tide of conversions to Christianity that lasted into the following century. The specific challenge of disembedding the masses of those who were newly and often nominally Christian from their Jewish social networks, the determination to

accelerate the conversions, and perhaps, paradoxically, the desire to re-
inforce a boundary between Jew and Christian that was being eroded by
the very success of the Spanish conversionary campaign—all these
spawned the first sustained drive to achieve residential segregation by
law.[24] Popular preachers like the Dominican friar Vincent Ferrer fanned
the flames of this campaign, arguing that "the neighbor of a Jew will never
be a good Christian." "So powerful was his reasoning," David Nirenberg
writes, "that it convinced the pope, the kings of Castile and of Aragon,
and innumerable town councils and municipal officers to attempt the
most extensive efforts at segregation in the Middle Ages."[25] The new
mood was epitomized in the 1412 Laws of Valladolid, the first article of
which required Jews and Muslims throughout King Juan II's Castile to
"dwell and live apart from Christians, in a separate part of the city, town,
and place where they reside, surrounded by a wall, having a single gate
for ingress and egress"[26]; the injunction was reiterated, albeit with somewhat milder terms, six months later.

To what degree these policies were implemented is disputed, although
it is clear that the mixing of the populations remained sufficient for the
Catholic monarchs Ferdinand and Isabella to rekindle the drive for forced
segregation of Jews later in the century, at around the same time they established the Inquisition to extirpate "Judaizing" among the New Christians. In 1480, after several edicts by the Crown ordering the segregation
of housing in specific cities, the Cortes (parliament) of Castile extended
this policy to the entire kingdom, resolving, "Since from continued conversation and common life of Jews and Moors with Christians great
damage and unpleasantness is caused ... we order and command all of
the Jews and Moors of all the cities, towns, and places in our kingdoms ...
that their quarters be separated from those of the Christians, and not be
in common." The state allowed two years for the execution of this resolution and appointed supervisors (visitadores) charged with traveling to
different cities to oversee and ensure its implementation. Thus began a
decade of uprooting and upheaval for Jewish communities throughout
the kingdom. Some of the cities hit hardest by the measure included Avila,
where the Jews were forced to live in the district of the leather tanneries,
"regarded as the worst place to live in the city"; Segovia, where the ex-
propriation of community property went so far that the Crown ultimately
stepped in to restrain it; and Guadalajara.[27] The process appears to have

been smoother in cities where the separation was already extensive, perhaps in part as a result of the segregationist push earlier in the century. The transfer of population was still ongoing twelve years later when the state reversed itself and decided on another tack for addressing its Jewish problem: complete expulsion, following in the footsteps of England, France, and an array of German cities. Evidently, housing segregation and other measures designed to separate Jews and suppress "Judaizing" had not achieved the goal of driving a wedge between Jews and conversos. That, at least, was the claim made in the edict of expulsion:

> You know well, or ought to know that because we were informed that in our realms there were some bad Christians who Judaized and apostatized from our holy Catholic faith, whereof the chief cause was the communication between the Christians and the Jews; in the Cortes which we convened in the city of Toledo in the past year of one thousand four hundred and eighty years, we ordained that the said Jews should be set apart in all the cities, boroughs, and places of our realms and dominions and to give them Jewish quarters and separate places where they might dwell, hoping that with this separation [the matter] would be corrected.

That it had failed to do so left the state, the edict went on, with no alternative but "to expel the said Jews from our kingdoms."[28]

The examples of Frankfurt and Spain indicate that the idea of the ghetto was already in the air when Venice interned its Jews in 1516. Even in Italy, the path to the sixteenth-century ghettos was paved in the second half of the fifteenth century by cities like Bari and Cesena, which segregated their Jewish populations in 1463 and 1487, respectively.[29] Yet the ghetto still lacked the status of a norm for how to deal with a Jewish presence deemed corrosive and regrettable, but for economic or theological reasons useful or necessary. Perhaps this might have emerged in time in Spain, considering the size of its Jewish population and the fact that ghettoization had the weight of the state behind it, but ultimately Spain took a different path. Even in Frankfurt, the foundations of the ghetto (or Judengasse) were not so secure some fifty years into the experiment. In 1515, just as the first discussions were taking place in Venice about segregating its newly acquired Jewish population, the Frankfurt city council (not for the last time) was openly debating the possibility of emulating the vast majority of German cities by expelling its Jews.[30] On the eve of Venice's decision in 1516, it was still expulsion—not ghettoization—that had the wind at its back in Western and Central Europe with respect to Jews.

Compulsory ghettos were generally established in one of two ways. The first and more common approach was to convert what was already a de facto Jewish quarter into a mandatory ghetto through the addition of gates and walls; this was the course taken in Rome and Prague. The other approach was to relocate the Jewish community to a new enclosed area, sometimes but not always on the periphery of the city. The Ghetto of Venice falls into this second category. It emerged as a result of the Senate's edict in March 1516 forcibly moving its Jews to a little island, in the outlying *sestiere* (district) of Cannaregio, known as the Ghetto Nuovo. Out of this came the convergence, and ultimately conflation, of the embryonic concept of a mandatory Jewish enclosure with a Venetian place name that, to that point, had no Jewish associations whatsoever. This initial arbitrary connection between word and thing has been disputed. To be sure, legitimate questions about the now broadly accepted Venetian etymology have played a part in the controversy over the term's origins. Yet there is also disbelief that a term seen as so fundamental to the Jewish experience was devoid of Jewish significance or even of a more generic connection to segregation. The history of the ghetto is full of attempts to endow the word *ghetto* with an etymology that links it semantically or thematically to the idea of the ghetto, as in the famous (and fallacious) folk interpretation that derives *ghetto* from *get,* the Hebrew term for a bill of divorce. Yet none of the alternative etymologies (and they are legion) have been able to shake the basic persuasiveness of the theory that traces the ghetto to the name of the Venetian island that became the site of the first enduring experiment with the residential segregation of Jews, at least in Italy. The Jewish history of the word *ghetto,* it seems clear, begins in 1516.[31]

Most believe that the name *ghetto* is connected to an earlier tenant of the two marshy islands in Cannaregio that were to become known as the Ghetto Vecchio (Old Ghetto) and the Ghetto Nuovo (New Ghetto). By the late thirteenth century, archival sources reveal, the Republic had centralized the melting and refining of all the raw copper amassed by the state in an official foundry, which in government documents from the fourteenth century onward is referred to alternately as the *geto, getto, gheto,* and *getho*.[32] Presumably, this term for foundry derived from the Venetian verb *gettare* (Latin *jactare*), meaning to throw or to pour, indicating the act of the casting of metal; alternatively, it may derive from *ghétta*, the slag or waste produced in the smelting process.[33] By osmosis, the word eventually became the name of the island on which the foundry was located.

By the mid-fifteenth century, the foundry was no more, having closed down decades earlier, but the place name endured. Two testimonies from 1458, given as part of a state inquiry into which of the nearby parishes the territory of the future ghetto belonged to, confirm the persistence of the name.[34] The deposed shared their memories of the area from their youth, clearly indicating that it was the site of the former foundry and providing the only eyewitness accounts of its operation and layout that we possess. The foundry itself, they testified, had been located on the southernmost of two islands, which was known as *el getto*. Perhaps in light of its military importance as the place where the cannons and shells of the Republic were produced, it was "completely enclosed with a sturdy wall."[35] The facility was a vast enterprise run by three state officials, with more than twelve furnaces in operation and hundreds of workers, many of them German, whom one of the witnesses recalled throwing stones at and calling *"Todeschi magnasonza"* (lard-eating Germans). There were two gates: an entrance to the foundry just off the Canale di Cannaregio immediately to the south and a kind of back door that opened to a little bridge that led to another island. The latter was a mostly "empty plot" that served as a dumping ground for all the refuse and rubble from the furnaces of the foundry. Later, apparently after the foundry was dismantled, it also was a place where weavers would lay out their wool to dry in the open air. This second, more northerly of the two islands was not referred to as *el getto,* but was considered part of the *terren del getto* (the "area of the Getto").

Over the rest of the fifteenth century the ties between these two islands, the getto and the terren del getto, began to wither and their fates to diverge. The erstwhile foundry site fell into disuse and disrepair, while the former dumping ground was sold separately and converted into a residential neighborhood, with a block of houses built around the perimeter of the island opening onto a courtyard shaped somewhat like a pentagon.

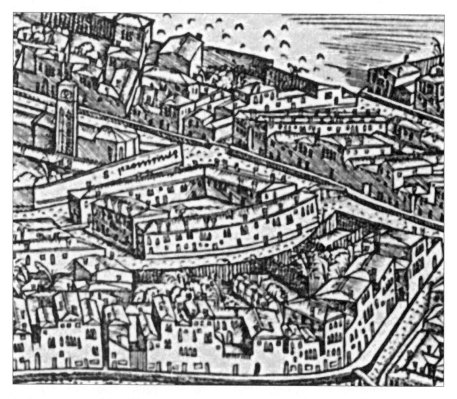

A close-up view of the Ghetto Nuovo from Jacopo de' Barbari's 1500 woodcut aerial *Map of Venice.*

In addition to the bridge that connected the newly developed island to the now dilapidated one to the south, a new bridge was built on the north side of the island, further linking it to the surrounding area. A text from the last decade of the century indicates that the old foundry site was still known popularly as *g(h)èto (jactum),* while the adjacent island was then commonly referred to by the slightly modified title of *g(h)èto nuovo (re-centioreum jactum).*[36] Both are visible in Jacopo de' Barbari's renowned perspective map of Venice from 1500. The Ghetto Nuovo is particularly well defined, with its two bridges and its central courtyard enclosed by a veritable wall of two-story houses with outward-facing doors and windows. The original Ghetto, or what would come to be known as the Ghetto Vecchio, is more difficult to make out, but it appears to be less developed.

The name *Geto Nuovo* was thus already in place by the time it became an all-Jewish area in 1516. *Geto* had no prior Jewish connotations or anything that would link it to the theme of segregation or enclosure. Yet just as this term once linked to the presence of a metal foundry had already come, by osmosis, to refer to the island complex that housed it, after 1516 it took two new associative leaps: first in becoming the name of the Jewish quarter of Venice (much like, later on, New York's Lower East Side or Chicago's Near West Side) and then, in transcending its Venetian origins, to emerge as the most commonly used name for the mandatory and exclusive Jewish district of any Italian city. As Emilio Teza, the author of one of the most important studies championing the ghetto-as-foundry etymology, wrote in 1904, "If the Senate had chosen [for Jewish residency] the Bràgora or Castello [another section of Venice] one of the two names would for centuries have sufficed to signify that part of a city reserved for Jewish occupancy."[37] It was mere coincidence that the word *ghetto* was grafted to the idea of enclosed Jewish space, but the operation succeeded. Knowledge of the prehistory of the site of *Il Ghetto* survived in the 1604 edition of Renaissance scholar Francesco Sansovino's 1581 masterpiece, *Venice, the Most Noble and Unique City*, which noted that the "common vestibule of the Jews is called Ghetto, because formerly artillery was cast there *(si gettavano l'artigliarie)*, as you can see from a painted cannon ball placed above the venerable gate, which is in the direction of Cannaregio."[38] The Venetian etymology did not appear again in print until Tomasso Temanza's 1781 *Ancient Map of the Noble City of Venice*, which brought the two testimonies from 1458 about the prehistory of the Ghetto Vecchio and Ghetto Nuovo to light for the first time.

Still, the tracing of *ghetto* to the Venetian *geto* only truly began to eclipse other interpretations in the second half of the nineteenth century and the early twentieth century. The chief objection to this etymology has been the fact that the Venetian Senate's deliberations refer to the area designated for Jewish settlement as the *Geto*, not *Ghetto*, and from the perspective of linguistics it is highly improbable that the soft *g* in *geto* could have evolved into the hard *g* in *ghetto*. Yet, whatever the spelling, the term was always pronounced with a hard *g*, and well into the sixteenth century "the distinction between the palatal *ge* and the guttural *ghe* had yet orthographically to emerge."[39] In the end, perhaps the strongest argument that the term *ghetto* was not coined in response to the segregation of the Jews, but was a relic of a history that preceded the arrival of the Jews altogether, is the fact that the original area to which Jews were

restricted was the Ghetto Nuovo, and not the Ghetto Vecchio. Were it
otherwise, one would expect that the first site of the Jewish enclosure
would have been known as the "Old Ghetto" and the subsequent addition as the "New Ghetto." In fact, when a final addition to the ghetto was
made in 1633, on a patch of land that had never been part of the *terren
del getto* of the former foundry complex, it was labeled the *Ghetto Nuovissimo*, the "Newest Ghetto." For by this time, after more than a century-
long circuit through Italy, *ghetto* meant "compulsory Jewish quarter"
and no longer bore the significance or even memory of "foundry."

Nevertheless, among those who believe the Jewish ghetto has its roots
in the word *geto*, there is one alternative to the ghetto-as-foundry consensus worth mentioning. In the early 1960s, the Italian Jewish historian
Joseph Sermoneta proposed that the path from *geto* to *ghetto* in the sense
of Jewish enclosure originated not in Venice in 1516, but a few decades
earlier in Genoa.[40] During the flight of Jews from Spain after their expulsion in 1492, there were several who traveled aboard a Genoese ship
heading eastward. The unexpected death of the captain en route forced
the ship to make an unplanned stop in Genoa and the Jews to disembark.
The Jews, however, were strictly barred from entering Genoa proper, as
a result of which they were effectively marooned for weeks on a pier, or
jetty, outside the city, and not permitted to leave. Conditions were deplorable: the Jews were completely exposed to the elements, without a roof
over their heads, and food and water were sparse. Many died, and others,
especially the young, converted, either of their own accord or under du-
ress. Sermoneta encountered this story in a book of responsa by Rabbi
David ben Hayim HaKohen of Corfu, published in the 1530s. There, R.
HaKohen referred to the site where the Jews were forcibly hemmed in as
the *geto*, or in Hebrew גיטו. If in Venice *geto* was primarily associated
with the *fonderia* or foundry, elsewhere in Europe—and specifically in
Genoa—this derivative of the Latin *jactus* also had the meaning of jetty.
Sermoneta's conjecture was that this Genoese *geto*, and not the Venetian
geto nuovo, was the true source of the word *ghetto*. The fact that R. Ha-
Kohen was still aware of the term *geto*-qua-jetty suggests that it had acquired an enduring notoriety in the collective memory of the Sephardic
exiles, some of whom eventually flocked to the ghettos of sixteenth-
century Italy. Moreover, Sermoneta believed that he had hit on a solution
to the conundrum of how the soft *ge* became the hard *ghe*. The Sephardic

exiles, Sermoneta assumed, would likely have identified the Italian *geto* with the Spanish *jeto,* whose first consonant they pronounced with a fricative [x] as opposed to a palatal *ge.* Italian, however, lacks the fricative [x] sound, and so when the term *geto* was reintroduced into the lexicon of Italian Jews by the refugees from Spain, the former converted the fricative to a hard *g.*

Sermoneta's theory is ingenious, but far-fetched. One problem with it is that Sephardic Jews, whether they hailed from the Ottoman Empire (the Levantine Jews) or had lived previously as Marranos and were coming directly from Spain or Portugal (the so-called Ponentine Jews), did not become a prominent constituency in the Italian ghettos before the late sixteenth century—in other words, well after the term *ghetto* had entered the general Italian lexicon as a term for a restricted Jewish quarter. Moreover, it is hard to explain away the fact that the Venetian *geto* is awfully close to the word *ghetto.* The most sensible conclusion remains that it was a Venetian foundry, not a Genoese jetty, that stands at the beginning of a semantic odyssey leading to the Italian Jewish ghetto. Still, Sermoneta's argument in the mid-twentieth century is a fascinating example of an attempt, in the aftermath of the Holocaust and its reinflection of the ghetto concept, to provide the word *ghetto* with an etymology rooted in a memory of death and mass suffering.

The story of how Venice came to ghettoize its Jews has oft been told.[41] In 1509, an alliance of armies known as the League of Cambrai, led by France, the Holy Roman Empire, and the papal states, attacked the Venetian Republic and overran its mainland territories (the so-called Terra Ferma). Many refugees from these areas fled to Venice, and Jews were among them. Until that time, aside from a relatively brief exception at the end of the fourteenth century, Venice had neither authorized nor encouraged the formation of a Jewish community within the city limits.[42] The government permitted individual Jewish merchants and doctors to settle in Venice, so long as they wore the required yellow badge (and eventually beret) and practiced their Judaism behind closed doors. Most of the Venetian state's Jews, however, were required to live across the lagoon in cities like Mestre and Padua and could only secure fifteen-day passes to stay in Venice when they had business to conduct in the city. These mainland Jews were among the hordes of refugees who sought asylum in Venice in 1509 to escape the advancing armies of the League of Cambrai. Their ranks included certain wealthy moneylenders from Mestre who had established a ten-year charter with Venice in 1503 granting them the right to come to Venice in case of war to protect themselves and safeguard the Christian pledges they had in their possession. But these moneylenders accounted for only a fraction of the Jews who took refuge in the city (who themselves were only a fraction of a much larger wave of migrants).[43] Venice thus found itself confronted not only with a massive refugee crisis that taxed its food supply and posed a danger to public health but also had to contend with an influx of Jews that put into question its traditional policy of maintaining at most a modest, under-the-radar Jewish presence.

After reclaiming some of the land that it had lost, Venice initially ordered all the refugees, particularly the Jews, to leave the city and return home. But soon the government reconsidered. The numbers of the urban poor, already high, had only swelled as a result of the war, and the city treasury was strapped. Allowing the Jews to remain in the city limits would kill the proverbial two birds with one stone: the Jews could be made to provide the Christian commoners with loans, thereby defusing potential social unrest, while also paying the state handsomely for the privilege of living and working in Venice. Accordingly, in 1513 the Council of Ten, one of the main governing bodies of Venice, established a new five-year charter with the leading bankers of the Jewish community that authorized the Jews to reside in the city and engage in moneylending in return for the substantial annual payment of 6,500 ducats. Two years later, in return for a three-year loan to the state, Jews gained the right to sell *strazzaria*, or secondhand goods, in a set number of stores on the Rialto.

The relaxation of the government's policy against allowing Jews to reside in Venice met with vociferous opposition. Many, especially friars and preachers, regarded the new Jewish presence as offensive, intolerable, and even dangerous. Venice had traditionally regarded itself as a "city of God" and a "new Jerusalem," whose emergence and survival in the face of so many obstacles, from the lack of city walls to the seas that threatened to engulf it, were due solely to divine protection: a belief that had already been shaken by the faltering war effort that had recently brought so many Jews to Venice.[44] By acceding to the existence of a Jewish community in Venice, the Republic was jeopardizing the very providential status that had been the city's pride and guarantee. Thunderous warnings of divine retribution from the pulpit, and calls for Jews to convert or be expelled made an impression. In a diary entry for Good Friday, 1515, the Venetian historian Marino Sanuto commented on "the evil practice resulting from the continuous contact with these Jews, who reside in this city in great numbers." Formerly, he claimed, they had remained in their homes and outside of public space during Holy Week, yet "now till yesterday they were going about and it is a very bad thing, and no one says anything to them, since because of the wars, one has need of them, and thus they do whatever they want."[45]

Certain Venetians began to explore the possibility of a middle-ground solution between acceptance and expulsion of Jews. In April 1515, a government minister proposed "that the Jews who were numerous in the city [living] in various houses and districts, and giving a bad example to all the Christians, should be sent to live in the Giudecca."[46] The motion failed, in part, because Jewish opposition was so forceful. But just short of a year later, the segregation of the Jews was called for by a Venetian senator named Zacaria Dolfin. Arguing that the Jews were corrupting the city by their presence and that they were the cause of the state's setbacks, Dolfin proposed "to send all of them to live in the Ghetto Nuovo [the new ghetto] which is like a castle, and to make drawbridges and close it with a wall."[47] This time, Jewish opposition—perhaps because of a sharp downturn in Venice's war fortunes—was unavailing.[48] The Doge of Venice and the Senate gave their support to this proposal, and on March 29, 1516, an edict was passed formally endorsing it. Admitting that "the urgent needs of the present times" had made it necessary to allow the Jews "to come and live in Venice," the preamble to the decree stated that nevertheless "no godfearing subject of our state would have wished them, after their arrival, to disperse throughout the city, sharing houses with Christians and going wherever they choose by day and night, perpetuating all those misdemeanors and detestable and abominable acts which are generally known and shameful to describe, with grave offense to the Majesty of God and uncommon notoriety on the part of this well-ordered Republic." As such, all the Jews living at present in the city, as well as those yet to come, were "to go at once to dwell together in the houses in the court within the Geto at San Hironimo [i.e., the Ghetto Nuovo], where there is plenty of room for them to live."[49] Christian inhabitants of this area were compelled to vacate their homes, and the Christian landlords of the houses on the site were to be permitted to raise the rents by one-third to induce them to comply with the order. Gates were to be erected in two places, to be opened in the morning at the ringing of the *marangona* (the largest bell in St. Mark's Campanile) and locked in the evening with permanent, round-the-clock surveillance (at the Jews' expense), and strict penalties were to be imposed on any Jew caught outside after curfew. Moreover, those areas of the courtyard open to the canal were to be sealed off with walls, and the outward-facing quays were to be bricked over, to close off the possibility of unsupervised entrance and exit. Thus the residential restriction of the Jews of Venice came into being, and the historic connection between the idea of segregation and the word *ghetto* was born.

The site of the former annex to the Venetian foundry would become the mandatory home of the Jews of Venice (at least, the first wing of that home) for 281 years. Yet there is every reason to believe that the Venetian Senate of 1516 would have been shocked and even scandalized if its members could have peered into the future and glimpsed that duration. For the creation of the ghetto did not resolve the issue of permitting a Jewish presence in Venice; it only tabled the matter. With the lapse of the original five-year charter of 1513 allowing Jews to live and work as moneylenders in Venice, the debate over whether to extend their settlement privileges (then restricted to the ghetto) or to return them to Mestre was taken up again, proving just as divisive. The forces that had opposed the admission of the Jews years earlier had not been mollified. Even Zacaria Dolfin, who had successfully pushed for housing the Jews in the Ghetto Nuovo a few years earlier, now argued for sending them all back to the mainland, noting that "if we keep them we must beware of the wrath of God, and that there are no Jews in France or Spain, and God prospers those kingdoms." (To which some senators responded that "the Jews were driven from Spain and exported great wealth therefrom," and after relocating to Constantinople "the Sultan Selim conquered both Syria and Egypt."[50]) In the end, the vote to extend the Jewish right of residence for a period of four years was much closer than the vote to restrict the Jews to the ghetto had been in 1516. Since the legal basis of the pre-emancipated Venetian Jewish community would always be the *condotta,* or temporary charter of no more than ten years, this touch-and-go status remained the norm well into the sixteenth and seventeenth centuries, even after the

Plan of the Jewish Ghetto of Venice, by Italian architect Guido Costante Sullam. The Ghetto Vecchio is the shaded area immediately to the south of the Ghetto Nuovo (dark shading), and the Ghetto Nuovissimo is directly east of the Ghetto Nuovo.

ghetto was expanded in 1541 to include the Ghetto Vecchio (the original foundry) to accommodate Levantine Jewish merchants and then again in 1633 to include the Ghetto Nuovissimo. Over the years, the moments in which the fate of the Jewish community of Venice appeared truly to hang in the balance became more infrequent. To the end of the Republic of Venice, however, the Jews, even at their most established, lived "on sufferance and not as of right."[51]

Although there was precedent for Venice's establishment of the ghetto, there is no evidence the Venetians drew on it. In none of the reports of the deliberations leading up to the edict of ghettoization were there allusions to prior instances of cities or states forcibly enclosing their Jews or even to church councils that promoted residential segregation. Indeed, it is possible that the template for the ghetto was taken not from older models of Jewish segregation, but from Venice's previously demonstrated interest in imposing residential restrictions on German merchants operating in the city. By the time the ghetto was established in 1516, Venice had already taken steps toward segregating most German merchants in the walled compound known as the *Fondaco dei Tedeschi,* complete with a curfew and a gate that was closed at sunset. Alternatively, the state may have been influenced by its earlier, relatively ineffective efforts to relegate prostitutes to separate quarters.[52] But all this is conjectural. In the end, Venice's decision to ghettoize rather than expel its Jews may have been unusual for the time, but it is difficult to credit it with a conceptual breakthrough in light of the genealogy of the "ghetto before the *ghetto.*"

Beyond even the existence of precedent for Jewish segregation and how it may (or may not) have influenced the Venetians, there is the issue of intent. The Senate did not set out, in 1516, to institute a new modus operandi for the treatment of Jews in Christian Europe. Its invention was a largely tactical, temporizing response to an unforeseen and generally unwanted development, a pragmatic balancing of economic and religious interests governed by local, short-term thinking. The Venetian Ghetto was, at its core, a compromise, in the sense of perpetually deferring a resolution of Jewish legal status. More germanely, it was a compromise between acceptance and expulsion.[53] For those who wished to see less of the Jews, the ghetto—while not really hindering Jewish mobility by day—relegated them to the northern fringe of the city by night. Yet it also made possible the emergence of a public, official Jewish community in Venice where none had existed previously.

If the Venetian Republic had no objective of establishing a new norm by creating the "first ghetto" in 1516, the same cannot be said of the papal states, which followed Venice in segregating its Jews some four decades later. On July 14, 1555, the recently installed and vituperatively anti-Jewish Pope Paul IV released a bull titled *Cum nimis absurdum* ("Since it is absurd"). As the former cardinal Gian Pieto Carafa, the pope had already demonstrated his anti-Jewish bona fides by overseeing the burning of the Talmud in the Campo di Fiori two years earlier, in 1553. Now came what was arguably the most noxious papal bull in all of Jewish history. It began by stating that it was "absurd and improper" that Jews, "whose own guilt has consigned them to perpetual servitude," should take advantage of Christian toleration by dwelling "side by side with Christians and near their churches, with no distinct habit to separate them," and even building homes in the best neighborhoods of the city. Since, however, the church only tolerated the Jews "to the end [*ad hoc, ut*] that they . . . should at length recognize their errors, and make all haste to arrive at the true light of the Catholic faith," they should be made to "recognize through experience" that "as long as they persist in their errors . . . they have been made slaves while Christians have been free through Jesus Christ, God and Our Lord."[54] Accordingly, the bull imposed a sweeping set of restrictions on the Jews of the papal states aimed at intensifying their segregation and stifling their economy. The Jews were to be reduced to one synagogue per city and to be prohibited from owning property. They were to be required, both men and women, to "wear in full view a hat or some obvious marking . . . in such a way that they may not be concealed or hidden." They were barred from employing Christian wet nurses or servants of either sex; they were forbidden from working in public on Sundays and Christian festivals; and they were not to associate with Christians on familiar terms. Jewish physicians were prohibited from taking care of Christian patients; Jewish loan-banks were to be constrained in their ability to compute interest and redeem pledges; and Jewish commerce in general was to be limited to the sale of strazzaria, secondhand clothing. Above all—and first on the list of impositions—the area where Jews (and only Jews) were to be allowed to live was to be meticulously sealed off. "In all future times in this city, as in all other cities, holdings, and territories belonging to the Roman Church," the bull stated,

> all Jews should live solely in one and the same location, or if that is
> not possible, in two or three or as many as are necessary, which are
> to be contiguous and separated completely from the dwellings of
> Christians. These places are designated by us in our city and by our
> magistrates in the other cities, holdings, and territories. And they
> should have one entry alone, and one exit.[55]

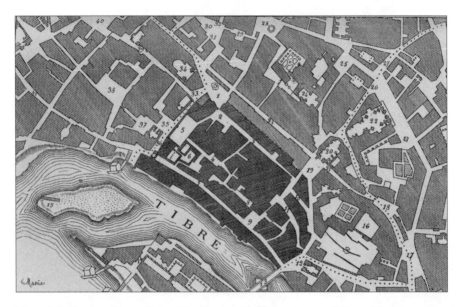

Map of the Roman Ghetto, from Giambattista Nolli's 1748 map of Rome. The ghetto is indicated with the darker cross-hatching.

Thirty-nine years after its emergence in Venice, the ghetto had come to Rome, and the Jewish efforts to avert the decree were just as futile as they had been earlier. Unlike in Venice, where the ghetto was created in an area with no prior history of quartering Jews, here the ghetto was established on the site of what had long been one of the main Jewish neighborhoods of Rome, the Rione (or district) of Sant' Angelo, on the left bank of the Tiber, not far from the Vatican on the other side of the river. On July 26— which coincided with the saddest day on the Jewish calendar, the Ninth of Av (Tisha B'Av), commemorating the destruction of the First and Second Temples—those Jews who did not already live in the area designated for the ghetto were driven there and the construction of a wall began. Ghettos were also established in other cities belonging to the popes, but fourteen years later, in 1569, after Pope Pius V expelled the Jews from throughout the church's dominions, only two ghettos were allowed to remain in the papal states—the Roman Ghetto and the ghetto of the Adriatic port city of Ancona.

Many of the decrees of *Cum nimis absurdum,* even if new to Rome and the papal states and shocking in their scope, were amply foreshadowed in the history of the church and Christendom. As early as the

Theodosian Code of 438 C.E. there had been an attempt to forbid the construction of new synagogues, even if the hard cap imposed by Paul IV was unprecedented. The ban on owning land and property had medieval antecedents. The Third Lateran Council of 1179 contained the prohibition on Jews employing Christian servants and wet nurses; the Fourth Lateran Council of 1215 introduced the notorious Jewish badge. The residential segregation of Jews also had precedent—in the proclamations of church councils and synods dating back to the thirteenth century, in the sporadic efforts to restrict Jews to particular quarters thereafter, and, above all, in the Venetian Ghetto. This continuity with the Venetian example would eventually come to be reflected in the place name. The earliest phrases used by the church to refer to the obligatory Jewish residence included *claustro degli ebrei,* the "cloister of the Jews" (or, in Latin, the *septus hebraeorum*), and the *serraglio degli ebrei,* "the enclosure of the Jews." Yet in 1562, Pope Pius V, in his bull *Dudum a felicis,* referred to the *septus hebraeoum* as a *ghectum,* presumably a Latinization of "ghetto": the first evidence of the use of the word *ghetto* to refer to a compulsory Jewish quarter in a generic sense. Starting at this point, it became possible to live not merely in "*the* Ghetto" (of Venice) but "*a* ghetto," and in the aftermath of the Vatican's decision to concentrate Jewish populations in the papal states, both the institution of the compulsory Jewish quarter and the labeling of such quarters as ghettos spread throughout Italy.

At its inaugural transfer, from Venice to Rome, the concept of the ghetto had undergone a mutation. In Venice, it was chiefly a compromise between religious ideals and the practical demands of providing credit to the poor and eventually, with the admission of Levantine and Ponentine (Spanish and Portuguese) merchants, maintaining Venice's foothold in maritime trade. The Roman Ghetto sought to hem in Jews physically and economically as never before, but still assigned them a place, however narrow and stigmatized, within the city. Yet the popes viewed the ghetto as more than simply a device for striking an equilibrium between acceptance and expulsion. Jews had lived in Rome from before the establishment of the Roman Empire. Unlike in Venice, the creation of the ghetto in Rome could not be conceptually linked to the construction of a community. If the Venetian Ghetto represented a move in the direction of greater (if still hedged) inclusion, the Roman Ghetto was just the opposite. The papal ghetto was a punishment of sorts, one (albeit major) component of a concerted assault on Jewish life designed to make Jews thoroughly miserable and reduce them to penury. Imbued with Catholic Reformation zeal, the popes of the second half of the sixteenth century saw the ghetto as part of a policy of "pious lashes" that, by subjecting the Jews to harsh discipline, might fulfill its purpose and accelerate their conversion.[56] This goal was clearly signaled in the preamble to *Cum nimis absurdum*, which effectively justified the ghetto along with the rest of the battery of the anti-Jewish measures it initiated on the grounds that the church only tolerated the Jews "to the end [*ad hoc ut*] that they ... should at length recognize their errors, and make all haste to arrive at the true light of the Catholic faith." The point of the papal ghetto was not to juggle religious and economic interests, but to insist on the utter primacy of the former; it was not to suspend or defer a final ruling on the legitimacy of a Jewish presence (while keeping Jews closed up so long as they were in the city), but to hasten a resolution of this problem once and for all. The cultural significance of the Roman Ghetto was thus different from that of its Venetian prototype. Its underlying motivation was conversionary as opposed to largely prophylactic. Rome is where the idea of the ghetto became an institution, one that most other Italian cities and states with Jewish populations would adopt in the following centuries.

The *Accademia della Crusca*, the oldest linguistic academy in the world and to this date Italy's main center for the study of the Italian language, was founded in Florence in 1583. It became especially well known for its dictionary, the *Vocabolario della lingua italiana*, which it published for the first time in 1612. The word *ghetto* appears in the *Vocabolario* for the first time in the third, 1691 edition. There, sandwiched between the entries for "Ghermire" and "Ghezzo," it is defined as "that collection of several houses, where the Jews live" *(quel raccolto di più case, dove abitano gli Ebrei).*[57] By 1691, ghettos had been established in most towns or cities in Italy where Jews lived. In the Medici state of Tuscany, ghettos were established in Florence (1571) and Siena (1572); in the Venetian Terra Ferma, in Verona (1600) and Padua (1601); in the Duchy of Mantua (1612) ruled by the Gonzagas; in cities annexed by the papal states, like Ferrara (1624) and Urbino (1634); in Modena (1638) and Reggio Emilia

(1670), under the ducal rule of the d'Este family; in Piedmontese Turin (1671); and in many other towns and cities. The creation of ghettos would continue, especially in Piedmont, well into the eighteenth century. The two major exceptions to what became the general pattern in Italy were the Tuscan port city of Livorno and Pisa, where ghettos were never established. The word *ghetto* was used as early as the Tuscan legislation establishing the obligatory Jewish quarters of Florence and Siena; it was also increasingly used by the Jews themselves, as the Hebrew minutes of the community organizations of the Jews of Padua from the 1580s (some two decades before a ghetto was finally created in the city) and of the Jews of Mantua from the 1610s indicate.[58] As was true in the case of Rome, the general adoption of the institution of the compulsory, segregated, and enclosed Jewish quarter throughout Italy—and of the term *ghetto* to denote it—does not mean that the motivations and meanings underlying the creation of a ghetto were entirely consistent from place to place. The ghetto of Florence was neither a Venetian-style compromise between economic and religious interests nor a punitive and conversionary measure in the mold of the papal ghetto of Rome. Rather, the Florentine ghetto was principally an expression of early modern "state-building," as the Grand Duchy of Tuscany sought to centralize and magnify its power through tighter control and spatial consolidation of the confessional communities that lived therein.[59] It may be the case that *ghetto* everywhere in Italy became the de facto term for "where the Jews live," yet this terse definition was only the common denominator of a concept with many associations.

Taking a closer look at this definition, we might wonder at its minimalism. Calling the ghetto "a collection of houses, where the Jews live" papers over the external force involved in keeping them there. Why simply the place "where the Jews live" as opposed to where they are restricted by law? There is a blurring of the line between "choice" and "compulsion" that would later characterize the fate of the word *ghetto*. Another striking feature of this 1691 definition is its matter-of-factness, even neutrality. This same emphasis on a general nonjudgmental description (mixed with local boosterism) is found in the Venetian scholar Francesco Sansovino's treatment of the ghetto. Sansovino depicts the "communal enclosure" or ghetto of the Jews in Venice as a noteworthy yet utterly normal feature of Venetian cosmopolitanism: "for as this state has been frequented by many peoples of every language and country, there were likewise Jews." In reportorial style, he describes, among other things, the creation of the ghetto in 1516, its spatial configuration, and the presence in it of a public official charged with overseeing the pawnshops and ensuring that the poor were not cheated. With considerable exaggeration, he characterizes the Jewish moneylenders as very opulent and rich, though the claim that "they dwell more willingly in Venice than in any other part of Italy"—this at a time when most Italian cities did not yet have ghettos—is plausible, considering the steady population increase that made the Venetian Ghetto so overcrowded. Situated between accounts of the Arsenale and the city's gardens, the entry on "ghetto" reads like a primer on "where the Jews live," without negative connotations or insinuations. If it is skewed, it is only to make the city's mandatory Jewish quarter appear happier and wealthier (and the city of Venice more tolerant) than it was in reality.[60] The absence of pejorative implications is similarly evident in the 1573 petition of Turkish merchants in Venice to be granted "a place of their own, as the Jews have their ghetto."[61]

While Christians may not have been permitted to live in the ghetto, it was hardly off-limits to them. As Donatella Calabi has written with respect to Venice, "shops of printers, booksellers, and jewelers, employing both Christian and Jewish workers and often housed in sublet rooms or attics, brought into the ghettos a virtual mob of casual laborers from both faiths—porters, street cleaners, water carriers, attendants of stalls and pitches, wandering vendors, and lackeys of the magistrates, all given the occasion and the pretext to crowd together, elbow to elbow."[62] Christians came to the ghetto to borrow on pledges, buy strazzaria, or cut deals with wholesale merchants. As we know from the autobiography of the seventeenth-century Venetian rabbi Leon Modena and from several travel accounts of Christian visitors, they even came to observe Sabbath services in synagogue and to listen to the Italian-language sermons. Indeed, "ghetto tourism," often thought of as something that began with middle- and upper-class "slumming" in late-nineteenth-century London and New York, has a much older pedigree. Several accounts of visits to the Italian ghettos have survived from as early as 1532, only sixteen years after the creation of the Ghetto of Venice and before the institution had spread throughout Italy. While there is extensive variety in the testimonies of visitors, which differ in everything from their length, detail, and accuracy to the degree to which they are clouded by anti-Jewish prejudice, together they offer a window into how the ghetto appeared to the foreign gaze that goes well beyond the early dictionary definition of "where the Jews live."[63] Visually, the travelers were struck by the dramatic height of the buildings, with their seven to nine stories in some cases and numerous subdivisions to accommodate the overcrowding of the ghetto. They commented (at times erroneously) on the color of Jewish headgear and on the physiognomy of the men and women. The English traveler Thomas Coryat, the first to use the word *ghetto* in English, was so taken by the noble bearing of the Levantine Jewish merchants in Venice that he concluded that "our English proverbe: To looke like a Jewe (whereby is meant sometimes a weather beaten warp-faced fellow, sometimes a phrenticke and lunaticke person, sometimes one discontented) is not true." Of the Jewish women he saw, he added that "some were as beautiful as ever I saw, and so gorgeous in their apparel, jewels, chaines of gold, and rings adorned with precious stones, that some of our English Countesses do scarce exceed them."[64] Less is said about the smells of the Jewish quarter, though one can imagine that "their strength and pungency were of course heightened by the shut-in nature of the ghettos."[65] Occasionally, travel accounts betray the unconscious influence of the stereotype of the *foetor judaicus*, "the stench of the Jew." Nicolas Audeber, a sixteenth-century French traveler who surveyed the Italian ghettos, wrote that "their men . . . have for the most part a bad mark, which is that they smell quite bad from a disagreeable, penetrating odor. I will guard my tongue on whether it is because of the garlic they use on all their meats or because of another secret reason that some allege."[66] For the most part, until the late eighteenth century, travel accounts do not portray the ghetto as a site of material filth and disorder. The figurative use of the word *ghetto* to denote a *Luogo sordido e sudicio* ("a sordid and dirty place") is only evident in Italian dictionaries from the nineteenth century onward.[67] Nevertheless, the association of the Jew with impurity, spiritual as well as physical, had deep roots in the Western Christian imaginary. Referring to the annual inundations of the Roman Ghetto by the overflow of the Tiber River, Filippo Maria Bonini, the vicar of Palestrina, said in 1663 that "the obstinate people get some benefit from the flood. They refuse to wash off the filth of the soul in baptismal waters, but at least those of the flooding Tiber wash off the dirt and stench of their bodies."[68]

Still, Jewish otherness had, by the late eighteenth century, entered the dictionary definition of *ghetto* with respect to one sense alone: sound. In 1798, as ghetto walls were being hacked to pieces and Jewish communities were being (temporarily) liberated throughout Italy, the Italian linguist Francesco Alberti di Villanuova provided the most elaborate definition of the word *ghetto* that had appeared in any reference work to that point. His entry on "ghetto," which appeared in the third volume of his *Universal Critical-Encyclopedical Dictionary of the Italian Language,* included the phrase *fare un ghetto,* literally "to make a ghetto," which, the author explains, "is said when many together want to say their piece, whence arises a tumult similar to that of the Jews when they sing in their synagogues."[69] Villanuova took this language verbatim from the notes to a 1729–1730 collection of Italian sonnets (the *Pleasant Rhymes*) by the satirical poet Giovanni Battista Fagiuoli. There, Fagiuoli uses this phrase to explain the following verse: "All at once the father-in-law would have spoken / And her sisters and brothers / Would have replied and made a Ghetto."[70] Fagiuoli's note implies that this colloquial usage of "ghetto" was unusual enough in the early eighteenth century to require clarification, though the phrase *si dice* ("it is said") suggests he did not invent it. Yet, the association of the ghetto with cacophony drew on a venerable link between Jews and noise in the Western Christian mind.[71] The phrase *fare un ghetto* echoed earlier medieval epithets such as *Lärm wie in einer Judenschule* (noise as in the synagogue) and *das geshray der Judischeit in irer synagog* (the cries of Jews in their synagogues), and indeed, the creation of the Frankfurt Judengasse in 1462 was at least premised on the need to protect the city's main cathedral from the clamorous, contaminating sounds of Jewish prayer in the nearby Jewish quarter. Coryat's description of the synagogue service he attended in Venice bore all the marks of this stereotype of the synagogue as the site of raucous noise. The public recitation of the Torah, he wrote, was characterized "not by a sober, distinct, and orderly reading, but by an exceeding loud yaling, undecent roaring, and as it were a beastly bellowing of it forth. And that after such a confused and hudling manner, that I thinke the hearers can very hardly understand him: sometimes he cries out alone, and sometimes againe some others serving as it were his Clerkes hard without his seate, and within, do roare with him, but so that his voyce (which he straineth so high as if he sung for a wager) drowneth all the rest."[72] With respect to the noise accusation, it was only a short step from the synagogue to the ghetto as a whole: for "outside the synagogue, but still within the compressed space of the ghetto, the demographic density could only accentuate the characteristic noisiness."[73] With the demise of Jewish segregation by law, the fear of Jewish noise pollution—now no longer restricted to the ghetto—was occasionally magnified. Thus in 1871, just months after the dismantling of the Roman Ghetto, Pope Pius IX grumbled of the Jews that "we have too many of these dogs in Rome these days, whom we hear barking up and down the streets, annoying everyone everywhere."[74]

Jews nearly always mounted some form of resistance (albeit varying in both intensity and effectiveness) to ghettoization when it was first proposed or legally enacted. They generally made an effort to forestall the decree, if not to scuttle it entirely. Yet in almost all cases, the thrust of the opposition was more practical than conceptual. The Jews' main concerns were the proposed location of the ghetto, especially if it was to be situated in a marginal, lightly populated area where they would be more vulnerable to mob violence and more distant from the city's commerce. They also worried about the financial losses they would incur as a result of moving into an area with limited housing and high rents that was cut off from their places of business. Such objections were raised in Venice, Verona, Padua, Trieste, and elsewhere.[75] In Frankfurt, the Jews sought to preempt the plan to relocate them to the easternmost edge of the city by suggesting that the more central area they were currently living in be legally and physically segregated. The Jews regularly complained (and, even after moving into the ghetto, continued to complain) about the size of the ghetto, its specific boundaries, degree of congestion, and quality of living conditions. Rarely, however, at least before the second half of the eighteenth century, did they charge the basic idea of the ghetto with being cruel and unjust. In the case of the Jews of Rome, for whom the ghetto came rapidly and without advance warning, the initial response was the height of understatement: "the Pope has ordered the Jews to live together."[76]

THE EARLY HISTORY OF THE GHETTO

Jewish historical writers of the sixteenth century, writing in the wake of *Cum nimis absurdum*, described the papal bull and the larger context of Paul IV's persecution of the Jews in muted terms. The bull contained several measures aimed at segregating and impoverishing the Jewish community, the first of which concerned the creation of a mandatory ghetto. Yet the initial Jewish descriptions of the bull often mix up the order of the stipulations, with the ghetto appearing out of sequence. In 1557, Immanuel Benvenuto prefaced his grammar *Graceful Wreath* with a dirge (*kinah*) on the events that had befallen the Jews of the papal states from the burning of the Talmud in 1553 to the martyrdom of twenty-four former Marranos in Ancona in 1556. Only after referencing in verse the requirement that Jews wear a special hat or badge, refrain from hiring Christian wet nurses, and maintain only one synagogue does the poem come to the ghetto decree. "Their dwelling is in garbage heaps—and in ruins and ravines," the verse reads, suggesting that what was objectionable was not so much the creation of a restricted quarter, but its location in a slum earmarked for dogs and prostitutes.[77] The chronicler Gedalyah ibn Yahya, in his 1587 *Chain of Tradition*, similarly placed the bull's demand "that all the Jews live in one neighborhood, whose gates are to be shut every night" after the order regarding distinguishing signs; the historian Joseph Ha-Kohen, in his 1575 *Book of the Vale of Tears*, did likewise.[78] In all three cases, the degree to which the ghetto now stood at the very foundation of the church's segregationist program seemed to escape notice; of far greater immediate concern were the mandatory badge and the closing of synagogues, not to mention the attack on the Talmud and the persecution of ex-conversos. Even Joseph Ha-Kohen's phrasing of the ghetto edict—"And he settled them on the edge of the land by themselves, so that neither the uncircumcised nor the impure live among them to this day"—implied that the restriction to one segregated neighborhood, by ridding the community of gentile pollution, was not without its benefits.[79]

The rise of a folk etymology in the late sixteenth century linking the word *ghetto* to the Hebrew term *get*, or bill of divorce, reflects the change that had taken place in how Jews related to the new reality of their spatial confinement. A Roman Jewish notarial document from 1589, rather than referring to Rome's compulsory Jewish quarter by the then-customary term *serraglio*, called it *nostro* (our) *ghet*, and this label became the new norm.[80] Roman Jewry routinely referred to the *ghetto* as a *get*, and while there are other linguistic reasons for why they may have initially shortened the term, the community's archives suggest that eventually they did come to connect it with the Hebrew גט *(get)*. The appearance of *get* some thirty-four years after *Cum nimis absurdum*, in the wake of measures taken by Pope Sixtus V to alleviate somewhat the overcrowding of the ghetto, reflected a critical change that had taken place in the collective mentality of Rome's Jews. Paradoxically, Sixtus V's slight relaxation of the restrictions and burdens on the Jewish community confirmed, for Jews, that the ghetto was no short-term separation, but a final rupture, and this recognition in turn gave rise to an association between the *ghetto* (which henceforth appeared in Jewish notarial documents with growing frequency, written alternately as *ghet, gete, gette, ghetto, and getto*) and a bill of divorce. Whether this in fact was proof of a tectonic shift in Roman Jewish consciousness, and not simply a pun on one Jewish notary's part, the association of ghetto with *get* had become ubiquitous.[81] Nor was this limited to Rome: documents from both Verona and Mantua indicate the use of *get* for *ghetto* was absorbed there too.[82] A connection between *ghetto* and divorce is found in Isaac Cantarini's 1685 *The Fear of Isaac*, which recounts an attempted sacking of the Paduan ghetto by a Christian mob a year earlier. Describing the forced segregation of the Jews of Padua decades earlier, Cantarini writes that they named the new restricted zone "Ghetto [גיטו], a *get* [גט] for a divorced woman, a poor, sad woman abandoned like a tamarisk in the desert."[83]

Coincidence or not, around the time Cantarini's work was published, the linkage between *ghetto* and *get* began to spread to the non-Jewish world. By the mid-seventeenth century, knowledge of the origin of the word *ghetto* had receded to the vanishing point. Leading scholars of the Italian language confessed to their ignorance of its etymology. In his *Origines linguae italicae* (1676), the philologist Ottavio Ferrari wrote *"ignotae originis"* in his entry for *ghetto;* nearly ten years later, Gilles Ménage, in his groundbreaking etymological dictionary of Italian, concurred, speculating that the word might derive from *Giudaicetum,* but admitting, "I don't know."[84] But it is just at this point that an etymology linking *ghetto* to the Hebrew term *get,* meaning deed of divorce, began to surface in print. Three years after the publication of Cantarini's *The Fear of Isaac,* Paolo Minucci explained the text's use of the term *ghetto* thus:

"*Ghetto* is a Chaldean word, which signifies *bill of divorce;* whence we say *Ghetto* to mean *a place of people [who are] segregated and cut off from commerce with other men.*"[85] This explanation (with Chaldean swapped for Hebrew) rapidly became the new orthodoxy, receiving the stamp of approval of several other linguists over the next two centuries.[86] Perhaps its most significant endorsement appeared in the German historian Ferdinand Gregorovius's *The Ghetto and the Jews of Rome* (1853), arguably the most famous work written about the Roman Ghetto in the nineteenth century. That was likely the high point of its credibility. In the decades that followed, the Venetian etymology made a comeback, and the ghetto-as-*get* theory began a slow decline.

As the years passed, and the ghetto became recognized as a central part of the Italian (and eventually more general) Jewish experience, the idea that the term had its source in the Hebrew for bill of divorce acquired a different sort of allure. It appeared to confer on *ghetto* a beginning commensurate with the meaning and importance of the phenomenon itself, uniting word and thing in a clearly motivated sign. By the late eighteenth and nineteenth centuries, it dovetailed neatly with an emerging "enlightened" outlook that attributed Jewish separatism principally to a long history of Christian hatred and rejection. While no longer compelling as an account of the origins of the word *ghetto*, the ghetto-as-*get* etymology is historically significant as a window into the adventures of the term itself. Likening the ghetto to a divorce suggested that it was the product of a rupture that took place at a particular moment. Confinement to a ghetto reflected a change in Jewish circumstances and their relations with gentiles, not a permanent condition of Jewish exile. There is a sense of "before" and "after," with the ghetto on the side of the latter, precisely the reverse of what would later occur in the age of revolution and emancipation, when the ghetto became seen as the quintessential "before" to modernity's "after."

The construing of the ghetto as a "bill of divorce" from Christian society would, over time, take on an increasingly tragic cast, but it is not at all clear that contemporary Jews understood their alienation in the same light. Some, at least, sought to impute positive meaning to their separation behind ghetto walls. Medieval Jews had long viewed their dispersed nuclei as "holy communities" *(kehillot kedoshot),* bound together by piety and the study of sacred texts. "The policy of Paul IV . . . bestowed upon the Jews in the form of the ghetto wall that which they had never before enjoyed during the entire tenure of the European diaspora, a physical boundary for their Holy Community."[87] The Roman Ghetto, at least in its initial stages, was fashioned by Jews into a sacred precinct, whose enclosure only magnified the intensity and vitality of Jewish cultural and communal life. Yet the most striking example of a ritual valorization of ghettoization comes from the Jewish community of Verona. Nearly a hundred years ago, the great historian of Italian Jewry, Cecil Roth discovered evidence, from the mid-eighteenth century, of a ceremony held by the Jews of Verona every year on the first day of the Hebrew month of Shevat. On that date, in 1600, the community had moved into the newly created ghetto of the city, where they still found themselves roughly a century and a half later, when Roth's source for the annual commemoration was written. Verona's Jews commemorated what they referred to as *kenisat hatser ha-geto*, the "entry into the enclosure of the ghetto" with a torch-lit procession of the Torah scrolls around the synagogue. They recited the Hallel prayer reserved for festive days of the Jewish calendar, along with special hymns. A rabbinic sermon composed for the occasion in 1765 connected the biblical exodus from Egypt to the entry of Jews into the ghetto, finding in both the hand of God. "On that very day," the sermon's author claimed, referring to the date on which Jews had entered the ghetto a century and a half earlier, "the Lord took the Israelites out from among the nations and performed for us miracles and wonders . . . and on that account we are gathered together to give thanks to His great Name, may He be blessed."[88]

Much remains obscure about this little festival, which faded from memory after the Jews of Verona were emancipated by French revolutionary armies in 1797. While we find other positive assessments of the restriction of Jews to a particular quarter in Jewish writing of the time, few other examples of special rites to celebrate the creation of a ghetto have come down to us. Perhaps other Jewries were less sanguine. Even the Verona festival, it has been argued, was a celebration not of ghettoization per se, but of the fact the community had been spared expulsion or relegation to an outlying slum.[89] Be that as it may, the Verona case suggests that there were Jews who regarded their spatial concentration as a blessing and not a curse. They associated segregation in a crowded neighborhood with survival, not attrition. The ghetto, in this view, was not the most recent of the many afflictions of *galut,* or exile. It was, on the contrary, a precursor of redemption, the influx of diverse communities of Jews into the ghetto foreshadowing the ingathering of exiles in messianic times.

The separation afforded by the ghetto might also be appreciated for easing the fulfillment of certain principles of halakhah. To permit the carrying of certain objects outside the home on the Sabbath, Jewish law requires the creation of an eruv, a kind of ritual enclosure that symbolically merges the "private" and "public" domains (between which the transferring of objects is forbidden) into one common area. By walling off the Jewish quarter from the rest of the city, the ghetto essentially became a private domain (*reshut ha-yahid*), within which carrying was allowed on the Sabbath. Yet some interpreted the space within which the ghetto permitted carrying more expansively. Traditionally, one of the ways Jewish communities have secured the right to carry on the Sabbath throughout a town or city is by "renting" the streets and public domains from the municipal government. Yet the requirement to rent non-Jewish areas to permit carrying only applies in areas where two or more Jews are living. According to the Talmud, a single Jew who lives alone in a courtyard of gentiles may carry on the Sabbath without paying rent. With the rise of mandatory Jewish quarters in the early modern period, some rabbinic authorities began to argue that the ghetto itself—by concentrating all the Jews of the city in one location—fell within this legal category of the single Jew surrounded by gentiles, and therefore permitted carrying throughout the city, even without the payment of rent to the non-Jewish rulers. That is the upshot of a remarkable *teshuvah* (or responsum) by a Rabbi Raphael Israel Kimhi, written to a petitioner from Ferrara in 1730:

> In years past [the Jews] were dispersed throughout the city and fulfilled the decree of the sages [with respect to carrying on the Sabbath] by rental. Thereafter, however, the gentiles and the government decreed that [the Jews] should all live together in one courtyard, namely, the ghetto. As a result, they were instantly converted by the government and the gentiles [to the status of] an individual [Jew] in the place of a gentile thus exempting them from [the obligation of] rental. And without question, this was from God, for God . . . saw

the poverty and sorrow [the Jews] suffered on account of having to rent the city from the king or ruler. . . . and therefore He, may He be blessed, took pity on his people to save them from sin and put in the heart of the government to decree that [the Jews] should be together in one courtyard, making them an individual in the place of a gentile and automatically freeing and exempting them from rental.[90]

Here, the placing of all the Jews in a ghetto is presented as an act not only of divine providence but also of divine mercy, because of its lifting of a legal and financial burden. A divorce, perhaps, but one that was devoutly to be wished for.

Over the past thirty years or so, scholars have increasingly questioned the degree to which ghettoization did in fact breed cultural isolation or "divorce." The thrust of this scholarship has been to portray the ghetto as a paradoxical space: a space of legally imposed separation and concentration, yet also of comings and goings and cross-cultural encounters; a space that united Jews of different backgrounds and at the same time frequently magnified their differences; a space that divided while also mediating between Jews and Christians, even as it also mediated between the medieval and the modern; a space in which, unexpectedly, Jewish culture and religion flourished. Far from simply representing the culmination and formalization of medieval segregation, the ghetto worked, by effect if not intent, to embed Jews within the fabric of the city by providing them with a place of their own, however limited and stigmatized: "a halfway house between acceptance and expulsion."[91] From a quasi-prison for Jews, the ghetto has come to figure in the latest research as a place of real, yet porous and permeable boundaries.[92]

We generally think of the ghetto as being of greatest relevance for Jewish life in the centuries before emancipation, a time that is often periodized in Jewish history as the "Age of the Ghetto" or "Ghetto Times." But this perception needs to be nuanced. The walled ghetto only emerged as the normative setting of Jewish existence in one place: the Italian peninsula. With few, albeit notable, exceptions (including, though not limited to, Frankfurt, Worms, Prague, and Metz), total residential segregation of Jews from Christians was not characteristic of England (after Jews were readmitted in the second half of the seventeenth century), Holland, France, or the Germanic lands; above all, it was not a distinguishing feature of the Polish-Lithuanian Commonwealth, where the vast majority of European Jews lived. Towns and cities occasionally placed restrictions on where Jews could live, designating certain streets and districts as off-limits, and as had long been their wont, Jews tended to congregate in particular neighborhoods of their own accord. But most European Jews in the early modern period lived in mixed communities and had Christian neighbors. If there was an "Age of the Ghetto" in Jewish history, it existed only in pre-emancipation Italy. Even there, moreover, it is difficult to find in the expansive Jewish literature of the age any evidence of a preoccupation with the ghetto, let alone an expression of acute distress caused by the experience of being forced to live in separate quarters. Not everyone celebrated it, to be sure, but few appear to have mourned it. The seventeenth-century Venetian rabbi Leon Modena's autobiography routinely refers to the Ghetto Nuovo and Ghetto Vecchio, and to the various accommodations he inhabited therein, but never once does he lament or even acknowledge the fact of Jewish residential restriction in the city. Nor, in his description of his travels throughout northern Italy does he deem it worthy of note to record when a Jewish community he visited had or lacked a ghetto.[93] A similar insouciance can be found in the work of Modena's contemporary, the Venetian rabbi Simone Luzzatto. In his 1638 *Discourse on the Situation of the Hebrews and in Particular Those Dwelling in the Illustrious City of Venice*, Luzzatto makes a case for the toleration of the Jews in Venice based on their economic utility to the Republic, grounded largely in the outsized role they played in the city's international trade. Only twice in his lengthy treatise does Luzzatto so much as mention the fact that Venice's Jews lived in a ghetto. In his calculation of the annual sum of ducats contributed by Jews to the state's treasury, Luzzatto notes, in addition to all the customs duties and the duties on imports, one final special tax: "the tax of one-fourth of the rents, which the Jews find very heavy, since the houses are appraised in proportion to the size of their dwellings, confined in the *cramped enclosure* of the ghetto."[94] Perhaps Luzzatto, for all his lavish praise of the Venetian government for its fair treatment of the Jews, and for all his assurance of the deep attachment of the Jews to the city, could not resist calling attention to a measure of injustice in the fact that Jews were forcibly concentrated in the "cramped enclosure" of the ghetto. Still, viewed in the context of Luzzatto's reasons for writing the *Discourse,* the ghetto—however cramped—barely registered as an afterthought. The year 1638 was extremely perilous for the Jews of Venice, when the future of the community appeared to hang in the balance. A major economic scandal, centered on a trove of stolen goods discovered in the ghetto, seemed to drive animus against the Jews to an all-time high and generated deep concern that the expulsion of the Jews not just from the ghetto but also from all of Venice's territories might be imminent. With possible expulsion looming, and with the ghetto now established as a part of Venetian Jewish life for more than a century, Luzzatto clearly had larger battles to fight. The ghetto may have shaped the horizons and possibilities of those who passed the bulk of their lives within it, but it was not as much a focus of obsessive attention as it would later become, perhaps because it was taken for granted. It is only in the late eighteenth century, when the liberalization of Jewish legal status was increasingly on the table in Western and Central Europe and the situation of Italian Jews being restricted to ghettos began to appear more anachronistic and anomalous, that we begin to encounter more evidence of Jewish and non-Jewish protest against the indignities of ghetto life.

2

THE NINETEENTH-CENTURY TRANSFORMATION OF THE GHETTO

THE WORD *GHETTO* WAS BORN in Venice, and for a brief time in the late eighteenth century, it appeared fated to die there. On the late afternoon of July 12, 1797 (though the parallel Jacobin date of 24 Messidor V, Year One of Italian Liberty, was far more suggestive of what was to come), a motley crowd congregated in the large square of the Ghetto Nuovo. Exactly two months earlier, the Venetian government, under the Doge, had abdicated in favor of a municipal council with Napoleon's armies encamped across the lagoon and poised to enter the city: the final act in the millennial history of the Most Serene Republic. On that afternoon, soldiers and civilians, men and women, and Jews and Christians gathered to carry out the municipality's order "that the Ghetto Gates . . . be taken down in order to eliminate that mark of segregation between the Jewish Citizens and the other Citizens, where none must exist." The spectacle that ensued had elements of both sober ceremony and spontaneous joy. Deeming the mere removal of the four wooden gates insufficient, the crowd tore them down to the ground, hacked them to pieces, and burnt them in a massive pyre in the middle of the Campo del Ghetto Nuovo. Throughout the demolition, men and women danced together, and even the rabbis "dressed in Mosaic garb" joined in, "producing a greater energy." The burning complete, the assembled, drawing on a script from many a previous revolutionary festival, planted a Liberty Tree in the center of the square, as if to declare the conquest of the ghetto by the ideals of *liberté, égalité,* and *fraternité* complete. According to the Venetian National Guardsman charged with directing the razing of the gates, all that remained to consummate the ghetto's makeover was to rename it. "O Citizens," he wrote, reporting on the day's events, "for the completion of your work it only remains to give a new name to the Ghetto in order to destroy this ignominious mark whose name still serves as a representation of the former separation, and I would suggest the substitution of the name Contrada della Riunione (Place of Meeting)." A day later, the municipal council voted to do just that. The legal segregation of Jews in Venice and the name that had become synonymous with it were officially no more.[1]

Place names, of course, are not so easily stricken from the popular lexicon and historical memory. Whether this particular name change would have proved effective in the fullness of time became moot shortly thereafter. On October 17 of the same year, the French ceded control of Venice to the Austrians in the Treaty of Campo Formio. With the formal entry of Austrian troops into Venice the following January, the political and civil equality the Jews had acquired in the short-lived period of French hegemony was largely rescinded, and many of the old restrictions on owning property and occupations open to Jews were reinstated. There was, however, a prominent exception to this rollback of rights: the Austrians did not bring back the ghetto, at least as a coercive institution. The roughly 1,600 Jews of Venice—though they hardly had time to leave in the months since the ghetto gates had fallen—were still free to settle elsewhere in the city.[2] Only one element of the Venice Ghetto was restored: the name itself. The Ghetto of Venice was no longer a technical ghetto, but it survived as a space and a name.[3]

What happened in Venice in 1797 was duplicated throughout Western and Central Europe toward the end of the eighteenth century. Venice's Jewish ghetto was neither the first nor the last to be liberated during Napoleon's Italian campaign.[4] The extent of the fanfare that greeted its fall may have been comparatively greater in Venice than in other cities, but the razing and burning of ghetto gates, the planting of a liberty tree, and even the renaming of a nearby street or quarter in honor of *concordia* or *libertà* were part of a ritual marking the sudden and far-reaching upheaval of the old order.[5] The desegregation of Jews that was celebrated in these pageants was rarely immediate, nor would it, in all cases, prove final. The revolutionary ideology that had imposed republican rule for all, including Jews, was typically forced into retreat along with Napoleon's armies. Nearly everywhere, Jews lost rights they had obtained as a result of the zigzagging course of the Napoleonic Wars; in a few instances they were even forcibly reghettoized. Still, the wave of liberations from 1796 to 1799 was the start of Jewish emancipation that went beyond France to the rest of continent, however protracted the attainment of legal equality would prove. And it was the death knell for the old Jewish ghetto.

From the late eighteenth century to 1870, when the last surviving official ghetto—the Ghetto of Rome—was dismantled, states progressively lifted residential restrictions that confined Jews to mandatory urban neighborhoods, and Jews, especially those with the financial resources to do so, steadily poured out of those cramped, dilapidated areas to form voluntary communities elsewhere. Urban renewal projects leveled the old, narrow alleys and rundown buildings of several ghettos (including, most notably, the Rome Ghetto, the Frankfurt Judengasse, and the Prague Judenstadt), to the point that only traces of the former Jewish settlements endured.[6] The road "out of the ghetto" was, in short, one that many a nineteenth-century Jew did travel. Still, the notion that the ghetto receded from most Western and Central European Jews' lived experience in the nineteenth century flattens a transformation that was in fact far more layered. This transformation involved an elevation of the word *ghetto* across multiple languages and an explosion of its range of meanings and insinuations at the very moment when the ghetto as a historical institution appeared to be everywhere on the wane. It was precisely when Jews began to leave the ghetto in ever greater numbers that the word *ghetto* came to loom ever larger in the Jewish mind as a site of memory that could be used as a rhetorical and ideological weapon. The "ghetto" gained a centrality in the Jewish imagination that, ironically, it had never really enjoyed in an earlier period. It emerged as a Jewish keyword that became, to quote Raymond Williams's definition of the keyword, indispensable not only for "discussing but at another level for seeing [their] most central experiences."[7] For modernizing Jews, the word *ghetto* came to play a role similar to that of the newly minted postrevolutionary term *"ancien régime"* for the French revolutionaries. It became the paramount metaphor for a premodern Jewish past destined for obliteration, but one that survived as a spectral presence. Wherever modernity and its package of promised goods—political emancipation, social mobility and embourgeoisement, cultural assimilation and acceptance—had yet to fully triumph, the image of the ghetto arose.[8] Indeed, the very elaboration of what Jewish modernity meant came to rely on a parallel construction of everything it was not, and that was increasingly subsumed under the rubric "ghetto." By the 1890s, a century after the revolutionary government in Venice sought to consign the word *ghetto* along with the ghetto gates to oblivion, the former had only grown in its semantic reach and signifying power.

That invading French armies would assign such importance to liberating ghettos in their victorious Italian campaigns reflected the rise of a new understanding, in eighteenth-century Europe, of the nature and sources of the "Jewish Question."[9] In the early modern period, the ghetto had been justified as a treatment aimed at curbing, if not curing, the threat that the toleration of a Jewish presence posed to Christendom. Some viewed the ghetto as an inoculation of sorts, a preventive measure that would protect society from contamination through careful regulation and enclosure of Jewish difference.[10] Others, like the popes, saw the ghetto as a more aggressive regimen whose ultimate goal was to dissolve Jewish difference, not simply contain it, by intensifying the pressure on Jews to convert.[11] Whatever the precise motivation for segregating Jews, it was Judaism itself that was the threat to the Christian body politic and the ghetto that was the antidote. In the last few decades of the eighteenth century, however, enlightened thinkers who continued to view Jewish particularity as problematic argued that the ghetto, far from fixing or alleviating the problem, was in fact one of its root causes. They advocated a remedy for Jewish difference centered on the razing of ghettos. This was part of a more general reformist discourse that pressed for the amelioration of Jewish legal status, on the grounds that the granting of civil parity to Jews was the surest route to erode their distinctive character and transform them into a productive segment of society.

A foundational text in this regard was the Prussian civil servant Christian Wilhelm von Dohm's *On the Civil Improvement of the Jews.* Written at the behest of Dohm's friend, the German Jewish Enlightenment philosopher Moses Mendelssohn, the 1781 tract anticipated arguments that would be made over nearly a century of literature devoted to championing Jewish enfranchisement.[12] While conceding that Jews were "more morally corrupt than other nations" as well as "more antisocial and clannish," Dohm claimed these qualities to be "a necessary and natural consequence of the oppressed condition in which they have been living for so many centuries." Jews were only contingently peculiar and contemptible, not essentially so. At bottom, Dohm asserted, "The Jew is even more man than Jew." If treated more humanely, Jews would naturally become "happier and better members of civil societies" and less obstinately different.[13]

Starting with the suggestion that Jews be given "equal rights with others subjects," Dohm proceeded to recommend additional means for the "civil improvement of the Jews." One practice he argued against was assigning Jews "separate districts" where they might be kept apart from other subjects. Noting that "the Jews, left entirely to themselves, would be strengthened in their prejudices against Christians, and vice versa," he wrote that the best recipe for diminishing this mutual hostility was to promote "frequent intercourse" between Jews and Christians and "sharing the burdens and advantages of the state." Dohm criticized the inhumanity of "restricted districts of Jewish residence," which were "remnants of the old harsh principles." Singling out the Frankfurt Judengasse as an especially egregious example of this callousness, he decried how Jews were "locked up every night" and "forced to build their houses many stories high and live under very crowded conditions resulting in uncleanliness, diseases, and bad policing, and greater danger of fire."[14]

Eight years later, on the eve of the French Revolution, the Jesuit priest Abbé Henri Baptiste Grégoire made his own plea for Jewish emancipation in his *Essay on the Physical, Moral and Political Reformation of the Jews*.[15] Like Dohm, Grégoire linked the granting of equal rights to Jews to the larger goal of advancing their "physical, moral, and political regeneration"; also like Dohm, he castigated the policy of the residential segregation of Jews. "It is very impolitic to assign separate quarters for the Jews," he titled one of the book's chapters, "as they ought to be dispersed among the Christians." Grégoire made a case against ghettos that was both more extended and more radical than Dohm's argument. By bottling Jews up in neighborhoods of their own, Grégoire claimed, the state only strengthened the bonds of Jewish collectivity and fanned the flames of Jewish hostility toward the Christian other. "To unite the Jews, with a view of freeing them from their prejudices," he wrote, "would be like throwing sulphur in a fire to weaken its activity. On the contrary, it will be necessary to separate them, and to destroy, as much as possible, all communication between them."[16] Liberating Jewish ghettos was thus less a humanitarian gesture than a means of removing a potentially lethal threat to the general welfare. The same prophylactic logic that once authorized the creation of ghettos now warranted their destruction. Proof that Grégoire cared more about dissipating Jewish particularism than any right to choose one's residence could be found in the lengths to which he went to avoid the emergence of de facto Jewish quarters. The state, he argued, should place a cap on the number of Jews permitted to settle in a particular street or neighborhood; "when this number is completed, the rest must be obliged to remove somewhere else." Integration, as opposed to simply desegregation, was the aim, even if the former entailed a new round of legal coercion.

Both the Prussian Dohm and the French Grégoire condemned the idea and institution of the ghetto. However, their critique indicates that the word *ghetto* had yet to become a general, pan-European signifier of Jewish segregation and solidarity. Dohm referred to *Judengassen,* or "Jewish streets" in German, noting in parentheses that these were known as *Juiveries* in France.[17] Grégoire did allude to the practice in some Italian cities of "shutting them [the Jews] up every evening in the *Ghetto,*" though he hastened to add that "the separate streets assigned them are thus named."[18] In Italy of the 1780s, there was no true equivalent to the discussion of the Jewish Question that erupted in that decade in Germany and France, at least in terms of its importance. Before the mid-nineteenth century, few Italians spoke out for expanding Jewish civil liberties with the zeal of a Dohm or Grégoire. Nevertheless, there were some Italian echoes of the emergent discourse on Jewish legal rights, and in this literature, not surprisingly, the word *ghetto* featured more prominently.[19]

The most salient example was a book titled *The Influence of the Ghetto on the State,* written by the Mantuan noble and political economist Count Giovanni Battista Gherardo D'Arco.[20] The first volume of the book, which was published in 1782, appeared amidst a wave of reforms enacted by the Habsburg emperor Joseph II between 1781 and 1789, aimed at an economic and cultural transformation of Jews throughout his Central European realm. An avid proponent of both enlightened absolutism and physiocratic and cameralist economics, Joseph II intended these measures, the so-called Edicts of Tolerance, "to make the Jewish nation useful and serviceable to the state."[21] Their thrust was to enlarge the scope of Jewish educational and economic opportunities, while eliminating some of the more humiliating discriminatory measures against them, from the body tax to the requirement that Jews visibly identify themselves through beards or some other distinguishing badge or garment. Yet, the edicts sought to severely circumscribe the juridical autonomy and self-governing powers of Jewish communities by banning the use of excommunication and limiting rabbinic and communal authority to purely religious matters. Because Habsburg territory, by the late eighteenth century, comprised parts of the Italian peninsula, the Jews of these lands, which included D'Arco's Lombardy, in addition to Gorizia, Gradisca, and the port city of Trieste, received their own Edict of Tolerance in late 1781. This changed the Jews' legal and communal status, along with inspiring debate between and among Jews and Christians over its intended scope, in some instances years before formal emancipation and the fall of ghetto walls at the hands of invading French forces.[22]

This was the background to D'Arco's *The Influence of the Ghetto on the State*. Written to support the reforms of the Habsburg monarch, whose enlightened absolutism and physiocratic economics D'Arco fully shared, the book was nevertheless sharply critical of the role of Jewish commerce and finance in the national economy, in areas such as the trade and resale of raw materials and manufactured goods, currency exchange, and moneylending. Like Dohm before him and Grégoire after, D'Arco questioned the impact of Jews on the economy. Unlike Dohm and Grégoire, D'Arco saw monopolistic greed, xenophobia, and misanthropy as essential to the Jewish collective character. "If stealing," he writes, "is not forbidden to the Jew, but, on the contrary, prescribed; if dishonesty is not to be avoided, but praiseworthy . . . who among the inhabitants of the Ghetto will not be led out of interest [to commit] every injustice, every fraud, every theft, as long as he can do it unobserved, and consequently go unpunished by the government?" At the same time, D'Arco argues that "the separation of the Ghetto from the state," which he repeatedly laments, is the result not only of Jewish particularism but also "of the laws and conditions, under which the Jews have generally been admitted by the nations to live among them."[23] He implies that, by reeducating Jews and emasculating their rabbinic courts and communal autonomy, "that corporate spirit" that divides and estranges Jews from the state may change as well.

D'Arco explains that his focus "on the influence of the Ghetto on the State" is restricted to Jews as a corporate entity, and is not on the small number of individual Jews who exist at a remove from the community. Ironically, this narrowing of his focus is connected to a broadened understanding of the word *ghetto*. For the sense of "ghetto" here is *not* limited to an enclosed space in certain cities where Jews are compelled to live. Metonymically, it refers to Jews as a nation or collectivity that resides as a separate body or society within the state. In D'Arco's Italian frame of reference, the two meanings may be intimately linked, but the reach of the latter definition is obviously much longer, extending as it does to Jewish communities that operate on an autonomous or corporate basis yet are not, strictly speaking, ghettoized. And indeed, in his survey of the Jewish role in the European political economy, D'Arco addresses many Jewries of this sort, from the Jews of Holland to the Jews of Poland.

By the late eighteenth century, this use of "ghetto," at least in Italian, as a metonym for the Jewish people was sufficiently common to be noted by dictionaries of the era. In 1798, the third volume of Francesco Alberti di Villanuova's dictionary included three definitions in its entry for "ghetto." After first identifying it as "an enclosure, or a collection of several houses, where Jews live in certain cities," the entry adds, "Ghetto is also taken to mean Jews collectively, that is, the inhabitants of the ghetto," and provides examples of this usage both from a seventeenth- and early-eighteenth-century Italian text.[24] The final sense given is also figurative: "to make a ghetto," which "is said when many together want to say their piece, whence arises a tumult similar to that of the Jews when they sing in their synagogues."[25]

Despite the evidence he provides of semantic expansion, D'Arco's use of the word *ghetto* did not escape criticism. The most aggrieved rejoinder to his tract came from Benedetto Frizzi, a Trieste-based Jewish physician and scholar who became a noted exponent of the Italian Haskalah (or Jewish Enlightenment).[26] In his anonymous 1784 *Defense against the*

Attacks on the Jewish People in a Book Entitled on the Influence of the Ghetto on the State, Frizzi gave a full-throated rebuttal to D'Arco's accusations, conceding nothing. He championed the Jewish role in the economies of Italy and of Europe, arguing that the trade and speculative practices of Jewish merchants had actually enriched the countries they lived in, not impoverished them. Similarly, he refuted the claim that the Talmud was an "anti-Christian" text, while defending the compatibility of Jewish communal autonomy and rabbinic jurisdiction with loyalty to the state.

Frizzi's polemic against D'Arco's treatment of the ghetto extended to the latter's invocation of the term itself. "He speaks always of the Jews in general," Frizzi complains on the very first page, "as opposed to the inhabitants of the ghetto in particular." In fact, the Jewish commerce that D'Arco derides is mainly conducted by Jews who live in places where they are not housed in ghettos, from port cities like Livorno and Trieste, to those located in Holland, to those of Germany and Poland: "Consequently, this is a work with a misbegotten name and with discordant ideas for the most part."[27] Frizzi argues for a limited understanding of the term *ghetto*, rejecting any associative leap from a mandatory urban quarter for Jews to the Jewish people and community in a broader sense. Here we have a debate over the meaning of "ghetto," with an elastic application of the term being answered by a demand for terminological exactitude. D'Arco's contribution to the burgeoning literature on the Jewish Question would quickly be forgotten, yet his slippery use of the term *ghetto* would ultimately prove prophetic.

Early in 1821, the French Jewish composer Fromental Halévy traveled to Rome on a fellowship, as a recent laureate of the prestigious Prix de Rome. During his sojourn of roughly a year and a half in the Eternal City, he kept a travel journal.[28] Six of the thirty-five pages of his journal narrate a chance visit, in what appears to be the spring of 1822, to the Ghetto of Rome. Halévy begins,

> I was about to leave Rome, when one day, intending to visit the Capitol, I got lost in the little streets near the Palazzo Venezia. Intending to find my way, I got more and more lost. Suddenly, I found myself in the middle of a rather dirty market; before me, I saw a large gate

with a guard in front. I entered and asked, "Where am I?" "In the *ghetto*," I was told. "What is the *ghetto*?" "The quarter of the Jews." "Of the Jews?" "Yes, they live in this enclosure, these are their buildings, and at the end of this little square, the building you see that is a little more ornate than the others contains two of their temples."[29]

With the air of a total neophyte to Jewish life in Rome—indeed to Jewish life period—Halévy describes walking through "narrow straits that do not deserve the name streets" and past "small, low, poorly lit houses teeming with women and children, whose clothing attested to their misery." Going inside a synagogue, he observes and is deeply moved by the solemnity of a service and then attends a Passover seder as an invited guest, where he quizzes his host (identified as Mr. Issakhar) about the scroll affixed to the doorpost *(mezuzah)* and reacts to the unleavened bread *(pain azyme)* given him as if it were his first time eating matzoh. (The latter scene in particular contains striking parallels with the seder depicted in Act II of Halévy's most acclaimed opera, his 1835 *La Juive*, which debuted some thirteen years after his visit to the Roman Ghetto.) While dining, Halévy asked his host about "the tolerance accorded the Jew by the Roman government." "You see how we are treated," Mr. Issakhar responded. "We are less miserable than our ancestors . . . but our lot is still rather grim. We may not live outside this quarter that the Romans call *ghetto*."[30]

Halévy was the son of a cantor. He had been brought up traditionally in the small but growing Jewish community of Paris, and, only two years before traveling to Rome, he had composed a *De Profundis*, in Hebrew, a liturgical piece for singers and orchestra that was performed in a Paris synagogue. It is curious then that he wrote about Jewish life in the ghetto with such detachment and ignorance. However false Halévy's tone may ring at times, the mandatory ghetto was still very much a reality for Rome's Jews in 1822, as it had been, with a few relatively brief recent interruptions, for nearly three hundred years. Venice may have held the "copyright" for the term *ghetto*, but by the nineteenth century if not earlier, it was Rome's Ghetto that had become most synonymous with the institution.[31]

By the late eighteenth century, the plight of the Jews of Rome was increasingly being commented on by foreign visitors and delicately protested by the inhabitants of the ghetto themselves. This heightened attention to the Roman Jewish predicament was prompted by a genuine exacerbation of their suffering, which stood in ever starker contrast not only to the improvement of Jewish legal and social status elsewhere in Western and Central Europe but also to the milder treatment of Jews in other ghettos in Italy (including in the papal states).[32] In 1682, Pope Innocent XI had outlawed all Jewish loan-banking, depriving the ghetto of one of the few occupations open to Jews other than trade in secondhand clothing. While the prohibition only affected some fifty families, it was these families who had been the economic "elite" of the ghetto and the main contributors to the coffers of the *Università,* or official Jewish community. Their demise was economically ruinous for the ghetto and spurred large numbers of families to accede to baptism.[33] The popes at this time also reinvigorated the conversionary drive that had motivated the creation of the Roman Ghetto from its inception. Cases like that of Anna del Monte—a seventeen-year-old Roman Jew who was abducted by the papal police in 1749 and held captive in the House of Conversions (*Casa dei Catecumeni*) for fourteen days—were uncommon only in that she managed to resist the unrelenting pressure to convert and was able to return to the ghetto in the end.[34] While the church had long opposed forced or secret baptisms, its growing anxiety about liberal trends in European politics and society strengthened its determination to demonstrate the success of the confessional state by bringing about the conversion of the Jews—and made it more amenable to narrow interpretations of what constituted coercion. Meanwhile, the papacy continued to bombard the Jews of the ghetto with restrictions. In 1775, a few months after his accession, Pope Pius VI issued a highly punitive bull that served to accentuate the segregation of the Jews. Among other things, it threatened Jews who violated curfew with execution and prohibited the Jews from maintaining shops outside the ghetto.

The Roman Ghetto on the eve of the French Revolution was thus increasingly starved of capital, bankrupted by communal debt, and on permanent edge about the rising conversionary threat. No wonder, then, that the French magistrate Charles-Marguerite-Jean-Baptiste Mercier Dupaty, in his 1785 *Letters on Italy,* described the lot of Roman Jews as "more miserable than anywhere else." If a Jew merely allowed to slip from his mouth the words, "I want to be a Christian," then he would be immediately confined for two years to the House of Converts, however much he might regret it. "People ask," Dupaty wrote, "when will the Jews convert to Christianity? I ask: when will the Christians convert to tolerance?"[35]

Even before the French Revolution officially reached Rome with Napoleon's troops in 1798, it had become for better or worse a lens through which the situation of the Jews of Rome was viewed. In his 1793 *Secret Memoirs and Criticisms of the Courts, Governments, and Customs of the Main Italian States,* the French revolutionary diplomat Joseph (Giuseppe) Gorani described the Roman Jews as "extremely poor," to the point that often an entire family was "wedged into" one room with one bed, which they took turns using. He added that on his last visit to the ghetto, his conversation with a particular group of Jews turned to the subject of the revolution:

> They were ignorant of everything that France had done in favor of their nation. They were well aware that there had been a revolution, but they did not have an exact idea of it. . . . But when I gave them a truer picture of what had taken place, when above all I explained to them that the goal of this revolution was to assure an absolute equality of rights to all men and to impose on them the same obligations; when I let them know that this equality was established between all men, whatever their religion or nation, and that the Jews were namely admitted to the same advantages, these unfortunates [the Roman Jews] exhibited an astonishment that is difficult to conceive.[36]

For Roman Jews living still under the papal regime, the association between the French Revolution and Jewish rights was a source of peril as much as of hope. In 1793, after word spread of the guillotining of Louis XVI and his consort Marie Antoinette, a Roman mob lynched a French Jacobin-leaning diplomat and then descended on the ghetto to attack the presumed sympathizers with the revolution. They laid siege to the ghetto for a week and managed to set it on fire, though papal authorities intervened to prevent it from being incinerated.[37]

During the Napoleonic Wars, Rome's Jews enjoyed intervals of civic equality. In February 1798, French soldiers entered the city, exiled Pope

Pius VI to France, and proclaimed the Roman Republic. Exchanging the yellow hat for the tricolor, the Jews welcomed their liberators with jubilation. As elsewhere, the ghetto was illuminated, a large liberty tree was planted in front of the synagogue (the Cinque Scuole), and there were processions with tricolor flags and drums in which Jews participated in great number.[38] On February 18, Antonio Pacifici, representing the new Roman Republic, addressed the Jews from the main ghetto piazza, stating, "From here on, if you are good citizens, you are also our brothers, our equals; one law will judge us and you."[39] This emancipation proved to be short-lived; two years later, in 1800, a Neapolitan invasion succeeded in ousting the French, and the papal states were restored under Pope Pius VII. Yet this restoration itself was soon interrupted. In 1808, Napoleon, now king of Italy, dissolved the papal states, annexed the territory to the Kingdom of Italy, and took Pius VII prisoner in Fontainebleau. Once again, the ghetto was legally disestablished, and the restrictions on the Jews of Rome were lifted. Six years later, this back and forth between legal emancipation and ghettoization came to an end with the final defeat of Napoleon and the reconstitution of the papal states under the rule of the restored Pius VII. The reversal was abrupt and nearly complete. Despite offering to pay Pius VII the high sum of one hundred thousand scudi to maintain their political and civil rights, the Jews were forced back into their old ghetto existence.[40] The obligation to wear the Jewish badge was reinstated, Jews were barred from public office and from the university, and they were forced to liquidate all their real estate holdings outside the ghetto within five years. Under the terms of the notorious 1775 bull of Pius VI, the stores they had opened outside the ghetto were closed, and the Jewish economy was reduced to *strazzaria*. Once again, the Jews were forbidden from hiring Christian servants and were obliged to attend conversionary sermons.[41]

Rome was not the only city on the Italian peninsula where the ghetto returned with the restoration of the old regime. Ghettoization was reinstated throughout the papal states, as well as in the Kingdom of Sardinia (which controlled the Piedmont region in the north) and in the Duchy of Modena. Yet Rome was where the ghetto and the whole arsenal of persecutory measures that went with it were enforced most assiduously. A French citizen like Halévy, despite his Jewish descent, might have been able to avoid internment in the ghetto during his stay in Rome, so long as he did not flaunt his Jewishness too openly, but for the vast majority of Roman Jews there was no exit. By the mid-nineteenth century, as a result of the 1848 revolutions and creeping Italian unification, legal ghettos had disappeared virtually everywhere from the Italian peninsula—except in Rome. Yet even Rome was not immune to change; in early 1848, Pope Pius IX dismantled the walls of the ghetto, but any hope that this would culminate in actual liberation was sunk by the failure of the revolution that ensued. The walls did not return, but the ghetto remained in place.

If the Ghetto of Rome was already attracting increased notice for its backwardness in the eighteenth century, by the mid-nineteenth century, as basically the last of its kind, it had become the very symbol of archaism. Both the champions of liberalism and Jewish emancipation and their critics had a stake in fashioning Rome and its ghetto as the ultimate foil to modernity and as a showpiece for the confessional state. In his 1848 call for Jewish emancipation throughout the Italian peninsula, Massimo d'Azeglio, even after describing the "narrow and unclean streets, the lack of air, and the filth that is the inevitable consequence of the forced ag-glomeration of too many people, nearly all of them miserable," claimed his depiction of the Roman Ghetto could hardly convey even "one thou-sandth of the woeful conditions that . . . are evident within its walls."[42] The German historian of medieval Rome, Ferdinand Gregorovius, was more lukewarm on the subject of Jewish emancipation, yet his long essay *The Ghetto and the Jews of Rome,* published in 1853—which became arguably the most well-known nineteenth-century portrait of the Roman Ghetto—gave a memorable description of the "yellow flood" of the Tiber that annually flowed through its streets: "What a melancholy spectacle to see the wretched Jews' quarter sunk in the dreary inundation of the Tiber! Each year Israel in Rome has to undergo a new Deluge, and like Noah's Ark the ghetto is tossed on the waves with man and beast."[43] D'Azeglio and Gregorovius were only two of a long list of non-Jewish writers who wrote about the Roman Ghetto in the nineteenth century with varying levels of sympathy and political engagement; others include Stendhal, Nathaniel Hawthorne, Jakob Burckhardt, Edmond About, Joseph Méry, and William Wettmore Story. Some, like the conservative Burckhardt and, to a degree, Gregorovius, viewed the ghetto with a kind of anthropological interest, as a curious relic of a then-vanishing old

Europe; others, like D'Azeglio and About, were more vocal in their denunciation of it. The mix of fascination and repulsion found in non-Jewish accounts of the Roman Ghetto was heavily tilted toward the latter in the Western Jewish press. There, the focus on the living conditions of Rome's Jews grew especially sustained and intense (and incensed) at mid-century.[44] From the pages of the largest circulating Jewish newspaper of the era, the German-language *Allgemeine Zeitung des Judenthums,* Ludwig Philippson, the liberal rabbi who was the paper's editor and chief writer, regularly decried the Roman Ghetto, calling its history "one of the darkest pages in the annals of inhumanity" and comparing it to an enclosure of wild beasts.[45] In the final, eleventh volume of his *History of the Jews from Antiquity to the Present,* Heinrich Graetz blasted the post-1814 and post-1848 papal restorations of ghettoization as a return to the "Middle Ages."[46]

Despite the often considerable difference in attitude toward the Jews and the Ghetto of Rome in the writings of nineteenth-century Jewish and non-Jewish writers, certain recurring images traverse this literature. The Roman Ghetto, with a population of around three thousand souls concentrated in an area of roughly one-tenth of a square mile, was a paradigm of Jewish abjectness and of the stubborn survival of the old in the new. In writings on Jewish Rome from this period, it stands in a relationship of both continuity and contrast with the rest of the city. On one hand, it is an antiquity among antiquities, an epitome of the "medieval" in a confessional state seen as itself quintessentially medieval. "What is this [i.e., the ghetto] but a ruin?" a contributor wrote in the *Calendar and Yearbook for Israelites in the Year (1847) 5607.* "A ruin that has stood unaltered for centuries, even as time has knocked down the old abodes of misery in all the other districts of Europe; a ruin among ruins, which the spirit of the century has ignored in its wanderings across the earth; a ruin, that eventually will collapse like all the others, when the tempest and thunder of world fate pass over it; a ruin, that posterity will eventually regard with the same astonishment as it does the others."[47] Yet, the Jews of the ghetto were viewed as "Rome's only living ruins," in the famous words of Gregorovius, possessed of an uncanny ability to endure even the most adverse conditions; "they alone out of the confusion of the countless religious sects of ancient Rome have remained alive and unchanged."[48]

Watercolor of *Via Capacciotto in the Ghetto,* by Franz Ettore Roesler, late nineteenth century. The painting was part of a series of portraits of the Roman Ghetto that Roesler composed in the period between the dismantling of the legal institution of the ghetto in 1870 and the knocking down of its old buildings and narrow streets beginning in 1885.

The conquest of Rome by the Italian army of General Raffaele Cadorna on September 20, 1870, brought the curtain down on the pontifical state and, with it, the longest surviving ghetto in Europe. The Jews who remained in Rome were now legally free. Fifteen years later, as part of a massive urban renewal project, the entire area of the ghetto was razed, leaving virtually no remnant of the decrepit buildings and maze of streets that had once existed on the spot. "Rome has become a modern world city," the German Jewish historian Abraham Berliner wrote on the eve of the demolition, reminiscing on the last days of the Roman Ghetto, "and a modern world city cannot tolerate a ghetto!"[49] The ghetto as an institution appeared to have come, at long last, to an end. By 1870, however, the word *ghetto* had already begun to transcend its Italian roots and to become a more general spatial concept and metaphor associated with premodern Jewish life. The surge of public concern at mid-century about the situation of a Jewish community for which *ghetto* was a 300-year-old place name helps explain why.

On discovering Rome's Jewish quarter in 1822, Halévy asked, "What is a ghetto?" It is altogether conceivable that Halévy was unfamiliar with the word *ghetto*. He certainly knew what matzot and mezuzot were, but he may not have known what a ghetto was. Indeed, the transformation of the word *ghetto* only began in earnest after 1822.

The first significant change in the nineteenth century was the word's migration into other languages. A term associated with immobility was, all of a sudden, very much on the move. Until roughly the 1830s and 1840s, the word *ghetto* was in wide use only in Italy. Certainly, there were Jewish streets and quarters, including streets and quarters where Jews were segregated by law, elsewhere in Europe. But these were typically referred to by labels native to the language of the place. Open an Italian-German dictionary from the eighteenth or even nineteenth century, and the entry for "ghetto" will likely read "Judengasse," "Judenstraße," "Judenviertel," or "Judenstadt"; an Italian-French dictionary, and it will read "Demeure des Juifs," "Carrière des Juifs," or "Juiverie."[50] In fact, these terms were not exact equivalents. Of the myriad names for the Jewish section of a city in European languages, *ghetto* alone entailed a conceptual package of legal compulsion, total residential segregation, and physical separation via gates and walls.[51] A "Judengasse" or "Judenviertel" *might* be mandatory, exclusive, and enclosed, though only rarely did each of these combine all three elements; an Italian "ghetto" was, virtually by definition, all three. It was only in the nineteenth century that *ghetto* began to emerge as a term for a restricted Jewish area across multiple languages. This was a gradual and uneven process, not a sudden shift. Well into the nineteenth century it was not uncommon for definitions of *ghetto* to continue to give priority to, or simply to stop at, the original Italian referent. To wit, the *Dictionnaire de la langue française,* in its 1873 edition, included the word *ghetto* within its French lexicon, but defined the term simply as the "name, in certain Italian cities, of the quarter where Jews were obliged to live."[52] One year earlier, in a sign of how synonymous with the ghetto the city of Rome had become, the great French encyclopedic dictionary of the nineteenth century, the *Grand dictionnaire du XIXe siècle,* defined "ghetto" as the "miniature quarter of Rome where the 4,000 [sic] Jewish inhabitants of this city, under the papacy, were clustered, in its narrow streets, which were closed up with chains at night, to prevent anyone from leaving."[53] The first edition of the *Oxford English Dictionary* (known as *The New English Dictionary on Historical Principles*) was more generic in its definition, but still placed Italy in the foreground: "The quarter in a city, chiefly in Italy, to which the Jews were restricted."[54] The term seems to have made its earliest and deepest inroads into German. In the eleventh edition (1857) of the *Brockhaus Encyclopedia*, the premier German-language encyclopedia of the nineteenth century, the entry spanned roughly two columns and distinguished between the "word," whose origins were clearly Italian but whose etymology was (so the author alleged) to be "found in no lexicon," and the "thing" itself, which had "spread over half of Europe from the earliest Middle Ages into modern times to some degree." The author claimed that the word's twofold meaning of a restricted Jewish street or urban quarter and a term for the Jewish community as a collective appeared frequently. Mostly, the *Brockhaus* entry was a jumble of scattered, often erroneous references to years and places where segregation was instituted; however, on a more thematic note, the author contended that the ghetto was a result not only of "Christian intolerance and overwhelming lust for subjugation" but also of the Jews' own "national corporate spirit," their "drive for exclusivity and consolidation." Strikingly, while including Venice in his list of examples, the author seemed ignorant of the fact that the term *ghetto* had originated there.[55]

Like many a migrant, *ghetto* provoked questions in its new languages about where, exactly, it had come from. While debate about the etymology of *ghetto* had begun in the seventeenth century, the term's rovings in the nineteenth century fueled a fresh wave of interest in the issue. Was the word *ghetto* originally derived from the name of the foundry (or *geto*) complex that antedated the all-Jewish district on the site of the Venetian Ghetto by more than a century? Or, as a popular folk etymology claimed, did it have its root in the Hebrew term *get* for bill of divorce? These two theories continued to compete with an increasingly legion number of conjectures in the late nineteenth and early twentieth centuries.[56] An 1869 article on the topic wondered why the term *ghetto* had yet to merit an entry in most German dictionaries and lexicons. "The ghetto, the (Italian) term for Judengasse," it began, "has been naturalized in many languages, but the meaning of this word seems to have found no right of citizenship *(Heimatsrecht)* in the dictionary. . . . once the refuge of castoffs, [the ghetto] is now itself denied a 'little place' there [i.e. in the dictionary], where otherwise so many [words] find refuge." In the course of its border crossings, the word *ghetto* began to appear stateless, without a homeland or *Heimat.*[57]

If the first change to the word *ghetto* was its absorption into other languages, the second was a significant broadening of its range of meanings and implications. The diffusion of the term throughout Europe, and, eventually across the Atlantic, yielded a "ghetto" that was, semantically speaking, more and more diffuse. In 1822, a ghetto was a compulsory and segregated Jewish quarter of an Italian city. There was, by that point, some figurative usage of the term, at least in Italian, but it was minimal compared to what would ensue. In the course of its nineteenth-century travels, the word *ghetto* became a basic, structuring metaphor of Jewish consciousness, routinely invoked by emancipated Jews to explain where they had come from and to contrast their past with the present. A crucial part in this development was played by the emergence, in the mid-nineteenth century, of what was initially a mostly German-language genre of Jewish fiction known as *Ghettoliteratur.* The German Jewish author Berthold Auerbach, who would eventually achieve fame in nineteenth-century German literature primarily for his "village stories," began his fictional career with two "Jewish" novels, *Spinoza* (1837) and *Poet and Merchant* (1840).[58] Auerbach had originally intended that these two books would headline a longer series of fictional works on the subject of "Das Ghetto," the title he gave to his preface to *Spinoza.* His foreword brings us close to one of the "turns" in the evolution of a word as he wishes for a previous definition of *ghetto:*

> In the Brockhaus Conversation Lexicon, vol. 2, p. 170, the article "Commerce" [Gewerbe] should have been followed by " 'Ghetto' (Ital. masc., in German commonly neut.)—the Jewish quarter in Rome and Venice."[59] I might then have been spared from having to include this definition for many readers. It would have sufficed simply to note my intention to present, under this title [i.e. "Das Ghetto"],

a series of historical portraits of Jewish life and mores, of which the following work constitutes the first installment. . . .

Jewish life is decaying little by little, as one piece of it after another falls by the wayside. Therefore, it seems to me that the time has come to let poetry and history and both together capture its movements in images. . . .

I would have preferred that this novel appear at the end of my ghetto [series], since in an ultimate sense it [the ghetto] came to an end with Spinoza. But I confess that I could not resist the impulse of the idea after it gripped me so. In addition, the ghetto still exists today, and will disappear with many others still.[60]

The whole unspoken thrust of Auerbach's introduction is that a minimalist definition of *ghetto* as "the Jewish quarter in Rome and Venice" would be inadequate. He proceeds to endow the word with much more general significance. It is not simply a question of extending the term to refer to compulsory Jewish quarters outside Italy. It is not even a question of expanding its reach to incorporate enclaves that are not, strictly speaking, coercive. *Ghetto* here evokes something considerably vaster: an entire gestalt of Jewish traditions, customs, folkways, values, and social types in the midst of disappearing. Auerbach knew well that seventeenth-century Amsterdam had no Jewish ghetto in the classical sense of a gated street or quarter with walls and curfews. Yet Spinoza, the excommunicated heretic, might still with justification be said to have blazed the trail out of the ghetto by virtue of his having been the first to leave the world of traditional and communal authority behind.

Auerbach abandoned the project outlined in "Das Ghetto" in the early 1840s.[61] Yet, far from petering out, the idea for a literature that would immerse itself in the *petit détails* of "old world" Judaism, and dramatize the fraught relationship between this world and those who had left it behind, would go on to blossom. The true pioneer in this respect was Leopold Kompert, whose series of stories and novellas about regional Jewish life in his native Bohemia, *From the Ghetto: Stories* (1848), became an almost instant sensation. While precedents for Kompert's literary evocation of traditional Jewish society certainly exist, he was the first, after Auerbach, to identify this milieu with the term *ghetto* and to give rise to a now-recognizable genre of *Ghettoliteratur*.[62] Considering his importance

Leopold Kompert, drawing based on a photograph by Wilhelm Hecht.

to the form, it is worth pondering some of the qualities of his work that would prove especially characteristic and influential.

The first notable attribute of Kompert's fiction was its continuation of Auerbach's reinvention of the ghetto concept. Kompert opted to label his miniature Bohemian strongholds of traditional Jewish life as ghettos. He did so even though the strict segregation and exclusivity of the original Italian ghettos, or of the Frankfurt Judengasse or the Prague Judenstadt for that matter, were not characteristic of these Bohemian Jewish districts, neither in historical fact nor in Kompert's literary reconstruction. With few exceptions, Kompert's "ghettos" were not mandatory, walled-off quarters that formed part of a much larger city, but more like Jewish streets

(Gassen) in towns surrounded by rural peasant villages, occasionally located on noble estates. While these streets were mostly Jewish, the very first story in Kompert's *From the Ghetto,* titled "Judith the Second," indicates that there were exceptions. One of the story's characters, Christoph Wirth (popularly dubbed "Reb Christoph"), was a gentile born in the ghetto who was "more Jew than Christian," spoke fluent *Judendeutsch* ("jargon"), and regularly stood outside his house as Jews left synagogue to wish them a "gut Schabbes" or "gut Jontef" (holiday).[63] Conversely, there were also Jews who lived outside the *Gasse,* like the "village Jews" of the long novella "The Randar's Children" who were part of a family whose head of household—the *Randar* in Yiddish, or *arrendator* in Polish and Russian—was responsible for managing the local noble's tavern and distillery. "If you love the perfume of the forest," "The Randar's Children" begins, "the verdure of the trees, and the singing of the larks, do not enter the ghetto! Larks fly in very small numbers above its walls, and in the ghetto the shade of the trees is not at all thick. There people have too many cares, and besides, there is not much space."[64]

The closest Kompert came to offering an account of his title came in the 1850 edition of *From the Ghetto,* which followed his publication of another set of ghetto stories, *Bohemian Jews,* in 1849. In a foreword, the author reflected on how much had changed since his first book had appeared two years earlier. As a result of the 1848 revolution, most of the remaining residential restrictions on Jews living in the Habsburg Empire had been lifted. These included the so-called Familiants Laws, which, since their institution in 1726 and 1727, had placed a cap on the number of Jewish families that might legally reside in Bohemia and Moravia.[65] To ensure compliance with the quota, the laws also restricted the right to marry and establish a family to only one son from each household—the subject of one of Kompert's stories in *From the Ghetto,* titled "Without Authorization." Kompert questioned whether his title, *From the Ghetto,* was still appropriate. He had given the book a title, that "some time after, thanks to the irrefutable idea of right and humanity, should have been stricken from the foreign-word dictionary *(Fremdwörterbuch)* of the German nation and our Fatherland." If he had nevertheless opted to preserve the title, it was not because he wished to express any doubt about whether the ghetto gates had truly been opened wide. Rather, it was "out of the feeling, that we should not simply visit the places, where we were previously happy, but also those where we suffered a great deal."[66] Kompert intimates that his choice of the Italian word *ghetto* from the German *Fremdwörterbuch* was meant to convey the external constraints endured by the pre-1848 Bohemian Jews, though this is hard to square with a depiction of the "ghetto" that only occasionally dwells on its oppressive aspect. Kompert titled a later, two-volume collection of novellas *Stories of a [Jewish] Street*, in which the "Gasse" of the title was essentially indistinguishable from the "Ghetto" of either his original *From the Ghetto* or his later *New Stories from the Ghetto* (1860). His enlargement of the term *ghetto* encompassed the looser concept of the gasse, or Jewish street.

Kompert's title *From the Ghetto*, an indication of the main setting of the stories, can also be translated as *Out of the Ghetto*, thereby alluding to the path taken not only by characters in this collection but also by the narrator himself. The preface conveys precisely this perspective of the narrator vis-à-vis his subject. He remembers, as a boy, climbing a small foothill outside his parents' home on Sabbath afternoon, from which he could look down on the entire gasse, including on his grandparents. Worried, they begged him to come down from the precipice. "I see," the narrator recalls, "many a head bent with alarm, many a beckoning finger; I can hear many a scream of worry as well. But I say: let me be! I must stay on the mountain!"[67] This was indeed the road Kompert had traveled. Born in the Judengass of Münchengrätz (Mnichovo Hradiště), a small town a few kilometers from Prague, Kompert had left home to study briefly at a university in Prague and then to work as a tutor in Vienna and Pressburg (Bratislava) before finally settling in Vienna for good in 1847. The narrator in Kompert's ghetto stories serves as something of a cultural translator capable of introducing non-Jews to an unfamiliar world or providing fellow Jewish emigrants from that world with an opportunity to return briefly, albeit in the realm of the imagination. Significantly, only the narrator uses the word *ghetto*. The characters themselves never identify their enclaves by this term. Invariably, they either refer to the "Jewish area" as the gasse or (more frequently) the *kille*, the Western Yiddish term for *kehillah*, or Jewish community. In this way, Kompert makes a sharp distinction between the language of the outsider, however sympathetic, and the lexicon of those who remain inhabitants of traditional society. The word *ghetto* is symbolically associated with the stranger or at least with one who has become estranged.

This distance from the world depicted in the stories goes along with an ambivalence on the narrator's part that would prove typical of the entire genre of ghetto literature. The ghetto lies on a spectrum between the extremes of revulsion and nostalgia: it repels and disgusts, even as it also at times pulls those who have left back in. Some ghetto authors leaned toward the pole of disdain, others—like Kompert himself—were more sentimental; yet a degree of alienation was never absent in the latter just as a scintilla of admiration was always present in the former. Arguably, the work that best illustrates this ambivalence in Kompert's oeuvre is his 1849 story "The Peddler."[68] The story concerns a young Jew, Emanuel (né Elijah), who left his hometown at the age of thirteen to study in gymnasium and university and now, living in Vienna, is on the verge of converting to Christianity to marry Clara, his former tutee. Before going through with it, however, he decides to pay a visit to his native Judengass for the first time since his departure years earlier, and for what will inevitably prove to be his last time. Yet rather than appear as himself, he returns incognito, in the guise of a *bettler* (beggar), with the aim of celebrating one final Sabbath with his family, albeit without being recognized. At least initially, his plan seems to work; his mother Chane, father Schimme, younger brother Benjamin, and sister Rösele, while strangely drawn to the "guest," take him for the beggar he pretends to be. "The Peddler" is consistently maudlin and strains credulity: would a parent really not recognize a child last seen at thirteen, even if he were dressed like a beggar and several years had passed? Yet Kompert's story is cleverly structured. In essence, it is written with two storytellers: the omniscient narrator who appears throughout Kompert's work but also Emanuel himself, the insider-turned-outsider. Emanuel not only stages the encounter with his family, on the basis of knowledge he is privy to but his family does not have. He also routinely reports on his experiences in letters to his beloved, in which information crucial to the reader's own understanding of the plot and background is often revealed. Over the course of the story Emanuel's narrative distance is gradually overcome. He goes off script and increasingly finds himself at the mercy of emotions and impulses he cannot control. Seeing his own, younger self reflected in his eleven-year-old brother, Emanuel writes to Clara, "It is as if ties that I thought I had cut off long ago are pulling me to remain here. There is something that I still have to do here, but I do not know what it is. . . . I have become an entirely different person."[69] An attempt to escape and return to Vienna is foiled when, early Sunday morning, Emanuel runs into his father, a traveling peddler, just outside the ghetto and agrees to accompany him on his weekly circuit of the peasant villages. During the week he spends wandering with his father, sleeping in barns and eating cold and moldy food (because his father refuses to eat the unkosher meals the peasants offer him), Emanuel learns much about Schimme Prager— about his mix of personal religious stringencies and laissez-faire tolerance, about his unspoken acts of kindness toward the gentile villagers, about his awareness of the world beyond the ghetto—that he had not known previously. He tries to convey his impressions in a letter to Clara from the road, comparing his peddler father to a book:

> Imagine a book that supplied you with the most beautiful things to read. You continue reading, on and on, amazed to hear the magnificent sound of powerful melodies. You do not know where they are coming from, or where they are headed. Everything tells you that you have discovered primal powers of humanity here, more beautiful and more splendid than you have ever seen before.
>
> But it is not simplicity or naiveté that you are finding here. It is a higher feeling, a sanctified biblical feeling, as it were. You read on—and suddenly you find the pages stuck together, and the melodies stop. You lose track of the wonderful living faith, and you cannot read further. The filth of life has bound the pages to each other, and the paste of vulgarity has cemented them together. It is a great misfortune for the inhabitants of the ghetto that you remain fixated on these passages. They jump out at you because initially they are an affront to your organs of touch and sight, and human beings never want to take the time to be thorough. You never read further into the book, and that is your loss. We are the ones who suffer from this.[70]

Emanuel's book metaphor is meant in context specifically to communicate something of his father's essence, yet his words might just as well be said of the ghetto itself. For Kompert's ghetto is a unique composite of muck and poetry, noise and music, yet only the sympathetic observer capable of moving past the first can hope to penetrate to the second.

In the end, Emanuel returns with his father for the Sabbath, reveals his true identity to his family, and—apparently—remains in the ghetto. Wisely, though, Kompert resists a conventionally happy ending and settles for something more cryptic. The story concludes with Emanuel's final letter to Clara: "The unfortunate one builds his hut close to the place where happiness resides. He strolls amid the happy ones, and his smile often seems as if it were borrowed from them. I shall smile, I shall be happy—but can I ever forget you, Clara?"[71]

Like Auerbach before him, Kompert justifies his literary endeavor as an attempt to preserve the memory of a vanishing world. Kompert's ghetto may not be as remote as the portraits of traditional Jewish society in other branches of ghetto literature—Emanuel, after all, returns home in the end—but over this site of memory as well, there hovers the threat of extinction. Should it not be permitted to the chronicler of the ghetto, Kompert asked in 1850, "to see once again the outgoing time in its loving, homey face, to capture its qualities, before they become unrecognizable to him? Should he not be permitted to press once again the hands of the figures who stood by his cradle, before grass overgrows their graves and a new age, heedless over whom it treads, destroys that grass, which was fertilized by the dust of their decrepitude?"[72]

The association of the ghetto with anachronism, with a disappearing if not yet extinguished past, gave rise to a fundamental ambivalence in attitudes toward it, as the ghetto came to serve not simply as a marker of the old and obsolescent—of a confining past Jews had to escape if they were to become modern—but also as a romanticized object of longing, for a world-in-miniature that would soon be no more.[73] It also made possible a respatialization of the ghetto, which was increasingly seen as residing wherever modernity and emancipation had not yet fully penetrated, from Spinoza's seventeenth-century Sephardic Amsterdam to the rural towns and townlets that were the main canvas of nineteenth-century ghetto literature. The late historian Reinhart Koselleck stressed the importance of the temporalization of concepts in the experience of modernity. Emancipation, to cite one of Koselleck's own examples, becomes more than simply an act of freeing slaves or even of the granting of equal rights; it becomes a universal historical process on the march, steadily advancing to include more and more groups.[74] The ghetto was likewise temporalized in the nineteenth century, in effect as emancipation's foil or (to use Koselleck's term) "counter-concept."[75] More than simply a place, the ghetto was now a metaphor for the medieval or premodern. To the idea of a spatial divide between Jew and Christian that was foundational to the ghetto concept there was now added the implication of a temporal divide between the premodern and the modern. Because Eastern Europe was seen as the foremost example of a region where tradition still held sway, it became, in the mind of ghetto poets and their readers, the pre-eminent setting of ghetto Judaism. Kompert had initiated the transposition of the ghetto image from the physically enclosed and exclusive quarters of Italy and Germany to the mostly small-town Judengassen of Bohemia. Those who followed in his wake would build on this migratory trend and carry it farther eastward.

Of Kompert's successors in the ghetto literature genre, it was the Galician-born Austrian author Karl E. Franzos who earned the greatest renown and arguably did the most to cement the association of the ghetto with the *Ostjude* ("East European Jew"). Whereas Kompert frequently neglected to identify the "ghetto" in his stories (we never do know the name of Emanuel's hometown in "The Peddler"), the main setting for Franzos's Jewish-themed stories and novels was Barnow, a fictionalized version of the Eastern Galician (or Podolian) townlet Czortków (Chortkiv), where Franzos was born and spent the first eleven years of his life. With Barnow, the idea of "ghetto" colonizes and usurps what is, today, recognized as an alternate site of Jewish life, itself laden with literary and mythical overtones; namely, the *shtetl*, Yiddish for "small town." The former Polish-Lithuanian Commonwealth, especially its easternmost sections, was dotted with hundreds of small towns *(shtetlakh)*, many of which were founded on the private estates of Polish nobles and were surrounded by countryside where Christian peasants, frequently of another ethnic background (e.g., Ukrainians), lived.[76] A sizable percentage, and often even a majority, of the population of these little towns was Jewish, distinguished from their neighbors not only by religion but also by occupation, language, dress, and culture. The shtetl was not a ghetto in the original sense of a compulsory, gated, all-Jewish, and only-Jewish quarter of the city: there was virtually no legally imposed segregation, and because of their demographic strength and even preponderance, provincial Jews often related to (or at least imagined) the shtetl in its entirety as Jewish space.[77] It was only as a result of a series of mental leaps and associations—the identification of the ghetto, the Jewish "street," and traditional Jewish society more generally as spatially confining and temporally lagging—that the Jews of Barnow could be considered "ghetto Jews." Like Kompert, Franzos makes clear that "ghetto" is an exonym foreign to the vocabulary of the place. In his debut 1868 story, "The Picture of Christ," the narrator introduces the "ghetto" as follows:

> It is always dark and gloomy there, however brightly the sun may shine, and dark pestiferous vapors fill the air, although the meadows beyond may be full of flowers. And this wretched part of the town is the most thickly inhabited of all, for it is the Ghetto, the Jews' quarter, or, as they call it in Barnow, the "Gasse."[78]

Perhaps without intending to, Franzos betrays a slight tonal artificiality in a set of portraits of Podolian life purportedly committed to unsparing realism, simply by virtue of the non-native quality of the term with which the genre of *The Jews of Barnow* is synonymous. The word *ghetto* once again serves to establish a certain distance between the author and his subject.

Like Kompert, Franzos could claim the identity of insider turned outsider, though he was far more of an assimilationist than his Bohemian precursor. Born in Czortków in 1848 to a Galician mother and a father of Sephardic descent who was the district physician, Franzos spent the first eleven years of his life in the Podolian shtetl at a remove from the Orthodox, mostly Hasidic Jews of the town.[79] From a young age, he recalled his father molding him into a German liberal nationalist. "By nationality," his father would tell him, "you are not a Pole, Ruthene (Ukrainian), or Jew—you are a German," though he hastened to add that "by religion you are a Jew."[80] Franzos's parents sent him not to a *heder,* that is, to a traditional Jewish school, but to a school in the Dominican monastery, where he was the only Jew. His father taught him German and arranged for a tutor in Hebrew. After the death of his father in 1858, the family moved to Czernowitz (Chernivtsi) in Bukowina, where he attended gymnasium and developed the goal of becoming a classical philologist. After that ambition was foiled by his refusal to convert (which, even in the post-1848 Austro-Hungarian Empire, was still virtually required of any Jew who aspired to an academic career), he resolved to study law,

Karl Emil Franzos, woodcut from 1880.

which he did first in Vienna and then in Graz. His discovery that his path to a career as a lawyer was also blocked by his Jewishness ultimately pointed him toward journalism. In 1872, he became a correspondent for the leading liberal newspaper in Vienna, the *Neue Freie Presse*. By that time, he had also begun writing the fictional portraits of "Barnow" that would eventually earn him acclaim as perhaps the most prominent ghetto writer of the late nineteenth century.

Franzos famously (or notoriously) labeled the territories of Galicia, Bukowina, southern Russia, and Romania "Halb-Asien" ("semi-Asia"), a label he claimed was justified not simply geographically but also on the grounds that there "European *Bildung* (education) and Asiatic barbarism, the European striving for progress and Asiatic indolence" were juxtaposed.[81] For Franzos, nearly everything about Jewish Barnow—its arranged marriages and superstitious rituals, its veneration of Hasidic wonder-working rabbis, its extreme rejection of those who dared to seek "Western" enlightenment and to challenge the authority of the old ways—appeared to belong to the "oriental" side of "semi-Asia." Here and there in his writings are some of the stock expressions of idealization characteristic of ghetto literature, as in this description of the arrival of the Sabbath in "The Shylock of Barnow": "It has grown dusk in the town, but there is no gloom in the hearts of its Jewish inhabitants. The dismal irregularly built houses of the Ghetto are now enlivened by thousands of candles, and thousands of happy faces. The Sabbath has begun in the hearts of these peoples and in their rooms, a common and unusual occurrence, and yet a mysterious and blessed influence that drives away all that is poor and mean in everyday life."[82] But these glimpses of the "poetic" dimension of ghetto life are considerably scarcer in Franzos than in Kompert.

While the weakening of the Italian referent for the ghetto and the displacement of its image onto Eastern Europe were mostly unself-conscious processes, those changes did not escape notice. In an 1878 feuilleton on Kompert and the new genre of ghetto literature titled "The Ghetto and Its Poets," the literary critic Wilhelm Goldbaum wrote, "If one thinks of a rectangle, with diagonals running from Moscow to Prague and from Odessa to Poland, then one has rather accurately delimited the current extent of the geography of the ghetto." Italy, he went on, may be where the name and entity originated, and on a recent visit to the dirty "tangle of streets" of the Rome Ghetto it seemed to him as if he had suddenly been transported to a "Russian or Polish Jewish town." But, he continued, "The spirit of the ghetto, that hazy, turbid spirit with the mark of martyrdom and a troubled air," was no longer to be found there. "Only in the East, among the Slavs, do the Jews still live in the Ghetto. They are not, to be sure, set apart from the natives by barriers, chains, and bridges, but spiritually and socially it is as if they are separated by a wide river."[83] As if to illustrate this point, the Austrian (gentile) writer Leopold Sacher-Masoch, opened one of his *Jewish Stories* from 1878 titled "Moses Goldfarb's House" as follows: "It was not actually a ghetto in which Moses Goldfarb lived with his own, but rather a bona fide Polish-Jewish tavern . . . standing a mere hundred steps outside the village on the Kaiserstrasse. Nevertheless, the ghetto is everywhere where an authentic pious Jew settles, and where the Torah thrusts its invisible, but insurmountable walls between him and the rest of the world, in particular where he lives as completely alone among Christians, separated from his brethren, as Moses Goldfarb."[84] One could be a "ghetto Jew," like Moses Goldfarb, despite living in a rural village virtually alone among Christians, in a setting that hardly resembled the Galician shtetl or "Gasse," let alone the historical ghetto. What mattered was that one still lived and breathed under the canopy of Torah. As the German-born American Jewish sociologist Louis Wirth would write fifty years later in his 1928 book *The Ghetto*, "The ghetto is not only a physical fact, it is a state of mind."[85]

In 1889, the centennial of the French Revolution, a liberal Austrian Jewish weekly of the era commemorated the anniversary with an article titled "Bastille and Ghetto." Calling the storming of the Bastille an act that "signified the destruction of absolutism, feudalism, and the entire dreadful medieval state of affairs and the gradual erection of the modern constitutional state," the author stated that, like the Bastille, "the Ghetto was an emblem of the Middle Ages, of barbarity and terrifying arbitrariness in the name of religion."[86] If not for the storming of the Bastille and the ideas of freedom and human rights the revolution heralded, "there might still be a ghetto in many a European state, not only a spatial [ghetto], but a political one, in which the Jews would be excluded from equal participation in the life of the state." Some equated the developing idea of the "ghetto" simply with injustice, intolerance, and cruelty; others identified it with community and authenticity. But however one construed the ghetto, by 1889, it had become the Jewish equivalent to the "Bastille," the metaphor par excellence in the Jewish experience for the "medieval" and "premodern," for all that came before emancipation.

In 1894, the American Reform rabbi David Philipson published *Old European Jewries*, the first effort to trace the rise and fall of the "officially instituted Ghetto." Three parts history, one part travelogue, the book was based on Philipson's wide-ranging reading and memories of his visits to what remained of three of the most famous of the former mandatory Jewish quarters—the Frankfurt Judengasse, the Prague Judenstadt, and the Roman Ghetto. Philipson approached the history of the ghetto as one would expect from an exemplar of classical Reform, with loathing for ideological separatism. For Philipson, the ghetto, along with other segregationist measures like the Jewish badge, belonged to the "dark, medieval days" of the confessional state and Christian fear of Jewish "pest-like" contagion. "What a picture the Ghetto recalls!" Philipson lamented. "The narrow, gloomy streets, with the houses towering high on either side; the sunlight rarely streaming in; situated in the worst slums of the city; shut off by gates barred and bolted every night with chains and locks, none permitted to enter or depart from sundown or sunrise! The solution at last had been found; the Jew was effectively excluded."[87] This exclusion lasted for some four hundred years, until the sun had finally set on the last of the old ghettos—the Ghetto of Rome—in 1870. As a result, Philipson wrote, "The Jews of the civilized world are as free as other men" and "the evil times that invented the ghetto are, it is to be hoped, gone forever." However, the continued plight of the Jews of Eastern Europe—and in particular of the Tsarist Empire—indicated that the ghetto system had yet to be vanquished:

> There, in barbarous Russia, the mediaeval spirit still rules, and a Ghetto exists whose condition is more horrible perhaps than ever that of any Ghetto of earlier days. It stands forth in a blackness the more intense because of the sun of tolerance that shines everywhere else. It is not the Ghetto with which we have become acquainted thus far, a street or section set apart in a town or city, but a district set apart in a country. The Jew is told, "only in certain sections of the land you may dwell." . . . This Russian Ghetto is known as the Pale of Settlement.[88]

Philipson identifies the physical boundaries of the ghetto in 1894 with the Russian "Pale of Settlement," the name given to a significant portion of the vast western borderlands of the empire. The Jews of Tsarist Russia were largely confined to this area (which comprised much of present-day Lithuania, Belarus, Ukraine, Moldova, and Poland); after the persecutory May Laws of 1882, they were mostly prohibited from settling outside its already overcrowded towns and cities ("a Pale within the Pale," in Philipson's words), though this ban was only intermittently enforced. There was thus some measure of legal restriction to warrant Philipson's stretching of the term, though the existence of a "Russian Ghetto" was purely metaphorical. Still, the thrust of Philipson's history was that the days of the involuntary ghetto were everywhere numbered. The ghetto might still exist, but it should not exist, and eventually—with the inexorable progress of emancipation—would no longer exist, because it was unjust and anachronistic.

While Philipson confidently prophesized that the end of the ghetto was at hand, a play called *The New Ghetto* was published by a prominent Central European Jewish cosmopolitan intellectual, the thirty-four-year-old Viennese journalist Theodor Herzl. His four-act drama was set in a contemporary Vienna of increasingly antisemitic politics that would culminate, in 1895, in the election of an antisemitic mayor—the Christian Socialist Karl Lüger—to run one of Europe's most artistically avant-garde cities. The play is best described as a tragedy of the "emancipated Jew" whose determination to get "out of the ghetto" is foiled by antisemitic rejection and the false messiah of assimilationism. It concludes with the Jew's own martyrdom. Jacob Samuel is a young, earnest, newly married lawyer who is a product of and has married into the Viennese Jewish upper middle class. His family, both native and acquired, is a kind of Jewish subculture filled with the stock types of anti-Jewish caricature: from his overprotective mother; to his superficial and materialistic wife Hermine, the daughter of a wealthy textile manufacturer; to his money-grubbing and morally dubious brother-in-law Rheinberg, a stock market speculator. Jacob alone appears to wish to remain formally Jewish (refusing the path taken by the formerly Jewish physician in the play, Dr. Bichler, who has opted for baptism) while still breaking free of stereotypically "Jewish" characteristics. He places immense value on his long-time friendship with the gentile doctor Franz Wurzlechner, and he expresses shame and regret at having, years before, backed out of a duel with an Austrian noble, Captain von Schramm, after a petty quarrel between them. Shortly after the wedding, the officiating rabbi, Friedhammer, mindful of the continued influx of Eastern European Jews into Vienna and of the mounting strength of the antisemitic movement, engages Jacob in a debate over the merits of the "ghetto," along with the possibility and desirability of escape:

FRIEDHAMMER: The ghetto was gloomy and unclean, but family values blossomed therein. The father was a patriarch. The mother . . . lived only for her children—who in turn lovingly revered their

parents. Do not vilify the Judengasse to me, my good friend. It is
our poor home.

JACOB: I'm not vilifying it! I'm only saying, we must get out!

FRIEDHAMMER: And I am answering you: we can't! When the real
ghetto still stood, we could not leave it without permission—at great
danger to our lives. Now the walls and barriers are invisible, as you
say. But this moral ghetto also is our prescribed abode. Woe to him,
who wants to get out. . . .

JACOB: Herr Doctor, we need only break these barriers differently
than the old ones. The outer barriers had to be pulled down from
the outside, but the inner ones we must uproot ourselves! We ourselves! From ourselves![89]

The remainder of the play dramatizes Jacob's failure to achieve this liberation. Franz coldly breaks off his friendship with Jacob, claiming that,
on account of his political ambitions, he cannot afford to be associated
with Jacob's new entourage of stock exchange Jews. Then Jacob becomes
entangled in a legal and financial mess that makes of the already contemptuous Captain von Schramm a sworn enemy. The rather convoluted
plot centers on a coal mine owned yet neglected by von Schramm and
his brother-in-law and coveted by Jacob's own brother-in-law Rheinberg.
Jacob reluctantly draws up the papers for a deal converting the mine into
a publicly traded company, giving Schramm the opportunity to acquire
much-needed capital and Rheinberg the right to purchase one-third of
the shares. Shortly thereafter, a representative of the mine workers visits
Jacob, who has developed a reputation as a workers' advocate, to complain about the deplorable conditions at Schramm's mine. Jacob agrees
to investigate, and in the aftermath of his visit the miners decide to strike.
When they return to work after a three-week walkout, disaster ensues.
Water that had backed up in the mine during the hiatus breaks through
its foundations, causing a massive loss of life. The value of the company
plummets, financially ruining Schramm yet providing Rheinberg (via his
agent, the unrefined yet *echt*-Galician Jew Wasserstein) with an opportunity to buy up shares on the cheap. Schramm barges into Jacob's office
and accuses him of having orchestrated the strike, in collaboration with

his "Judenpack" ("Jewish rabble") of partners, to destroy him. Jacob slaps him in response, and as a result he finally gets the duel he had earlier avoided—and dies of his wounds. His final, stammering words are a testament to his foiled aspirations: "Jews, my brothers, they will first let you live again—when you. . . . Why do you hold me—so firmly? . . . I want—out! . . . Out—out—of the—ghetto!"[90]

The contrast between Herzl's and Philipson's works from 1894 was stark. Philipson was confident that the Owl-of-Minerva moment of the "ghetto" had arrived with the triumph and spread of emancipation. Its final dissolution was not yet a reality, but the end was visible and growing nearer on the horizon. Simply by his choice of title *The New Ghetto*, Herzl put this confidence into question.[91] The ghetto was not limited to the now-dismantled "old European Jewry" that the modern Jew had escaped and could safely regard from a distance. Nor was it, in a looser sense, the spiritual setting of all the not-yet emancipated or acculturated, the continued denizens of the East European *shtetlakh*. It was, on the contrary, a shadow that even the most zealous assimilationist and would-be foil to the "ghetto Jew" could not shake. Through *The New Ghetto*, Herzl worked through his growing doubts over the viability of emancipation and assimilation that would, a year later, lead him to embrace political Zionism. Only with the emergence of a "new Jew" disabused of the fantasy that assimilation could solve the Jewish Question and convinced of the need to redeem Jewish honor through the creation of a Jewish homeland would Jews be able, finally, to leave the ghetto behind.[92]

The attitude toward the ghetto of early Zionists was, in fact, ambivalent. This was especially true of Zionists of Western backgrounds, like Herzl or his lieutenant in the Zionist Organization, the writer, physician, and critic Max Nordau, who embraced Jewish nationalism only after growing disenchanted with a cosmopolitanism they had once championed.[93] Zionism, like other modernizing Jewish movements, rejected the ghetto and promised to heal its supposed pathologies. Nordau's famous call in 1903 for a "Jewry of muscle" was predicated on the claim that centuries of confinement in the ghetto had contributed to an atrophying of the Jewish body. "All the elements of Aristotelian physics—light, air, water and earth—were measured out to us very sparingly. In the narrow Jewish street our poor limbs soon forgot their gay movements; in the dimness of sunless houses our eyes began to blink shyly." Yet times had changed: "now, all coercion has become a memory of the past, and at least we are allowed space enough for our bodies to live again. Let us take up our oldest traditions; let us once again become deep chested, sturdy, sharp-eyed men."[94] Nordau's opinion of the "ghetto," however, was by no means purely negative. In his speech to the First Zionist Congress (1897), Nordau surprised the delegates by coming to the defense of the ghetto Jew, whom he compared favorably to his emancipated successor. "The word 'ghetto,'" Nordau pronounced, "is today associated with feelings of shame and humiliation. But students of national psychology and history know that the ghetto, whatever may have been the intentions of the peoples who created it, was for the Jew of the past not a prison, but a refuge." The ghetto Jew was legally without rights, but psychologically free, because his values and role models were proper to the little Jewish world—"the spiritual and moral equivalent of a motherland"—that he inhabited to the full. The spiritual serenity and security of the ghetto Jew lay in stark contrast to the abject confusion and neurosis of the self-hating emancipated Jew. For the latter, having severed and sedulously concealed all his former ties with the ghetto, staking all on acceptance by and imitation of the gentiles, the cold shoulder of his "countrymen" came as a devastating blow: "He has lost his home in the ghetto yet the land of his birth is denied to him as his home."[95] The ghetto Jew, in short, possessed something the emancipated Jew sorely lacked: a national pride and psychological wholeness that Zionism, without resorting to the coercion and confinement characteristic of the ghetto, promised to recapture. For Nordau, the emancipated Jew—"insecure in his relations with his fellow man, timid with strangers, and suspicious even of the secret feelings of his friends"—was more in need of therapy than the ghetto Jew who, for all his crudeness and foibles, never sought to hide from his Jewishness. We might say that Nordau viewed Herzl's "new ghetto" of nouveau riche parvenus—the invisible, intractable ghetto of those most confident of having left the ghetto—with far more disdain than he did the original "ghetto."

Over the course of the nineteenth century, an Italian term for a restricted Jewish quarter became a general symbol of pre-emancipated Jewish society. The ghetto as a place and institution appeared to be receding into the past as the century progressed; the "ghetto" as a word and concept, by contrast, was more widely used and diversely applied than had ever been the case in the ghetto's heyday. Herzl's phrase the "new ghetto" was the ultimate product of the path from place to metaphor blazed by the term. It indicated how deeply the notion of the ghetto as a counter-concept to emancipation and assimilation had taken root in the modern Jewish imagination, even if the whole thrust of his play was to question this opposition. At the very moment Herzl was writing of a "new ghetto" of the inward-looking Viennese Jewish bourgeoisie, observers were increasingly struck by the presence of densely packed neighborhoods of mostly poor Jewish immigrants from Eastern Europe in the cities of the West (including Vienna), living in what were either entirely new urban enclaves or expansions of previously existing ones. By 1894, the word *ghetto* was increasingly used to designate these quarters as well. The "new ghetto" of the late nineteenth century was not only a psychological space of the socially snubbed but was also, once again, a physical place in the big city. And this was connected to the greatest geographical leap the word *ghetto* had taken to date: its crossing of the Atlantic to America.

3

THE GHETTO COMES

TO AMERICA

ONE DAY IN THE 1880S, an aspiring author and recent Russian Jewish immigrant set out for the office of the New York *Sun* with an article he had written in his pocket. His name was Abraham Cahan, and the article he was carrying was "a set of vignettes of life in the Jewish quarter" of New York. Summoning the courage to submit the article for consideration in person, he walked into the Lower Manhattan office of the *Sun*, a newspaper "then at the peak of its reputation and influence," and was directed to the chief manuscript reader for the Sunday edition. "We'll print this next Sunday," he told a delighted Cahan, encouraging him to "bring him more such copy." But when Cahan was about to leave, the editor called him back. "Pardon me," he said. "You use a word about which I must ask. What is a ghetto?"[1]

Recalling this episode in his memoirs some forty years later, when he had become a giant of Yiddish journalism as editor of the *Forward* and a renowned author of immigrant fiction, Cahan remembered thinking, "Was it possible for an educated man not to know the meaning of that word?" A more charitable interpretation would be that the term *ghetto* was not yet part of the American lexicon. By the 1920s, however, this unfamiliarity was a distant memory. "Today," Cahan asserted confidently, "every major American city has a Jewish quarter, some of them as large as a city. . . . And every American understands the meaning of the word ghetto. He knows that it is not the part of the city in which Jews are compelled to live; that kind of ghetto does not exist. It is merely the neighborhood in which large numbers of Jews have settled."[2]

Of all the turns in the conceptual history of the ghetto, one of the most significant, in terms of both the physical and mental distance traveled, was its migration from Europe to America in the late nineteenth and twentieth centuries. Yet it is fair to ask whether the ghetto was ever "merely the neighborhood in which large numbers of Jews have settled." At most, it can be said that if it had become possible by the late 1920s to define "ghetto" as "the neighborhood in which large numbers of Jews have settled"—in other words, as a voluntary Jewish quarter—it was only after an extended process of redefinition in which multiple individuals, Cahan prominently among them, had played a part.[3]

As the old mandatory ghettos and Judengassen in Western and Central Europe were dismantled—culminating in the liberation of the last surviving ghetto in the West, in Rome, in 1870—the focus of the struggle for Jewish emancipation was directed to holdouts like Romania and the Russian Empire. With respect to legally imposed segregation, it appeared to many—including to the American Reform rabbi David Philipson, author of the 1894 *Old European Jewries*—that the only remaining "ghetto" in the world was the largest in the history of the idea, the Pale of Settlement in Tsarist Russia. To the degree that "ghetto" had also become synonymous with traditional Jewish society—a society depicted as at once isolated and backward, yet also as a vanishing world of authentic Jewishness, in the new genre of ghetto literature—the perception of an eastward migration of the ghetto to Bohemia and Moravia, or to Galicia and Bukovina, received further confirmation. The "ghetto Jew" in the nineteenth-century Jewish mind became a bearded, Yiddish-speaking, caftan-wearing Eastern European Jew.

The return westward of the "ghetto" in the late nineteenth and early twentieth centuries was principally a result of the mass emigration of Jews out of Eastern Europe. Much of the old conventional wisdom about this exodus—most notably, that it began promptly in the wake of the 1881 pogroms in the southern Pale and that it was motivated above all by a desire to escape political violence or conscription in the tsar's army—has been demonstrated to be false.[4] Though the magnitude of the wave certainly grew substantially in the 1880s, the migration of Russian and Polish Jews had begun earlier in the nineteenth century and was in fact consistent with a westward shift starting in the seventeenth and eighteenth centuries.[5] And the chief motivation for this outflow, as in most cases of mass immigration, was economic, not political. Over the course of the nineteenth century, the size of the Jewish community in Eastern Europe (including not only the Russian Pale but also Austrian Galicia and Romania) more than quintupled, yet the Jewish economy—hemmed in by residential restrictions that grew ever stricter, confronted by the competition of surrounding nationalities that were developing their own nascent commercial and professional classes, and limited mostly to light industry and an itinerant peddling that was increasingly outmoded—was unable to keep pace.

As a result, by 1914 more than three million Eastern European Jews had left their country of origin and created new immigrant colonies in cities in the West.[6] Typically, the newcomers settled initially in districts that had long been the site of Jewish neighborhoods and in some cases, at an earlier point, even compulsory ghettos. Vienna's Jewish population was mainly concentrated in Leopoldstadt, the Habsburg capital's second district. The site of a mandatory Jewish enclosure in the seventeenth century, before most Jews were expelled from Vienna for the second time in their history in 1670, Leopoldstadt reemerged as a voluntary Jewish neighborhood in the decades after 1848, with the lifting of the remaining curbs on Jewish residence.[7] In 1880, nearly half (48.3 percent) of Vienna's Jews lived in Leopoldstadt, accounting for just shy of one-third (29.6 percent) of the district's total population; by 1910, Leopoldstadt's total share of Viennese Jews (whose number had climbed from roughly 73,000 to 175,000 in that thirty-year span) had fallen to one-third (32.4 percent), though they accounted for a slightly larger percentage of the second district (33.9 percent). By the end of the nineteenth century, the poorer sections of Leopoldstadt (including the section to the north known as Brigittenau) were largely occupied by immigrant Jews from the provinces (especially from Habsburg Galicia), and the district "became a 'Jewish ghetto' once again in the popular imagination."[8] This reputation remained intact through the 1930s, especially because the area was further inundated by an influx of Jewish refugees from Eastern Europe in the 1910s and 1920s uprooted by World War I and the numerous wars and pogroms in Poland, Ukraine, and Russia that followed in its wake.[9]

If Vienna had its Leopoldstadt, Paris had its *Pletzl* (Yiddish for "little square"), located in the fourth *arrondissement* on the right bank and centered around the Rue des Rosiers. The site of one of the oldest juiveries established in Paris before the expulsion of Jews from France in the fourteenth century, the area became a Jewish quarter once again in the early nineteenth century, when it attracted immigrant Jews from Alsace-Lorraine.[10] A century later, its Jewish character remained intact, but the residents were then largely Yiddish-speaking Russian and Romanian Jews. "Its narrow streets," Paula Hyman writes, "displayed signs in Yiddish, harbored kosher butcher shops and Jewish restaurants, and gave shelter to the petty commerce of immigrant peddlers." Paris attracted some 30,000 Eastern European Jewish immigrants between 1881 and 1914. That number climbed to 150,000 in the interwar years, after the United States and Great Britain had essentially closed their doors.[11] While East European Jewish immigrants also settled in Montmartre and between the wars in an area known as Belleville, the Pletzl remained the area of densest concentration and the most slum-like conditions. "The alleys are frightfully dirty," A. Frumkin wrote in the *Jewish Daily Forward* of New York in 1912, and "the houses mostly old ruins," with "twelve to fifteen persons" often "living in two small rooms."[12] As earlier immigrants moved out of the Pletzl in the 1920s and 1930s, new immigrants moved in, and the representation of the Pletzl as a "ghetto" spread beyond the borders of France. In an article titled "An Evening in the Parisian Ghetto," written for the *Prague Daily Paper* in 1925, the author noted, "Like all great cities, Paris, in one of its oldest and filthiest corners behind the Hotel-de-Ville, has its singular ghetto. It is not large, one can traverse it in a quarter of an hour; but the Rue des Rosiers has nonetheless its own, self-contained imprint and from the first house smells completely different from the rest of Paris."[13]

Berlin's Jewish quarter could not compare to Leopoldstadt and the Pletzl (not to mention London's East End or New York's Lower East Side) in size, in part because East European immigrants to Imperial Germany faced more acute and sustained pressure from both non-Jews and native German Jews to disperse and integrate into German life—or leave the country.[14] Yet there too a miniature immigrant "ghetto" took root before World War I in the streets of the *Scheunenviertel* ("Barn Quarter"). In 1904, Jacob Thon, a Galician rabbinical student in Berlin, portrayed a stark contrast between the "broad, airy, clean streets" of Berlin where one could "breathe freely" and the "small, filthy alleys" of the "former Jewish ghetto," where the "characteristic *Judengassen*" remain in place and "all the foreign Jewish immigrants concentrate."[15] Most of these immigrants in pre–World War I Berlin moved out of the Scheunenviertel as soon as they had the chance; in 1910, only 25 percent of Eastern European Jews in Berlin proper lived in the quarter. Still, the "Jewish" reputation of Scheunenviertel endured and was enhanced by the migration of tens of thousands of East European Jews both during World War I (as refugees or forced laborers) and in the Weimar period.[16] "Wherever Eastern European Jews migrate and settle," one contemporary observer wrote in 1920, "there is formed without any external compulsion, with more or less sharp contours, a ghetto, the tightest clustering in a territorial sense. Berlin has in the Hiertenviertel, the earlier Scheunenviertel, its typical ghetto." The author noted that the area was known in the local jargon as the "Jewish Switzerland" and that one of its main streets, Grenadier-straße, was 95 percent Eastern European (and mostly Galician) Jewish and in its language, mores, and customs was cut off from the rest of "great, booming Berlin." Yet, the Jewish quarter of Berlin was nothing like the great immigrant ghettos of London and New York, in part because the absence of a common "Jewish" industry like the garment trade made it difficult to keep the immigrants clustered together. "The Eastern European Jews," she conceded, "are distributed across the center [of the city] to the outermost periphery, and over the years the dispersion within the city divisions has grown stronger."[17] Despite including Berlin in his overview of "Ghettoes in the West" Joseph Roth also downplayed the degree to which it truly contained a vibrant Jewish neighborhood. Because Berlin was a "point of transit" from which immigrants generally wanted to move on to America, and because the city made more concerted efforts to assimilate newcomers, Berlin's "ghetto" was hardly a ghetto at all, but "just a couple of small Jewish streets around the Warschauer Brücke and in the Scheunenviertel."[18]

None of these Jewish ethnic enclaves compared in size to London's East End, which was the largest in Western Europe. And no one did more to cement the identification of such enclaves with the word *ghetto* than the Anglo-Jewish humorist, journalist, and writer of fiction Israel Zangwill. His 1892 *Children of the Ghetto: A Study of a Peculiar People* was a literary sensation that effectively inaugurated a new kind of ghetto novel, one whose setting would be the new, largely immigrant "ghetto" of the big city. The novel went through numerous reprints, was translated into several languages (including German, Hebrew, and Yiddish), and made Zangwill perhaps the most prominent, widely recognized English Jew of his day. It contained two parts. The first, "Children of the Ghetto," was a series of thematically linked portraits of the culture and folkways of London's East End immigrant Jews. The second and shorter of the two, "Grandchildren of the Ghetto," explored the lives and dilemmas of identity of the "West End" upper- and middle-class English Jews who had either personally escaped the ghetto or were at least a generation removed from the East End. The two sections are linked not only by recurring personas but also by a kind of bidirectionality, as characters not only leave the ghetto, but in some cases return.

Zangwill himself was a "child" of the ghetto, born to immigrants from Latvia and Poland, though at the time of his birth in London's East End in 1864, the steady inflow of Eastern European Jews had not yet become the flood it would be after 1880.[19] From the time Portuguese and then Ashkenazic Jews began resettling in London in the second half of the seventeenth century, some four hundred years after their formal expulsion from England in 1290, they settled mainly in the City of London and in the streets immediately to the east. There was no mandatory ghetto for the new population of Jews; the community itself was organized on voluntaristic foundations, without the corporate status that made it easier for most communities on the continent at the time to punish religious laxity and enforce discipline. Well into the eighteenth and early nineteenth centuries, the east side of the City of London remained home to nearly all Jews: rich and poor, native born and immigrant, Sephardic and Ashkenazic alike. Starting around 1825, wealthy Jews began leaving for leafier, more upscale areas like the West End, even as, with the decline of the City of London as a residential area, the nearly two-thirds of London Jews who remained in the "old" neighborhood throughout the nineteenth century continually pushed its boundaries farther east (into Whitechapel) and south.

Photo London Stereo.

Israel Zangwill, undated.

Between 1881 and 1914, as many as 150,000 Eastern European immigrants settled in Great Britain. This more than doubled the size of the
country's Jewish population and dramatically transformed the character
of English Jewry, which before this influx had become largely middle class,
fully emancipated, and enthusiastic citizens of the British state. Most of
the immigrants—some 60 to 70 percent—settled in London, especially
in the East End. "Long a point of arrival for newcomers," Todd Endelman
writes, "the East End offered opportunities for employment, was home
to synagogues and other institutions necessary to lead a traditional Jewish
life, and, above all, was the chief residence of fellow Yiddish-speaking
Jews who had arrived earlier in the century."[20] Almost two-thirds of male
workers in London in 1901 were concentrated in the clothing, footwear,
and furniture trades, with almost half of the total in tailoring and the garment industry. By 1914, London was third only to New York and Chicago in its population of Eastern European Jewish immigrants. They lived

clustered together in a two-square-mile East End neighborhood that contained one of the most densely populated areas in England.[21]

By the time of the 1880s immigrant influx, Zangwill had abandoned Jewish observance and was no longer a "child" of the ghetto. After studying and winning a prize for scholastic achievement at the East End's Jews' Free School—one of the premier institutions dedicated to "Anglicizing" Jewish immigrant youth—he had proceeded to the University of London, from which he graduated with triple honors in 1884. During the 1880s, he began his career as a writer and journalist, earning particular renown for satiric columns and short fiction that portrayed and sometimes lampooned the two later subjects of *Children of the Ghetto*: both East End working-class and West End middle-class Jewish life. He was a big enough name in Anglo-Jewish letters by 1890 that the newly formed Jewish Publication Society of America would commission him to write *Children of the Ghetto*. It was that work that would set Zangwill on the path to transatlantic fame and earn him a reputation as an expert on the Jewish ghetto past and present.

Zangwill began *Children* with a "Proem" containing a point-blank acknowledgment of how the term *ghetto* itself was being defined, or perhaps redefined. "*Not here in our London Ghetto the gates and gaberdines of the olden Ghetto of the Eternal City; yet no lack of signs external by which one may know it; and those who dwell therein*. . . . The particular Ghetto that is the dark background upon which our pictures will be cast, is of voluntary formation." The survival of the ghetto following the removal of legal coercion reflected the internalization of the constraints and isolation it imposed. "People who have been living in a Ghetto for a couple of centuries," Zangwill wrote, "are not able to step outside merely because the gates are thrown down, nor to efface the brands on their souls by putting off the yellow badges. The isolation imposed from without will have come to seem the law of their being." Moreover, the constant flow of poor, devout Jews into East London contributed to the preservation of the area's character: "Such people are their own Ghetto gates; when they migrate they carry them across the sea to lands where they are not."[22]

The representation of the ghetto in literature lay on a spectrum with, on one end, alienation from a setting seen as miniature in size, narrow in its horizons, and embarrassingly behind the times and, on the other, nostalgia for a vanishing world, often a former home, whose emotional thickness of Jewish life would perish along with it. Zangwill's novel is closer to the pole of nostalgia. The opening "Proem" is mainly a eulogy for the East End of the eighteenth and early nineteenth centuries, when the wealthy *Takif,* or "man of substance," lived in the same neighborhood (if not the same street) as the needy *schnorrer* (beggar), when rich and poor alike converged on Petticoat Lane ("the stronghold of hardshell Judaism") and the "Great *Shool.*"[23] Zangwill laments that "only vestiges of the old gaiety and brotherhood remained; the full al fresco flavor was evaporated." Yet even the pale substitute that was the mostly impoverished, overworked, and underfed immigrant "ghetto" was not without its charms and poetry. "[T]*his London Ghetto of ours is a region where, amid uncleanness and squalor, the rose of romance blows yet a little longer in the raw air of English reality.*"[24] The "grandchild of the ghetto," ensconced in her West End refuge, was separated not only from the East End that endured thanks to continuous replenishment by traditional immigrants but also from a time when the "children" and the "grandchildren," as it were, dwelled side by side, in one community.

Zangwill's nostalgia does not prevent him from shining a light on the extreme poverty of the ghetto. The book opens by introducing us to the desperate straits of the family of the young Esther Ansell—the figure who, over the course of the novel, will come closest to resembling a protagonist. She lives with her widowed and financially inept father, her four younger siblings, and her old grandmother in a one-room garret apartment. Beyond dramatizing the destitution of the East End, Zangwill also evinces a disdain for the aesthetics of ghetto Orthodoxy that frequently crosses into snark. To the degree a plot line can be discerned in the first part of *Children,* it involves a kind of tragicomedy of Jewish law at its most rigid and absurd. When, at a party, a young fellow named Sam Levine jokingly places a ring on the finger of Hannah Abrams, the daughter of the pious and genial ghetto rabbi Reb Shemuel, and recites the traditional formula of Jewish marriage, an elderly man in attendance gravely informs Sam that he has unwittingly married her and will have to give her a *Gett* (a "bill of divorce") to annul it, which Reb Shemuel ultimately arranges. Hannah, who inwardly chafes under the restrictions of the law, falls in love with an assimilated Jew, and to her surprise, her father gives his blessing to their proposed marriage. All then appears well, until the fiancé mentions offhand to Reb Shemuel that he is a *Cohen,* or member of the priestly caste, whereupon the father sadly but sternly revokes his sanction of the marriage, since a *Cohen* is forbidden by Jewish law from marrying a divorcée and Hannah, however technically, holds that status. Hannah initially plans to elope with her fiancé, but in the end leaves him hanging and remains with her family, submitting to her father's wishes.

If Zangwill's ghetto is a site of ugliness, indigence, and a confining legalism, it is also, paradoxically, a site of plenitude. Even sapped of the diversity it had before the dispersion that turned the ghetto into a neighborhood of the immigrant poor, it teems with life and color in a way that forms a stark contrast with the comparative elegance yet also dullness of the "English Judaism" beyond the ghetto. Describing the spectacle of the Petticoat Lane market just before Passover, when the rich graduates of the ghetto briefly return to the East End to buy familiar foods for the festival ("ladies in satins and furs . . . jammed against wretched looking foreign women with their heads swathed in dirty handkerchiefs"), Zangwill paints the scene with a prose that is quasi-Dickensian in its abundance: "It was impossible to think of aught but humanity in the bustle and confusion, in the cram and crush, in the wedge and the jam, in the squeezing and shouting, in the hubbub and medley. Such a jolly, rampant, screaming, fighting, maddening, jostling, polyglot, quarrelling, laughing broth of a Vanity Fair!" Zangwill's reservations about "Anglicization" are legible when he portrays the streaming of a motley crew of students to the East End's Jews' Free School, Zangwill's own alma mater, "all hastening at the inexorable clang of the big school-bell to be ground in the same great, blind, inexorable Governmental machine."[25] Even when invoking categories of students whose disappearance would hardly be cause for disappointment—who would wish to see the preservation of "sickly children" or "cold and famished children"?—Zangwill, through the sheer force of his accumulating litany and with his somewhat Victorian view of the school as a "great, blind, inexorable Governmental machine," manages to convey a sense of loss at how "Anglicization" seems to swallow up and homogenize a whole array of types.

Zangwill's ambivalence about "Anglicization" moves to center stage when the focus turns to the English Jewish upper middle classes and the identity conflicts of the twenty-something crowd and their different visions of postghetto Judaism. Strikingly, two years before Herzl authored his *New Ghetto*, Zangwill notes that for all their meticulous emulation of English high society, the economic Jewish elite are hardly integrated. "For the history of the Grandchildren of the Ghetto," he writes, "which is mainly a history of the middle-classes, is mainly a history of isolation."[26] Social separatism remains the touchstone of the Jewish experience, even of those who have gotten out of the ghetto.

"Grandchildren" examines three different responses to this condition. First, there is the option of returning to the ghetto, represented by Esther Ansell. When we first meet her in Part II, the former ghetto denizen is a melancholic, headache-prone woman in her early twenties. Mordantly critical of the materialism and insularity of Anglo-Jewish society, she expresses her views only in an anonymously published novel widely panned by the Jewish community. Eventually, unable to tolerate the discrepancy between her public and private self, she takes leave of Jewish high society to return, at least temporarily, to the "unspeakably sordid and squalid" ghetto. Zangwill homes in on two male characters, both in love with Esther, who also seek to overcome the isolation of the ghetto and its "grandchildren," albeit in sharply different ways. The Oxford-educated Raphael Leon, a product of the West End, seeks a revival of English Judaism by stumping for a refined, idealistic, intellectually justified Orthodoxy confident of its mission and continued relevance to humankind. Rev. Joseph Strelitski is a Russian immigrant and child of the ghetto who defects to become the pulpit rabbi of a Kensington congregation; eventually he can no longer tolerate defending an Orthodoxy he sees as outmoded and comes to espouse the creation of a postrabbinic, postceremonial Hebraism that will be "all-inclusive" and provide the world with the "broad simple faith" it needs. The novel ends with Esther, Raphael, and Strelitski standing on the deck of a steamer about to leave for America: Strelitski is traveling in hopes of realizing his cosmopolitan vision in a more auspicious setting, and Esther to visit her family and attend her sister's wedding in Chicago. It is implied, but not assured that Esther will ultimately return to London to marry Raphael. The final vision is of Raphael "waving his handkerchief towards the throbbing vessel that glided with its freight of hopes and dreams across the great waters towards the New World."[27]

The voyage to America with which Zangwill's book concludes was prescient and perhaps not entirely coincidental, as we will see. England, after all, was a major point of transit for Eastern European Jews traveling on to America. Because of the fierce competition on Atlantic emigrant routes, it was often cheaper to travel from northern Europe through England to America than to make the trip directly.[28] England, then, could be said to have performed a part in the ghetto's migration from the Old to the New World. And Zangwill's best-selling book would play a not-insignificant role in the story of how "ghetto"—the word itself, as both a generic term and a place name—came to America.

For most of the nineteenth century, the word *ghetto* was foreign to Americans. Literally, it was an Italian loanword of uncertain etymology that was just beginning to usurp the equivalent term for the quarter to which Jews were restricted in other languages. Figuratively, it was even more alien. For nineteenth-century American Jews, the ghetto functioned in much the same way as it did for their coreligionists in Western and Central Europe; that is, as a counterimage, a symbol of a place and mentality left behind. Yet, in America, there was another negative resonance added to this cluster of connotations. The ghetto was not only a marker for the "premodern" and "pre-emancipated." It was also a marker of Europe, the "Old World" vis-à-vis the "New." The word *ghetto* certainly appeared in the nineteenth-century American Jewish press; newspapers like the *American Hebrew* and the *Jewish Messenger* furnished a steady account of the decline of the ghettos of Italy and Central Europe, just as they joined in the growing representation of the "Pale of Settlement" as a ghetto on a grand scale. But the ghetto was always something over there, across the ocean, as distant spatially as it was temporally.

The few challenges to this conventional wisdom before the late nineteenth century testify mainly to just how discordant the juxtaposition of "ghetto" and "America" would have sounded. In late April 1862, the *Jewish Messenger,* a New York-based weekly known for its anti-Reform line, ran a column titled "Our 'Judenstrasse.'"[29] No byline was given, although the author of the piece was undoubtedly the newspaper's editor, Samuel Isaacs, who had founded the weekly back in 1857 to be the voice of Orthodoxy in America.[30] "What an idea—a 'Judenstrasse' in New York and in the 19th century," the article began—"the 'Ghetto' is but the fanciful emanation of some novelist's brain—the 'Judenstrasse' is a fallacy. . . . Possibly there is no place on the continent [i.e., Europe] where our coreligionists dwell in any considerable numbers, but memorialises their sojourn by a street named after them." New York's Jews had no such officially named street: "Our *Judenstrasse* is not so designated, but it might with propriety be termed so at least one day in seven." The Judenstrasse the author had in mind was not Chatham Street, located on the southern edge of the notorious Five Points neighborhood, though this street—which formed the heart of America's secondhand clothing trade—had acquired a reputation as a Jewish street already in the 1830s and 1840s.[31] Nor was he referring to the Little Germany ("Kleindeutschland") enclave east of the Bowery, later to become known as the Lower East Side (and "New York Ghetto"), even though Jewish immigrants from Central and Eastern Europe already formed a considerable percentage of the area's residents by the 1850s.[32] Rather, "our *Judenstrasse*" was the Broadway of "elegant buildings," "stately banking establishments," and "commercial palaces" north of Canal Street on a Saturday afternoon. This apparently was where and when upwardly mobile and fashionable Jews liked to promenade ("always provided the weather is propitious"), turning Broadway for one afternoon a week "into a *Boulevard* graced by the presence of young Israel." The author's contempt for this crowd was not far from the surface. "Undoubtedly," he wryly concluded, "we are a great people."

The author alternates throughout between the terms *Judenstrasse* and *Ghetto*. If anything, given the title, he favors the former, which is not surprising when one considers the dominant place of immigrants from German-speaking Europe in the Jewish community of mid-nineteenth-century New York, especially within the rapidly acculturating middle class the author is skewering. He is less interested in conferring a new (or, for that matter, old) label on a particular area than in hitting the target of his moral and religious critique where it will hurt most, by suggesting that the New York Jews who like to congregate on Broadway on Saturdays "to see and to be seen"—the very group most likely to see themselves as having left the "ghetto"—have brought the Judenstrasse with them.

A less ironic application of the ghetto label to an American neighborhood would have to await the surge in Jewish immigration starting in the last quarter of the nineteenth century. Between 1881 and 1924, more than two-and-one-half million Jews left Eastern Europe for America. On arrival, they tended to settle in cities and to cluster in downtown neighborhoods, and the sheer size of the immigration wave ensured that these enclaves—from the Lower East Side of New York to Brownsville in Brooklyn to the Great West Side of Chicago—rapidly became known for their extreme congestion and distinct ethnic character. At its height in the first decade of the twentieth century, when it housed more than a half-million inhabitants in an area of roughly half of a square mile, the Lower East Side was the most densely populated space in the world.[33]

It is impossible to determine with certainty when these emerging enclaves were originally labeled ghettos. But in 1878, by which time the replacement of German Americans by East European Jewish immigrants on the Lower East Side was already far advanced, the author of a profile of New York's Jewish quarter, in the October edition of *Harper's,* wrote that it was strange "that there should be a 'Ghetto' in an American city, and especially in New York. But there certainly is on the east side of the Bowery, below Canal Street, almost as distinctive a Jewish quarter as is to be found in any of the old European cities where the Jews for centuries have been a proscribed race."[34] In late September 1878, around the time of Rosh Hashanah, the *New York Herald* ran a feature titled "New Year in the Ghetto," which described the "decorous and impressive" services in the "fashionable temples of the Reformed Jews uptown." The author noted, "Such scenes were representative of only a small proportion of the 80,000 Jews who constitute the Jewish population of New York." The "more interesting side" of "the picture" was provided "by the denizens of what is known as the New York Ghetto," which the author defined as "a quarter of the city inhabited almost exclusively by Russo-Polish Jews and resembling in many respects the old 'Judengasse' of Frankfurt. It lies in the lower part of town, east of the Bowery, and takes in part of Allen, Ludlow, Baxter, Chrystie, Henry and Clinton Streets, East Broadway and Chatham Street."[35]

While references to ghettos in an American context became slightly more common throughout the 1880s, the term was still very novel and, even in New York, might have drawn a blank. Ten years later, ignorance of the word would have been unthinkable, because the "ghetto" truly came to America in the 1890s. References proliferated in that decade, especially in newspaper articles, but also in the titles of books and their chapters. Notable examples of its naturalization include Charles Zeublin's study of Jewish Chicago titled "The Chicago Ghetto," which formed

NEW YORK
LOWER EAST SIDE

Map of the Lower East Side, 1905.

a chapter of Jane Addams's landmark *Hull House Maps and Papers* (1895); Abraham Cahan's fictional debut *Yekl: A Tale of the New York Ghetto* (1896), which became a classic of immigrant literature; or Morris Rosenfeld's collection of Yiddish proletarian poems translated as *Songs of the Ghetto* (1898). In an 1897 article titled "Pictures of the Ghetto," the *New York Times* offered its first feature-length story on the Jewish quarter "south of Houston street and east of the Bowery." "It is quite unnecessary," the author began, "to go to Europe to see a genuine Jewish ghetto. There is one, a large one, the largest in the New World in fact, right here in New York."[36] In 1899, a serialized newspaper column called "Desk Studies for Girls," under the heading "New Words and How to Use Them," listed, alongside terms like "resumé" or "radical" or "bourgeois," the word "ghetto," which it defined as "the part of the city or town formerly set apart for the Jews, as in Rome or Frankfort-on-the-Main," adding that "at present this name is a synonym for 'Jewish quarter.'"[37]

Of all the works written in the 1890s that featured the word *ghetto* in its new sense as a synonym for "Jewish quarter," it was Zangwill's *Children of the Ghetto* that arguably did the most to popularize it. Indeed, Zangwill's novel had an American history from its conception. As mentioned, the newly founded Jewish Publication Society of America, eager to publish popular Jewish fiction for an American audience, looked across the Atlantic to commission what became *Children of the Ghetto*. The book was marketed heavily (and effectively) to an American readership from the start. Released in two volumes in 1892 as *Children of the Ghetto, Being Pictures of a Peculiar People,* the book proved rapidly successful, if controversial.[38] One reviewer, writing for *The American Hebrew,* the leading New York Jewish newspaper of the day, called *Children* a "complete presentation of every phase of Jewish life in a modern city, so that it is all mirrored before us in one comprehensive picture"; he added, "This is valuable to every one of us, however varied be our experience."[39] Another reviewer argued that, despite the book's East End London setting, it had captured the general ambience of modern-day ghettos everywhere. "The Jewish character," he wrote, "is of such strongly-marked nature that wherever the same class be found, in every large city of civilization . . . the same types may be recognized by those who have any knowledge of a ghetto anywhere."[40] The Jewish critical response, however, was far from universally positive. Many faulted Zangwill and the Jewish Publication

Society (JPS) for furnishing antisemites and the enemies of Jewish immigration with grist for their mill with the book's portrait of the "alien" ghetto and its "contemptible" grandchildren.[41] Whether loved or loathed, Zangwill's novel was a hit on both sides of the Atlantic, so much so that, three years later, Macmillan bought the rights from JPS and published a second, single-volume edition of *Children of the Ghetto*.

In a letter describing the kind of book he wanted, Judge Mayer Sulzberger, the chair of the publications committee of JPS, had suggested to Zangwill that he might opt to have his "hero or heroine . . . emigrate to America—'the land of the free and the home of the brave.'"[42] While Zangwill seemed to compromise on this request—ending the novel with his protagonist on a ship departing from Britain for the United States, though perhaps only for a temporary stay—he gave evidence of his high hopes for America as the setting for the final millennial drama of the Jewish "ghetto." Through the figure of Strelinski, the ghetto-bred Russian immigrant and West End rabbi turned utopian dreamer of a cosmopolitan Judaism of the future, Zangwill gave voice to the vision of London's East End as only a pit stop on a story destined to cross the Atlantic: "It is in America . . . that the last great battle of Judaism will be fought out; amid the temples of the New World it will make its last struggle to survive."[43]

In 1898, Zangwill undertook another foray into ghetto literature, albeit of a different sort. *Dreamers of the Ghetto* was a portrait not of one specific Jewish neighborhood, but of "the Ghetto from its establishment in the sixteenth century to its slow breaking-up in our own day."[44] The dreamers of the title were a mix of invented and historical heretics, mystics, messiahs, poets, activists, and politicians, among them Baruch Spinoza ("The Maker of Lenses"), Sabbetai Zevi ("The Turkish Messiah"), the Baal Shem Tov ("The Master of the Name"), Heinrich Heine ("From a Mattress Grave"), and Ferdinand Lassalle ("The People's Saviour"). For all their striking differences, these rebels shared an intellectual and spiritual restlessness that led them to break, in some cases tragically, with the constraining provincialism of the "Ghetto" in pursuit of a more capacious and universalist vision. For Zangwill, the "dream" of the title had "not yet come true," because modern-day Jews, torn between a ghetto stuck in the past and a sterile bourgeois Judaism, had yet to achieve a meaningful synthesis of the old and the new. To that end, he closed *Dreamers* with a special appeal that he titled "To the American Jew." Zangwill urged "you [to] whom the sparkling air of the New World has infused with the energy to give yet another expression to the Dream of the Ghetto," to consummate the long-sought ambition, by bringing about "an immense strengthening of the Jewish spiritual consciousness, a burning conviction of some great world-part to play, some great world-end to serve, and one that can be better served by diffused isolation than concentrated isolation."[45]

If Zangwill hinted that the ghetto was coming to America, if only to meet its end, Cahan confirmed its arrival. *Yekl,* Cahan's fictional breakthrough, portrayed the desperate desire of "Jake," a recent immigrant to New York, to become a true American by abruptly and clumsily breaking with his Russian Jewish past as "Yekl." Yet the true protagonist of Cahan's novella was, in many ways, not a person, but a place: "that part of the East Side which has within the last two or three decades become the Ghetto of the American metropolis, and, indeed, the metropolis of the Ghettos of the world." Cahan introduced this area to the reader in one of the most iconic passages in all of American immigrant fiction:

> It is one of the most densely populated spots on the face of the earth—a seething human sea fed by streams, streamlets, and rills of immigration following from all the Yiddish-speaking centers of Europe. Hardly a block but shelters Jews from every nook and corner of Russia, Poland, Galicia, Hungary, Roumania; Lithuanian Jews, Volhynian Jews, south Russian Jews, Bessarabian Jews; Jews crowded out of the "pale of Jewish settlement"; Russified Jews expelled from Moscow, St. Petersburg, Kieff, or Saratoff; Jewish runaways from justice; Jewish refugees from crying political and economic injustice; people torn from a hard-gained foothold in life and from deep-rooted attachments by the caprice of intolerance and the wiles of demagoguery—innocent scapegoats of a guilty Government for its outraged populace to misspend its blind fury upon; students shut out of the Russian universities, and come to these shores in quest of learning; artisans, merchants, teachers, rabbis, artists, beggars—all come in search of fortune.[46]

What seems at first to be simply a teeming, undifferentiated mass ("a seething human sea") turns out to be varied beyond measure, with virtually

Abraham Cahan, 1937.

every type of East European Jew—indeed, with virtually every type of human—contained therein. No sooner has the narrator meticulously cataloged the variant populations than he returns to the original image of a kind of primeval chaos, explaining how all this diversity is "thrown pell-mell into one social cauldron—a human hodgepodge with its component parts changed but not yet fused into one homogeneous whole." In short, the ghetto itself functions as an assimilative "melting pot."

Such nuances in the makeup of downtown Jewish New York were mostly lost on contemporary observers of the ghetto. Works like the "muckraking" journalist Jacob Riis's classic *How the Other Half Lives* (1890), which pictured the "Hebrew quarter" east of Chinatown—or "Jewtown"—as a nightmarish zone of filth, disease, penury, money-grubbing thrift, and "low intellectual status," fed a growing anxiety about how, if at all, the ghetto could be "Americanized."[47] For all his rhetoric, Riis, himself a Danish-born immigrant, was neither a racial antisemite nor an immigration restrictionist; his point was to indict the tenement system ("the evil offspring of public neglect and private greed") in which three-fourths of New York's population lived. In later writings he expressed greater appreciation for the values, patriotism, and pluck of the immigrant Jews. "Their slums are offensive," he wrote in an 1896 essay, "but unlike those of other less energetic races they are not hopeless unless walled in and made so on the old world plan. They do not rot in their slum, but rising pull it up after them. Nothing stagnates where the Jews are."[48] Yet Riis's words were seized on by opponents of the recent mass immigration from Southern and Eastern Europe as evidence of the need for restriction.[49] Increasingly, nativists alarmed by the immigrant influx attributed the urban clustering of Jews to inherited instinct and expressed skepticism that they could ever be assimilated.[50] Writing in 1914, the American sociologist and eugenicist Edward A. Ross, a race-conscious restrictionist hostile to the new ethnic diversity, said of the immigrant Jews, "Centuries of enforced Ghetto life seem to have bred in them a herding instinct. No other physiques can so well withstand the toxins of urban congestion. Save the Italians, more Jews will crowd upon a given space than any other nationality. As they prosper they do not proportionately enlarge their quarters."[51] Seemingly, the Jews, like other "later aliens" in their miniature, overcrowded ethnic neighborhoods (Little Italy, Little Hungary, Little Armenia) concentrated in the Northeast, formed "insoluble clots," stubbornly resistant to dissolution through geographic dispersion and absorption.[52]

Against this backdrop, concern mounted among the so-called uptown Jews, earlier immigrants from Germany and Central Europe and their descendants who had shed much of their ethnic distinctiveness in the course of their assimilation. Though alienated from the culture of the East European newcomers and anxious about the threat they posed to their own tenuous social status and to the perception of American Judaism, they still generally opposed efforts to restrict immigration. Mindful of the nativist and increasingly racist ethos that underlay such proposed measures, and of the desperate plight of Jews in Russia and Romania who were their coreligionists, the German Jewish elite retained their loyalty to the idea of America as a haven for the oppressed with a unique capacity for assimilating foreigners. Some, however, hoped to break up the ghetto before it became further entrenched in the cities of the north.

In the fall of 1891, the *Jewish Messenger*, which had become an advocate of Reform Judaism, published a series of articles on "The New York Ghetto." There, the editors "solemnly protest[ed] against the tendency to form a Ghetto or Jewish quarter on the East Side of our city," insisting that "there is but one course open, that is, so to disperse of these immigrants on arrival as to relieve the congested condition of the ill-housed myriads on the East Side." The newcomers "must be Americanized, in spite of themselves. They must not be able to care or think for themselves until such time as amalgamation with their neighbors in the rural districts fits them for the amenities of decent society and the duties of citizenship."[53] The call to disperse the ghetto to "rural districts" had more than practical considerations behind it.[54] A small and overcrowded urban enclave flew in the face of America's self-concept as the land of "spacious skies." "Where are the prairies?" a contributor to the *Reform Advocate* wrote in 1913, in a review of the growing genre of immigrant ghetto literature. "The answer that immediately suggests itself is that the prairies—the freer and larger American life—are shut out from the view of these writers by the tall, dismal, and overshadowing tenement houses, which barely permit of a small glimpse of the day. The wide vistas of the open and freer American life are far away."[55] Kaufmann Kohler, the German-born American Reform rabbi and president of Hebrew Union College, the Reform rabbinical seminary, was unequivocal in his rejection of the voluntary segregation of the newcomers, stating point-blank in 1911, "There is no room for Ghetto Judaism in America."[56]

A different attack stemmed from communists who pictured the ghetto as a nightmarish milieu of capitalist exploitation. Michael Gold's indignant memoir of growing up on the Lower East Side, *Jews without Money* (1930), was a "tale of Jewish poverty in one ghetto, that of New York," though "[t]he same story can be told of a hundred other ghettos scattered over all the world." Gold portrayed the "East Side" as a filthy, noisy den of poverty and prostitution oppressed by "the sweatshops, the bawdy houses and Tammany Hall." Through Mikey's father, a painter with fantasies of material success who as a result of a workplace accident ends up futilely hawking bananas on the street, Gold dramatizes the alleged failure of the capitalist "American dream" to rescue the denizens of the

ghetto from their misery. Though there is some wistfulness for the camaraderie of his street "gang of little yids" and for the "free enormous circus
of the East Side," the dominant emotion of *Jews without Money* is a simmering anger—toward Mikey's father for his illusions, toward social
workers and slum tourists for their condescension to the inhabitants of
the ghetto, and toward organized religion for its materialism and duplicity.
The book closes with a paean to the "workers' Revolution," which "will
destroy the East Side when you come, and build there a garden for the
human spirit."[57]

The ghetto, however, had its apologists. The defenses typically were advanced by the Russian Jewish immigrants themselves, and they varied
considerably in their justifications of neighborhood concentration. Some
focused on the essentially temporary nature of the ghetto, arguing that
the newcomers themselves or at least their descendants, by virtue of their
own efforts, would emigrate in time from the immigrant slums without
the need for external intervention. Others trained a spotlight on the virtues and eclecticism of the ghetto as it was, or on the value of Jewish concentration per se, including in ways that challenged the equation of
Americanization with melting-pot assimilation.

For proponents of the American ghetto, it was best understood as a
transit zone or way station, a kind of absorption center that housed immigrants after they had arrived in America, but before they truly entered
American life. The earlier notion of the ghetto as a historical anachronism, out of place in modern society, endured, but with something new
added. In the nineteenth-century Jewish imagination, emancipation was
a one-way road out of the ghetto. The very fact that the ghetto had been
revived, so that now one could speak of movement in *and* out of the
ghetto—of Jews arriving and Jews leaving—indicated that something had
changed. The ghetto was no longer simply before modernity; it was between tradition and modernity. In "The Russian Jew in the United States,"
Abraham Cahan portrayed East European Jewish immigrants as a sober,
industrious lot devoted to acquiring English and "Americanizing" themselves with all due haste. Writing of the popularity of the evening schools
of the New York Ghetto, Cahan proclaimed that "nothing can be more
inspiring to the public-spirited citizen, nothing worthier of the interest of
the student of immigration, than the sight of a gray-haired tailor, a patriarch in appearance, coming after a hard day's work at a sweat-shop, to

spell 'cat, mat, rat,' and to grapple with the difficulties of 'th' and 'w.'"[58] Nor was the existence of a vibrant and diverse Yiddish press and public culture proof of any determination to remain separate and isolated. "The Yiddish periodicals," Cahan contended, "are so many preparatory schools from which the reader is sooner or later promoted to the English news- paper, just as the several Jewish theatres prepare his way to the Broadway playhouse, or as the Yiddish lecture serves him as a stepping-stone to that English-speaking, self-educational society, composed of workingmen who have lived a few years in the country, which is another characteristic fea- ture of life in the Ghetto."[59]

Perhaps the most striking illustration of the view of the New York Ghetto as a transitional site appeared in an article from 1904, in the Cincinnati-based *American Israelite*, at the time the leading organ of Re- form Judaism in America. Titled "The New Jewish Quarter of Harlem," the piece was mainly concerned with contrasting Harlem, as an area of second settlement for Jews, with the original "New York Ghetto" of Lower Manhattan. Reflecting on the emergence of "a new element in the Ghetto, a new vitality" with the rise of a younger generation, the author writes,

> The new generation, educated in American schools, perceiving that their own conditions in the congestion of the Ghetto caused by the tenement life were far away from the modern American notion of "sweetness and light," with almost their earliest conscious resolve determined to escape the Ghetto. The first generation lived together for mutual protection, the second saw in the segregation of the race many undesirable conditions. . . . The Jewish people did not come first to America, but to a sort of purgatory in the ghetto; later will they come to America.[60]

Not all of those who pictured the new immigrant ghetto as a transit zone and transitional space were as enthusiastic about the transition or as crude in their contrast of the old and the new.[61] Yet this perception of the American ghetto as a "purgatory" or "way station" or "preparatory school" would emerge in time as a master narrative of the immigrant ex- perience that would reverberate from popular fiction to academic writing. The squalor of the ghetto could be tolerated, because it was des- tined to be temporary, thanks to the herculean work ethic and passion for education and Americanization of the immigrants themselves and their sons and daughters.

Yet another defense of the ghetto sought to justify it less as a fleeting, generation-specific phenomenon than as a beacon of both cosmopolitanism and community. Ironically, one of the first contributions in this vein came from the pen of a gentile journalist. In 1902, Hutchins Hapgood assembled several articles he had published earlier on "the Jewish quarter of New York" into a book titled *The Spirit of the Ghetto: Studies of the Jewish Quarter in New York*. "No part of New York," he wrote, "has a more intense and varied life than the colony of Russian and Galician Jews who live on the East Side and form the largest Jewish city in the world."[62] Without suppressing the squalid and seamy side of Lower East Side life, he focused his study on the culture that had emerged amidst the sweatshops, pushcarts, and tenement houses—a culture shaped in large measure by the tension between the beckoning "new" American scene and the "old world" values the immigrants had brought with them. Thanks in large measure to his friend and fellow journalist Cahan, who served as something of a guide and translator, Hapgood immersed himself in the nuances of Yiddish New York. Hebraist intellectuals without readers and Talmudic scholars without influence, Yiddish poets of varying modes and moods, the burgeoning Yiddish stage and Yiddish press, even Cahan himself—all formed part of Hapgood's meticulous and sympathetic survey, accompanied by numerous moving charcoal sketches of the historical personas and social types interviewed and discussed by the "ghetto" artist (later turned acclaimed British sculptor) Jacob Epstein. While at times critical of the quality and aesthetic limitations of the work produced, Hapgood was rarely condescending. Indeed, he believed Anglo-Saxon America had something to learn from "the distinctive thing about the intellectual and artistic life of the Russian Jews of the New York Ghetto, the spirit of realism." Like some of the apologists for the ghetto, Hapgood viewed it as ephemeral. "In spite of the fact that the Jews have been at all times and in all countries tenacious of their domestic peculiarities and their religion," he acknowledged, "the special character of the Ghetto will pass away in favorably conditioned America."[63] And the rising out of poverty and escape from the tenements and sweat-shops were developments ultimately to be welcomed. Still, Hapgood never staked his defense of the ghetto on its ultimate demise. If anything, his profile memorialized precisely what would be lost with its disappearance: a "picturesqueness," an "infinite variety, vitality, and life," that made the Ghetto the quarter the most "peculiarly rich in interesting persons" in all of New York.[64]

Hapgood focused on the "certain kind of beauty" that the sympathetic observer could find in what was "generally supposed to be a place of poverty, dirt, ignorance, and immorality," and in that he was certainly an anomaly among outsiders, let alone gentiles. Other defenses, however, rebutted more directly the idea that the "ghetto" was a site of disproportionate crime and pathology while championing Jewish voluntary segregation on its own terms. In a two-part article for the New York weekly *The American Hebrew* in 1903 titled "Concentration or Removal—Which?" the Russian-born Jewish economist and social worker Isaac Max Rubinow argued that the efforts of organizations like the Industrial Removal Office to extract or divert immigrant Jews from their urban enclaves not only ran counter to the general trend of internal migration from farm to city but also was fundamentally antithetical to American principles of religious liberty. "If the newly arrived Jew," he wrote, "is to feel the difference between the oppression of his old country and the freedom granted in the new, he can only feel it in the large city—in the Ghetto, if you will. There he receives his first political lesson, which is also the most important one, that in this free country of Washington and Lincoln a Jew may look like a Jew, think like one, act like one, pray and speak like one, and yet be a respected and free citizen of a republic!" Rubinow scoffed at the notion there was anything unique about the propensity of the Russian Jews to cluster, asking, "Do not Germans, Italians, Poles, Frenchmen, Syrians, Greeks, etc., live in separate quarters of their own? Why do we not hear all this talk of the evils of German, Italian, or Irish concentration?" The prospect that, by virtue of continued immigration, the percentage of the New York population that was Jewish would keep rising was to be welcomed, not lamented, for this increase was the surest route to political clout and influence. Rubinow concluded,

> We may live to see New York 10,000,000 people strong. And if a large percentage of it will be Jewish, why, in the name of reason and common sense, should the Jew be sorry and worried? . . . Has the Irishman ever regretted that there were too many Irish people in the

city? Or has he made as much use of it as he could? Why shouldn't the Jew? Ah, but the Jew is different. Why is he different? Is he? Well, if he is, it is his own fault, for he needn't be; for votes are votes, and political power is political power.[65]

While suggesting some reservations with the term itself ("the Ghetto, if you will"), Rubinow had no beef with the phenomenon it designated. Dense Jewish neighborhoods in the major cities were an asset, not an obstacle, to Americanization.

Defenses of the ghetto also emerged with regularity from the Yiddish press. In a November 1909 article titled "The Ghetto of Yesterday and Today," which appeared in the Orthodox-leaning *Morning Journal,* the author conceded that the "Jews of the East Side are more or less separate from the general population." Indeed, he wrote, "The Jewish quarter, although not surrounded by the walled and closed gates of the erstwhile ghetto, is nevertheless a ghetto in the broad sense of the term." This isolation came at a cost, because it helped give rise to slanderous and erroneous claims about the Jews: to wit, the New York Police Commissioner Theodore Bingham's allegation, in an article on "Foreign Criminals" for the 1908 *North American Review,* that half the criminals in the city were Jews. (He later issued a retraction.) On the other hand, the German Jews who responded by calling for the dispersion of New York's Jewish inhabitants throughout the country to promote their assimilation, however well intentioned their efforts might be, demonstrated only their profound ignorance of Jewish history and the reasons Jews preferred to live clustered together. The ghetto may once have been a forced enclosure that embittered Jewish life and made it difficult for Jews to breathe freely. Yet it also had a counter-effect on the Jewish spirit: it made Jews aware that they had to remain together, to live like brethren, to feel the other's pain and try to lighten it. "In the ghetto," the author wrote, "a Jew felt among his own people, to whose destiny he was bound. This feeling has remained with the Jew up through the present day, when, in civilized lands, the walls of the ghetto have been broken down, and even in free America." Jews preferred the "suffocating air of their own quarter to the free air of a place where they are foreign and far from their brethren." To dissolve Jewish quarters by force would be to tamper with a deeply rooted Jewish feeling of collective responsibility and a yearning to live among one's fellow Jews.[66]

In the debate over the immigrant ghetto, the appropriateness of the word itself—*ghetto*—often stood in the dock. Criticisms came from various quarters. In December 1898, an article in the leading Yiddish weekly of the period, the Orthodox New York-based *Jewish Gazette*, blasted the latest initiative of the Baron de Hirsch Fund to resettle Jews in the suburbs by offering an $800 loan to any Jew who would invest $400 of his own money in buying a house outside the Lower East Side (excluding the Brownsville neighborhood of Brooklyn, which already by that point had become densely Jewish). In addition to expressing skepticism that the fund would in fact deliver on this promise, the author, identified only as Ben Amitai, questioned the very need to depopulate the New York Ghetto. "Why," he asked, "are the quarters where only Christians live not called ghettos? Why is the Jewish quarter a ghetto?"[67] Ben Amitai noted that all the different nationalities in New York seek to live together: Germans with Germans, Frenchmen with Frenchmen, Italians with Italians, Arabs with Arabs, and "Yankees" with "Yankees." Such was also the case with members of the same profession, be they actors, dancers, musicians, or secondhand dealers. Indeed, Fifth Avenue could be considered a "ghetto" of millionaires, and 34th Street a "ghetto" of artists. Ben Amitai suggested that calling the Jewish East Side a "ghetto" was both misleading and libelous, because Jews were no different than any other group in their desire to form distinct neighborhoods.

While Ben Amitai's was the protest of a seeming ghetto dweller, liberal Jews also, at times, objected to the "ghetto" label. In a 1908 column titled "The Word 'Ghetto'" that appeared in the *American Israelite,* Mollie Eda Osherman, a Chicago resident, decried what she alleged was the misapplication of the term that had become normative in newspapers and everyday language. Osherman rejected the eliding of the difference between the medieval European ghetto and the American immigrant enclave that writers like Zangwill and Cahan had done much to foster. "There is no valid reason why our Jewish section must be stigmatized with the word 'Ghetto,' she claimed, adding, "I am led to believe that our people, as a whole, it matters not what the condition of their finances or the division of the city in which they live, the state of their general culture or intellectuality, should co-operate in eliminating from the daily vocabulary that grating, unnecessary term, the 'Ghetto.' In that way we will tend to discourage its use from the press also."[68] In fact, an American Jew with far better political connections than Mollie Osherman had already succeeded in pressuring one major newspaper to do just that. In 1904, Louis Marshall, a prominent lawyer and American Jewish leader, wrote Adolph Ochs, the editor of the *New York Times,* requesting that the newspaper "adopt a rule banning the word" ghetto. That "a lot of Jewish citizens live in a certain portion of the city," Marshall explained, "is not a sufficient reason for applying to them a word which in history has been identified with contumely, oppression, ridicule, and hatred." Ochs agreed to this request, noting in his reply to Marshall his "instructions to prohibit the use of the word Ghetto with reference to the Jewish quarters of the East Side."[69] A search of the archives of the *Times* reveals no reference to various permutations of the phrase "New York Ghetto" from 1903 to the 1920s, precisely when this label was at its most popular.

The idea of the congested, yet legally voluntary Jewish urban enclave as a "ghetto" was originally a literary conceit. It was popularized by writers like Israel Zangwill and Abraham Cahan and derived from a longer history of supplementing the definition of the ghetto as a compulsory, segregated, and enclosed Jewish section of an Italian city with the notion of the "ghetto" as a way of life characterized by cultural isolation and living in the past. With Louis Wirth's 1928 book *The Ghetto,* however, the "ghetto" was assimilated into a new discourse within the rising field of urban sociology. The German-born Jewish Wirth was a student of Robert E. Park, one of the central figures of the Chicago School of sociology, which received its name from its association with scholars at the University of Chicago in the first half of the twentieth century. It became renowned for its detailed ethnographic studies of myriad aspects of modern city life, including ethnic neighborhoods and low-income "slum" areas. Chicago School researchers understood the city as a dynamic organism that cycled through various evolutionary stages and grew through recognizable and repetitive patterns. Ernest W. Burgess, along with Park another of the Chicago School's charter members, famously divided the city of Chicago into concentric zones, placing the different groups of poor, newly arrived immigrants in the "zone of transition" closest to the

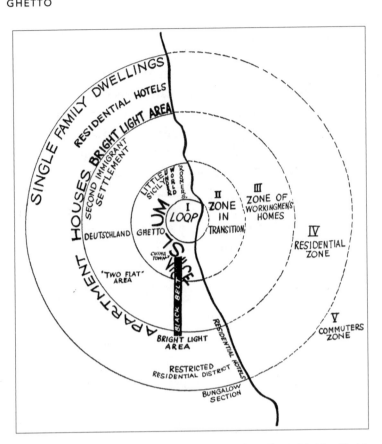

Ernest W. Burgess's concentric zone model of Chicago. The "Ghetto" is identified here as a slum neighborhood in the "Zone in Transition" immediately adjacent to the downtown business district ("The Loop"), alongside other ethnic enclaves such as Little Sicily and Chinatown.

central business area (in Chicago, the Loop) while demonstrating how acculturation and ascent up the economic ladder correlated with migration to successively outlying districts.[70]

Park in particular became famous for developing a theory of immigrant assimilation that relied heavily on the same "way station" paradigm that had characterized some of the earlier defenses of the ghetto.[71] In 1925, he described the inevitable process by which "the keener, the more energetic, and the more ambitious soon emerge from their ghettos and immigrant colonies and move into an area of second settlement, or perhaps into a cosmopolitan area in which the members meet side by side."[72]

Wirth's book, which originated as a University of Chicago dissertation advised by Park, was a pioneering attempt to transform the ghetto from a Jewish site to a sociological concept.[73] The book sought to show that the emergence of the ghetto in America, which struck most nineteenth-century observers as utterly incongruous, was an entirely natural and even predictable development. Contra those, like Mollie Osherman or Louis Marshall, who viewed the application of the word *ghetto* to Jewish ethnic enclaves as a historical falsification meant solely to defame, Wirth was determined to show that the same social forces that had given rise to ghettos in Europe in medieval times were also at work in the formation of immigrant colonies in twentieth-century America. Calling these quarters ghettos—modern ghettos—was not a priori slanderous, nor was it purely metaphorical. At the same time, despite arguing that the ghetto was deeply rooted in the Jewish historical experience, Wirth also vouched for its universal sociological significance and denied that it formed an insuperable barrier to Americanization. Mixing history with ethnography, combining insights gleaned from his reading of recent historical works, ghetto fiction, and first-person immigrant narratives with ideas about the evolutionary nature of immigrant migration, settlement, and integration absorbed from his Chicago School mentors, Wirth sought to bring cutting-edge social science to bear on the ghetto's peregrinations and above all on its move to America. At times, Wirth appeared certain that the ghetto in America imposed, at most, a temporary stay on an inevitable assimilation. At other times, this confidence seemed to waver.

Wirth sought to dispel the notion that his investigation of the ghetto was relevant to Jewish history alone. Robert Park, who penned a foreword to Wirth's book, described "our great cities" as "a mosaic of segregated peoples," each attempting to "preserve its peculiar cultural forms and to maintain its individual and unique conceptions of life." To the degree that "segregation becomes for them a means to that end, every people and every cultural group may be said to create and maintain its own ghetto." As a sociologist, Wirth claimed to be interested in the ghetto only to the extent that it might provide a case study of long-term "social isolation." His was a "natural history" of the ghetto, aimed at teasing out "universal truths that hold good irrespective of time and place." Wirth asserted that "while the ghetto is, strictly speaking, a Jewish institution, there are forms of ghettos that concern not merely Jews. There are Little

Louis Wirth, undated.

Sicilies, Little Polands, Chinatowns, and Black belts in our large cities, and there are segregated areas, such as vice areas, that bear a close resemblance to the Jewish ghetto."[74] The ghetto was a conceptual entity, the study of which represented nothing less than an inquiry into "human nature."

For Wirth, the first obstacle to understanding the ghetto was the belief that it had originated with legal coercion. The medieval ghetto took shape not out of "design," but as the "unwitting crystallization of needs and practices rooted in the customs and heritages, religious and secular of the Jews themselves." The first ghettos, then, were effectively voluntary ghettos: "Long before it was made compulsory the Jews lived in separate parts of the cities in Western lands, of their own accord." While Jewish religious law may have contributed to this self-segregation, at bottom Jews settled in separate areas for the same reason alien, stigmatized groups had done so throughout history. Doing so was a way of accommodating their strange way of life to a society that needed but did not necessarily want them and that they themselves viewed with suspicion. The introduction of the compulsory ghetto in the late medieval period mainly formalized and further ratified this preexisting accommodation: "The ghetto wall, the gates, the Jewish badge . . . became the physical symbols of the social isolation which manifested itself in the social distance between Jews and Christians."[75]

From this vantage, the Jewish neighborhoods that had arisen in slum areas of American cities could be seen as a return to the historical foundations of the ghetto concept as a voluntary enclave. Yet, time was not on the ghetto's side. In Europe, legal emancipation had already succeeded in razing the physical walls of the ghetto. The "invisible walls" were slower to fall, and the constant tide of Jews emigrating from Eastern Europe and creating new ghettos in the large cities of the West had only further impeded their dissolution. Yet "in countries where the contact between Jew and non-Jew has been continued for a few generations, and where no new immigration from other countries in which Jews retained their old status has taken place," Wirth claimed, "The ghetto has, to a large extent, disintegrated. Under these circumstances, not only does the ghetto tend to disappear, but the race tends to disappear with it." If this could happen in Europe, it would certainly also happen in an America that had no tradition of the ghetto, voluntary or coercive. Wirth, like Zangwill, was confident that if the American ghetto was a "mere continuation" of a "long history," it was also destined to be "a last scene of the final act," its function limited to that of a "transitional stage between the Old and the New worlds."[76]

Wirth's goal in writing *The Ghetto* was to explain not only the "natural history" of the institution but also the physical and psychological effects of the isolation it had imposed on the Jews. His main concern was to rebut the view of racists and eugenicists that the Jewish "physical type" and the "Jewish mentality" were the product of a pure and distinct racial inheritance. He insisted that space—not race—was the constitutive factor, relying heavily on the work of Maurice Fishberg, a Russian-born American Jewish physician and anthropologist then considered a leading authority on the ethnology of the Jews. In his 1911 *Jews: A Study of Race and Environment,* Fishberg conceded that, with respect to the Eastern European Jew, "the inferior hygienic, economic, and social conditions under which he was compelled to live in the Ghettos have left their mark on his body; he is old prematurely, stunted, decrepit; he withers at an early age. He is emaciated, his muscles are flabby, and he is unable to hold his spinal column erect." This alleged crookedness of the Jewish posture—for which Fishberg's book furnished an adjoining illustration—was already known at the time as the "ghetto bend," and, according to the author, was "one of the most important stigmata of the Jew's long confinement in the ghetto."[77]

Yet all these were acquired features, as opposed to hereditary characteristics, that vanished among the children of emigrants from the "ghetto." What was true of the Jewish physical type, according to Wirth, was likewise true of the Jewish social type. All the Jew's objectionable social behaviors—"that keen sense of self-consciousness which is often expressed in his awkwardness and lack of poise when in the company of strangers," the way "he is either shy and self-effacing, or . . . overcompensates in the direction of aggressiveness"—were residues of ghetto sequestration. As for the "Jewish mind," Wirth argued that the ghetto had a largely stultifying effect, cutting the Jew off from the "culture of the world" and restricting his education largely to the "Talmud and rabbinical dialectics."[78] Still, once liberated from the ghetto, the honing of the Jew's mental powers within this "dialectical training school" prepared him well for university study and entry into the professions. Ultimately, Wirth wished to demonstrate the degree to which the ghetto—and not an inborn biological blueprint—had molded the Jewish physiognomy and character. With the exit from the ghetto, the seemingly distinguishing features of the Jew would soon dissipate, and by all logic he or she would ultimately assimilate.

Wirth traced the Jews of Chicago from their modest mid-nineteenth-century beginnings and German Jewish heyday, to the emergence of the West Side Ghetto with its center on Maxwell Street ("the Rialto of the ghetto"), bursting with Eastern European Jewish immigrants, and to the accelerating flight from it. "If you would know what kind of Jew a man is," Wirth famously wrote, "ask him where he lives."[79] "The zones of settlement of the Jews," he claimed, "correspond roughly to the various generations of immigrants. Those who came earliest are now farthest removed from the original ghetto. They are also farthest along in the process of assimilation and in the departure from Old World customs and

Illustration of "The Ghetto Bend," by Ismael Gentz.

orthodox ritual." Yet Wirth was also keenly sensitive to just how difficult getting out of the ghetto might be. For "in their attempt to flee the ghetto, the partially assimilated groups have found that the ghetto has followed them to their new quarters," from areas of second settlement like Lawndale to new frontiers like the North Shore and Hyde Park. The barrier that remained to full acceptance in the gentile world became increasingly intolerable with every step of the journey away from the original ghetto and presented the now-estranged and deracinated "modern" Jews with a dilemma. They could either reaffirm their ties to the Jewish community and reenter the "tribal fold," which for Wirth meant a "return to the ghetto" as a "state of mind," if not actual place, or in effect, they could keep moving. Amidst the anomie of contemporary urban life, the ghetto provided "as near an approach to communal life as the modern city has to offer." Wirth was not devoid of appreciation for the ghetto as a "cultural community that expresses a common heritage, a store of common traditions and sentiments." Still, the fact that Wirth could conceive of a rekindling of Jewish consciousness only as an arresting of a natural progression that should lead to assimilation, intimates where his ultimate sympathies lay. The Jew, Wirth wrote, only "becomes human" when he or she leaves the "closed community" and forms "contacts with the outer world, encounter[ing] friction and hostility, as well as familiarity and friendship."[80] What value could there be, then, in a "return to the ghetto?"

For all of Wirth's suggestions that progress was neither linear nor irreversible, the gist of his argument was that the ghetto—weakened by a constant tide of defections and, with the enactment of legislation in the U.S. Congress restricting immigration in 1921 and 1924, cut off from its former source of replenishment—was bound ultimately to disappear. Yet the assumption of Wirth and the Chicago School more broadly that with every move away from the original immigrant enclaves the degree of Jewish concentration decreased concomitantly was being upended even as he wrote. In New York City, as Jews departed Lower Manhattan and other poor immigrant areas like Brownsville and Williamsburg in droves beginning in the 1920s, they moved to middle-class sections of Brooklyn and the Bronx that were frequently more, not less, densely Jewish. If in 1920, only 54 percent of New York's Jews lived in neighborhoods that were at least 40 percent Jewish in population, by 1925 that percentage had climbed to 64 percent and, five years later, to 72 percent.[81] Likewise, by 1930, Lawndale's Jewish population of 75,000 accounted for roughly two-thirds of the total neighborhood population and contained nearly one-third of Chicago Jewry in all. Outside the "Black Belt" on Chicago's South Side, it had the highest population density of any Chicago community.[82] Were these new Jewish neighborhoods ethnic ghettos? Writing for the English section of the *Forward* in 1926 on the subject of "The Future of the Ghetto in the United States," Nathaniel Zalowitz claimed that "the voluntary Ghetto . . . is in full sway today and I am not sure but that it will remain a permanent feature of Jewish life in the United States." Preempting the argument that there was "not a town, village, or hamlet in the whole length and breadth of our country, from Maine to California, where Jews are not found" and that "there is no law on the statute books of any of the 48 States limiting or regulating the residence of Jews," Zalowitz countered that "for reasons best known to themselves, the Jews have settled in several large cities, and, what is even more significant, in each of these cities they inhabit certain sections only. That, I urge, is the true hallmark of Ghetto life." The ghetto was not "vanishing," but, on the contrary, proliferating. In each of the boroughs of New York, Zalowitz wrote,

> There are Ghettos large and small, new Ghettos springing up almost overnight. There are Ghettos for foreign born Jews and Ghettos for native-born Jews; Ghettos for poor Jews and Ghettos for middle class and for rich Jews, for Russian Jews and for German Jews. The East Side is one kind of a Ghetto, Washington Heights another kind, West Bronx a third, Riverside Drive a fourth, Broadway between 72nd and 96th Streets a fifth, upper Fifth Avenue a sixth, and Brooklyn has a dozen different kinds and styles of Ghettos of its own.[83]

Zalowitz's understanding of the continued phenomenon of the "Jewish neighborhood" as a survival of the ghetto pattern was broadly shared in the Jewish press. A 1931 portrait of the New York Ghetto in the *Jewish Advocate* asserted that, even as the "mother Ghetto" was being abandoned, the "new generation . . . migrates across the river to Brooklyn, or travels far uptown to the Bronx, and there it begins to establish a new

Ghetto. For the Ghetto is a spiritual condition, not a matter of brick and mortar, and it is always rises anew, like the fabled phoenix."[84] Writing about the emergence of a Jewish enclave with kosher meat markets, delicatessens, and restaurants closed on Saturday on the Upper West Side of Manhattan in 1935, columnist Helen Worten went so far as to embrace the ghetto label. "If the west side has become the new ghetto," she claimed, "it is a different kind of ghetto. There was a time when American Jews might resent the idea of calling a Jewish residential area a ghetto. But there is no reason to do so now. Jews in New York find it is far more comfortable, for individual dignity and social pride, to reside in quarters where one is on a plane of equality."[85]

In the late nineteenth and early twentieth centuries, the word *ghetto* retained an almost exclusively Jewish referent and became embroiled in controversies over what, exactly, becoming a modern "American" required of its newcomers. The path "from place to metaphor" was to an extent reversed with the migration of Jews out of Eastern Europe and the emergence of ethnic enclaves in the West, above all in London, New York, and Chicago. Once again the ghetto became a place name. Postcards with images of pushcarts and packed crowds on Hester Street were commonly identified as scenes from the "East Side Ghetto" or simply the "Ghetto." The back of one, from the 1910s, explained, "The Ghetto, also known as 'Judea,' covers a large section of the East Side between Third Avenue and the river from Chatham Square to 10th Street. It consists of 6 and 7 story tenement houses, crowded to their eaves with humanity. A certain square mile of this section is said to contain a quarter of a million people. The narrow streets all through the Ghetto are thronged with push cart vendors, who deal in fruits and food stuffs of every description." A colorful painted map of Manhattan from 1926 identifies the area north of Delancey Street matter-of-factly as "The Ghetto."

And yet, even with the restoration of a toponymic dimension to the name *ghetto,* the metaphorical nature of the label was never far from the surface, and its usage and application remained contested, often bitterly. It drew on certain features that had become magnified in the nineteenth-century Jewish imagination—the association of the "ghetto" with all forms of Jewish separateness and with a highly concentrated, disorderly,

THE GHETTO, NEW YORK CITY.

The Ghetto, also known as "Judea" covers a large section of the East Side between Third Avenue and the river from Chatham Square to 10th Street. It consists of 6 and 7 story tenement houses, crowded to their eaves with humanity. A certain square mile of this section is said to contain a quarter of a million people. The narrow streets all through the Ghetto are thronged with push cart vendors, who deal in fruits and food stuffs of every description.

THIS SPACE FOR WRITING

R-43971

POST CARD

THIS SIDE IS FOR THE ADDRESS

PLACE STAMP HERE

THE AMERICAN ART PUBLISHING CO. NEW YORK CITY. 174

Top: Postcard from the 1910s identifying a street scene from the Lower East Side as part of "The Ghetto, New York City."

Bottom: Back of postcard, which claims that New York's "Ghetto" is also known by the name "Judea."

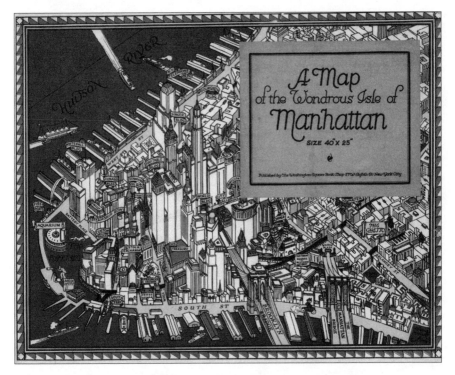

Detail of colored 1926 map titled "A Map of the Wondrous Isle of Manhattan," by Charles Vernon Farrow, published by Fuessle & Colman. The neighborhood just north of Delancey Street is labeled "The Ghetto."

overcrowded space—while neglecting or marginalizing the original aspect of legally coercive enclosure. For a revival of the ghetto as a site of mandatory segregation, albeit as a grotesque caricature of its late medieval and early modern prototype, we must travel back across the Atlantic to Nazi Europe of the 1930s and 1940s.

4

THE NAZI GHETTOS OF
THE HOLOCAUST

IN A MEMOIR ABOUT HIS YEARS AS A CHILD in the Warsaw Ghetto, the Polish Jewish literary scholar Michał Głowiński recalls hearing the word *ghetto* for the first time. It happened "at the very beginning of the war, right after the defeat" of the Polish army, when he overheard people around him debating, "Will they lock us in the ghetto or not?" The author writes, "I didn't know what this word meant, yet I realized that it was connected with moving." Out of this mystery he spun a fantasy that the ghetto was a "many-storied carriage riding through the streets of the city, pulled by some umpteen horses." Głowiński imagined that this carriage would contain "all kinds of staircases, so that one could run freely from one floor to the next, and many windows as well, so that nothing would stand in the way of looking out over the unknown world." Only with his family's confinement in the ghetto would he learn "the precise meaning of this word." What had initially "sounded so mysterious, so exotic, so intriguing" would be revealed as a chaotic, "discolored" labyrinth where the near-ubiquitous corpses "belonged to the permanent landscape, as the street was a place of death."[1]

The revival of officially segregated Jewish quarters by the Nazis had significant implications for the history of the ghetto concept as the Nazi segregation of Jews and how Jews experienced and represented this segregation evolved. From the beginning of the Third Reich to the eve of World War II, from 1933–1939, amid mounting legal and social exclusion of German Jews from German life and rising antisemitism throughout East Central Europe, an intra-Jewish discourse about the "ghetto" coalesced that extended well beyond German Jews to include an international cohort of Yiddish writers. During this period, the ghetto metaphor that had taken shape in the nineteenth century and had become a constituent element of Jewish consciousness reached the peak of its cultural prominence. The creation of obligatory and exclusive ghettos in Nazi-occupied Eastern Europe marked a new phase in the Nazi war against the Jews. During the Holocaust, the Nazi ghetto underwent a process of defamiliarization, as what were in most cases sites of mass starvation and disease and ultimately deportation to the death camps and killing fields became unmoored from any convincing historical precedent or prototype. This was followed by a partial refamiliarization of the ghetto after the war, as the ghetto experience was reinserted into a meaningful framework of events with heroes and martyrs and a message for future generations.

In her discerning study of how middle-class German Jewish families from 1890 to 1932 typically constructed their life stories, the German historian Miriam Gebhardt writes the following:

> The emancipation story was the most important element in the individual historical narratives. It formed the horizon, against which the particular family story played out. On the basis of the emancipation epoch a before-and-after story was established. "Before" was the traditional world. Discriminatory laws restricted the Jews' room to move and their possible career choices. Though it was a long time since they had lived in ghettos, the word "ghetto" was metaphorically applied to this time in the sense of spiritual and social isolation. The ghetto was an ahistorical and unchanging space. Intellectual closure above all was seen as characteristic of the premodern era. . . . In contrast, the transition to the modern [was represented] as an abrupt reversal.[2]

While there were certainly German Jewish observers in the latter years of the Weimar Republic who took issue with the mythic structure of this modernization story—including not only Zionists skeptical of emancipa-

tion to begin with but also some liberals who remained broadly committed to the idea of progress—this master narrative was still basically
intact on the eve of 1933.[3] The Nazi seizure of power appeared to pose
a threat not only to German Jewish legal and social status but also to the
fundamental story German Jews had been telling themselves about their
past, present, and future. It raised the prospect of a reversal and a return
to the "ghetto."

Over the next six years, in an uneven yet inexorable process, German
Jews saw their emancipation revoked and their removal from every niche
of German public life steadily magnified. Legally, the 1935 Nuremberg
Laws, in addition to outlawing mixed marriages, redefined German citizenship as a matter of German blood and reduced German Jews (previous
converts to Christianity included) to state subjects. Earlier, the civil service had banned all "non-Aryans,"[4] and a growing number of professional
and voluntary associations followed suit by barring Jews from membership. Businesses of Jewish entrepreneurs had begun to suffer due to Nazi
boycotts and harassment and the loss of "Aryan" clientele; some businesses had already been "Aryanized" as their owners were effectively
forced to sell at below-market prices. In the arts, stage companies and
orchestras had dismissed all their Jewish actors, directors, musicians, and
conductors.

The persecution of German Jewry had a clear spatial dimension as well.
Even before the state in the late 1930s began to prohibit Jews from at-
tending public schools, entering public parks, and shopping during all but
a few circumscribed hours, German Jews had grown accustomed to being
turned away from municipal swimming pools, restaurants, hotels, spas,
and even entire towns and villages. Signs and placards with variations of
Juden nicht erwünscht—"Jews not wanted"—had become a regular part
of the built environment and social landscape throughout the Reich. The
proliferation of spaces from which Jews were excluded was, to a limited
degree, compensated for by the creation of distinctively "Jewish spaces."
Early on, the Nazi authorities agreed to the creation of a Jewish *Kulturbund* (Cultural Federation) that would consist of the tens of thousands
of then-unemployed Jewish performers and would be permitted to stage
a censored repertoire of theatrical performances, concerts, operas, and exhibitions (with most German classics forbidden) to a "Jewish-only" audience. But the trade-off was not equal: the spaces that were designated

off-limits to Jews easily outnumbered the shrinking number of spaces available to them.[5]

Scholars commonly invoke the word *ghetto* to convey the snubbing and growing seclusion of German Jewry in the Nazi period. Avraham Barkai has described Nazi Germany as a "ghetto without walls" for Jews; one of the chapters of Saul Friedländer's *Nazi Germany and the Jews, Volume 1: The Years of Persecution* (1997), is titled "The New Ghetto"; and Michael Brenner has repeatedly depicted German Jews after 1933 as living in a "cultural ghetto" or "modern ghetto."[6] Such language echoes how German Jews at the time thought about their predicament.[7] For liberals who identified primarily as "Germans of the Jewish Faith," the efforts to exclude Jews from German culture and society came as an especially hard blow. Some counseled patience and a refusal to concede German identity. Writing in August 1933 in *The Morning,* the principal periodical of the Central Organization for German Citizens of the Jewish Faith, Heinz Kellermann portrayed Jewish history as a perennial seesaw "between the two poles of emancipation and ghettoization" and the present moment as simply a swing in the latter direction that was bound to be temporary. While acknowledging that the "external emancipation" of German Jews had come to an end, Kellerman urged his coreligionists to hold fast to their "internal emancipation," their sense of themselves as deeply German irrespective of the state's current attitude toward them.[8] A year and a half later, a contributor to *The Morning* sounded a more pessimistic note on the ability of Jewish youth in Germany to retain this inner consciousness. The author, Karl Julius Riegner, distinguished between two generations of Jewish youth: those older than twenty who had already acquired an immersion in German high culture (Goethe, Dürer) before the Nazis came to power, when "they didn't have to ask whether it was permitted," and a younger crowd that felt estranged from a "world of education *(Bildungswelt),* in whose development they could no longer have an undisputed share." Around this second group there "rose inconspicuously the walls of an invisible ghetto," a "frightful image" for those who had already widened their horizons. "The older [generation] play in the meantime Beethoven and seek to fathom Bach and Händel—the younger shrug their shoulders and retreat, only half consciously and without resignation." Yet the latter group could plausibly ask just how enmeshed in German culture even their elders could boast of being: "does a ghetto cease to be a ghetto, because one takes the German classicists within it? Can we escape it?"[9]

Perhaps the most famous example of a reworking of the ghetto metaphor to apply to the German Jewish plight came in a sermon by Rabbi Joachim Prinz in April 1935. Prinz was, by the standards of the day, unconventional: a young, brash liberal rabbi in Berlin who was simultaneously an avid Zionist.[10] In 1933, he had made a stir in German Jewish letters with a tract, *We Jews*, that turned the abovementioned "emancipation story" on its head. Prinz treated the modern Jewish break with the past and quest for assimilation not as a triumphant narrative, but as a sickness, a form of self-denying, even self-hating, pathology that had resulted only in marginality and a blindness to antisemitism and the nationalism of others. "The history of the Jews of the last century and a half," he wrote, "is in good measure a medical history, indeed the history of a strange patient: the fever chart is identical with the chart of the development of the world." It was actually the medieval ghetto Jew who belonged to the pantheon of authentic Jewish heroes. "The ghetto did not always breed the humpback and a beggarly humility," Prinz opined, "but the valiant Jew, who preferred to go to the pyre than to betray his Judaism." Beyond that, there was a question of the degree to which the modern Jew had truly escaped the ghetto. The Middle Ages had shut the Jew up in a ghetto, but this was a reflection of where things truly stood between the Jews and the peoples among whom they lived. Liberalism, however, had created an "anonymous ghetto."[11] Anonymous, in that it demanded of Jews a certain discretion, that they be emancipated as "cultivated Europeans" but not as Jews; yet anonymous also in the sense that it was only a narrow segment of the host population—not the peasantry, not the civil service, not the petit bourgeoisie—that was willing, conditionally, to accept the Jew as "one of them."

Prinz's 1935 sermon can be seen as a reflection, based on the experiences of the previous two years, of what happens when this façade of "anonymity" collapses. Excerpted in an April edition of a Zionist newspaper, it was titled "Life without Neighbors: A First Attempt at an Analysis. Ghetto 1935." "That we live in the ghetto," Prinz opened, "now begins to penetrate our consciousness." This ghetto was different, both conceptually and practically, from how the term had traditionally been understood. As a state of mind, "ghetto" captured a general feeling of unwantedness: *"that we live in a country, we Jews in Germany, where it is made clear to us in many places that our existence is a burden to the German people."* The previous two years, Prinz went on, had demonstrated that regardless of our intentions or our positive qualities, our abilities, or anything we might do or not do, many people of this country perceive us as an albatross on their national life. Our race, spirit, religion, the physiognomy of our faces, our basic way of life—all these make the *Volk* unhappy. This sense of being unwelcome almost everywhere had changed the very location of the "ghetto" in German Jewish consciousness:

> The medieval ghetto was sealed at night. The gate was shut harshly and aggressively; the bolts were forced carefully into place. One left the "world" and entered the "ghetto." Today the situation is reversed. When the door of our house closes behind us, *we leave the ghetto and enter our homes.* This is the basic difference. The ghetto is no longer a *geographically defined district,* at least not in the medieval sense. The ghetto is the "world." It is outside that the ghetto exists for us. In the markets, in the street, in hotels—everywhere is the ghetto. It has a sign. The sign is: being neighborless.[12]

The flipping of inside and outside when it came to the ghetto had resulted in a profound disorientation. For the Jews of the Middle Ages, Prinz had insisted, the ghetto, its gates and walls notwithstanding, had been a miniature homeland. For German Jews of 1935, pariahs everywhere, the open German landscape and culture they thought was their homeland had been transformed seemingly overnight into a ghetto, retaining only the isolation the word connoted and none of the comfort of being among one's own. In a "life without neighbors," Prinz maintained, "the ghetto is the 'world.'"

By the second half of the 1930s, the crisis of emancipation had metastasized to other parts of Europe. The situation in Poland, which with its three million Jews (10 percent of the total Polish population) had the largest Jewry in interwar Europe, was especially grim. Antisemitism, simmering from the moment Poland grudgingly approved a constitution in 1921 that gave Jews full civic and political equality while also recognizing their rights as a national minority, reached an outright boil after 1935. A confluence of factors, stemming from the example of Nazi Germany to the need for a scapegoat for the prolonged economic slump to the death in 1935 of Marshal Józef Piłsudski, the de facto leader of the Second Polish Republic who generally resisted antisemitism, opened the door to a vast escalation of antisemitic propaganda and anti-Jewish violence. Openly antisemitic parties like Roman Dmowski's National-Democratic (Endek) Party, with its slogan "Poland for the Poles," renewed their crusade for a cap on the number of Jews who could study in universities, arguing their representation should not exceed their percentage of the whole society—and the Ministry of Education largely capitulated as universities began to adopt quotas on their own. Universities, long hotbeds of anti-Jewish demonstrations, became the site of the most concerted effort at segregation. The phrase "ghetto benches" entered the Polish lexicon, as radical nationalistic students rioted and demanded—successfully in several Polish universities—that Jewish students be restricted in lecture halls to special sections reserved exclusively for them. The word *ghetto* played a pivotal role in antisemitic propaganda and discourse from 1935 to 1939, arguably more so in Poland than in Germany itself. The anti-Jewish clerical press was especially enthusiastic about restoring the ghetto "as an age-old Catholic tradition dating from the Middle Ages."[13]

Poland was far from the only East Central European state where reactionary right-wing antisemitism was ascendant in the interwar period. The second half of the 1930s in Hungary witnessed a tightening alliance with Nazi Germany and the rising clout of the fascist, vituperatively antisemitic Arrow Cross Party led by Ferenc Szálasi. In 1938 and 1939, the more conservative, established (though still antisemitic) right-wing government of the former Habsburg admiral Miklos Horthy, seeking to co-opt the extreme right, passed two successive anti-Jewish laws aimed at curbing the high percentage of Jews in Hungarian commercial, industrial, and professional life. The 1939 law, though unevenly enforced, was especially draconian; among other things, it called for limiting Jewish membership of the liberal and academic professions to 6 percent, excluding Jews from the civil service, compelling Jewish professors and teachers to retire within four years, and abolishing the right of Jews to buy or sell land. Moreover, the definition of "Jew" in both laws was at least partly racial; the first law excluded Jews who had converted to Christianity, but only if they had done so before 1919, while the second regarded children one of whose parents was a nonconverted Jew as Jews. In Romania, meanwhile, one of the most virulent antisemitic fascist movements in Europe, the Iron Guard, flourished in the 1930s, and as in Hungary, a moderate right-wing government increasingly took steps to appease the extreme right by implementing aspects of their antisemitic program. In 1937, the Romanian king went so far as to appoint a government led by two stalwarts of the Iron Guard, who proceeded to issue sweeping measures against the "Jewish enemy," targeting their role in Romanian economic and cultural life and even their citizenship. While this government lasted a mere two months, the moderates who replaced it did not completely revoke the anti-Jewish campaign the Iron Guard had initiated. A country that had long been regarded as among the most antisemitic in all of East Central Europe was increasingly living up to its well-deserved reputation as the 1930s drew to an end.[14]

In March 1938, German troops marched into Austria without resistance and to cheering crowds. The Anschluss—the annexation of Austria to Nazi Germany to form the Greater Reich—had begun. While this represented yet another violation of the Treaty of Versailles on Germany's part, the Allies responded with barely a whimper. The Austrian Nazis quickly set about expropriating Jewish assets, eliminating Jews from the economy and public life, and driving a wave of emigration so massive that it resembled—and in some cases was—an expulsion. A campaign to isolate and segregate the Jews that had been rolled out over a period of years in the so-called *Altreich* (Germany within the 1937 borders) and was far from complete by the time of the Anschluss was basically accomplished in Austria in a matter of months. Moreover, scenes of public humiliation of Jews erupted immediately following the entry of German soldiers into Austria. Cameras and newsreels recorded images (promptly suppressed by the Nazi propaganda authorities) of Nazis or simply ordinary Austrians forcing Jewish men and women to scrub pro-independence slogans from the streets and walls of Vienna. Some used toothbrushes, others their bare hands.[15]

A month later, Jacob Glatstein, one of the foremost Yiddish poets of the day, published his most searing and memorable poem, "Good Night, World." Four years earlier, Glatstein, from his home in New York, had traveled across the Atlantic and the European continent to visit his native Lublin—a trip he would later fictionalize in his two autobiographical novels, whose portrait of a Jewish Poland in its "autumnal phase" would prove eerily prescient.[16] Whether he wrote "Good Night, World" as a response to the Anschluss specifically, or to the sheer accumulation of antisemitic legislation, activity, and violence rampant throughout the Greater Reich and East Central Europe in the 1930s, is unknown. But the poem was clearly a *cri de coeur* that conveyed profound disenchantment and even disgust with the modern world. It began,

> Good night, wide world.
> Big, stinking world.
> Not you, but I, slam the gate.
> In my long robe,
> With my flaming, yellow patch,
> With my proud gait,
> At my own command—
> I return to the ghetto.[17]

Glatstein's poem was a farewell to the "big, stinking world" that continued to treat Jews so abominably and to "flabby democracy" that responded to such oppression in muted terms. It was also, by implication, a secession from the entire project of Jewish modernity. Since the Enlightenment, advocates for Jewish modernization had tirelessly fought to dismantle the barriers that hemmed in premodern Jewish society and had pinned their hopes on acceptance by the gentile world, whether as individual citizens, a national minority, or even a separate sovereign entity. Turning his back on all these aspirations, Glatstein seemed to be turning back the clock. His poem trafficked in various metaphors of Old World Judaism—the "long robe," the "flaming, yellow patch," the "humpbacked Jewish life," the "stray papers" of the "Twenty-Four-Books" (the Hebrew Bible) and the "Talmud," the "Law"—but the line that made the deepest impression and would ultimately inspire a whole literature was the defiant claim: "At my own command/I return to the ghetto." No symbol better captured the image of Jewish separation from the world and the extent of Glatstein's seeming resolve to take leave of Jewish modernity by "go[ing] back to my four walls" than the word *ghetto*.

The poem evidently caused an immediate stir, to the point that Glatstein felt compelled to clarify his vision in an essay that appeared in the next edition (May 1938) of the Yiddish periodical *Introspection,* which had published his poem the month before. In a short article, "Among One's Own: In Defense of the Ghetto," Glatstein fleshed out his understanding of "ghetto." He opened by expressing surprise that the mention of "ghetto" would cause such shock to Jews at a time when antisemitism was violently uprooting and destroying Jewish life in many lands. In response to the "masochistic Jews" who deemed the worst setback to Jewish life to be the "cultural ghetto" into which Jews were being forcibly driven, Glatstein disagreed strongly. Yiddish writing itself was as good a parallel as any to "ghetto life," he retorted. "In a Jewish business, in a purely Jewish neighborhood, a Christian customer will occasionally drop by, but in the Yiddish literary environment, no 'Aryan' ever comes in—it's a purely Jewish territory." Glatstein thus indicated that returning to the ghetto was less about reclaiming an abandoned rabbinic observance than it was about affirming a mother tongue that the outside world did not know. Referring to his long-time residence on the Lower East Side and his abiding commitment to a Yiddish literature deemed by many to be doomed to extinction, Glatstein wrote, "When one lives for a long time in a ghetto the terrifying nature of the word disappears instantly. It is perhaps a great tragedy for those who have left to return, but for people who live and will end their lives among their own it is difficult to conceive [of this] as such as tragedy." Glatstein added, "Of all the blows to fall on the shoulders of the German and now the Austrian Jews, the least of them for me is the fear of the ghetto. For them this must be the peak of misfortune, because it is a retreat from the heights of secular culture, but for me, the ghetto-professional, I have no sympathy for this kind of fright, and, if I can put it this way, for the fear of this fright." It was not that he failed to see the horror of forced confinement: "it is a tragedy," he wrote, "when one violently grabs and shoves people together in crowded conditions among themselves alone."[18] But absent the coercion, Glatstein had spent his entire life in such crowdedness and had made it his task to glorify his "four walls" as finely as possible.

If Glatstein indicated that his poem's call for a return to religious law and practice was not to be taken literally, the poet did not step away from the general thrust of a call for separation. The fallout in the press was not immediate, but after the colossal failure of the Évian Conference in July 1938 to address the plight of Jewish refugees and then the appeasement of Hitler in the Munich Agreement that September, the "return to the ghetto" question rapidly became a central topic of discussion among Jewish and in particular Yiddish writers. It provoked a host of articles in the press; served as the focus of a special evening forum in Yiddish in Paris in December 1938; and even underlay the creation of a new and short-lived Yiddish journal, *At the Crossroads*, in early 1939.[19] What did it mean to go back to the "ghetto"? The word *ghetto* was so malleable that no one could agree on exactly what it meant. As a result, participants in the debate invariably had to provide some kind of definition of the term in the course of staking out a position.

Those who supported, broadly speaking, the idea of a return to the ghetto—including the founding editors of *At the Crossroads*, the former Yiddishists and Diaspora nationalists Elias Tcherikower and Israel Efroykin—shared several features.[20] These supporters' mood tended to be one of profound pessimism, at times to the point of resignation. They were disenchanted with the Western democracies, which they saw as having failed to mount any kind of meaningful resistance not only to Hitler's assault on Jewish life but also to the virulent, at least indirectly state-sanctioned antisemitism of states like Poland and Romania. Equally, they had lost faith in the ideology of emancipation, with its promise of individual rights and full citizenship. Emancipation, by encouraging assimilation, had sapped the Jews of their national character and solidarity. They saw the ghetto as a site of asylum, where the Jews could at the very least survive the coming storm, while also insulating themselves from external influences and thereby achieving a national regeneration. The researcher Shmuel Feigin, writing from America, offered one of the most unwavering defenses of Glatstein's separatist vision. In a Hebrew article titled "Let Us Be Ready for the Middle Ages," which, somewhat surprisingly, appeared in the official Zionist organ *The World* in October 1938, Feigin asserted the need to return to the ghetto of our own will. "It is better," he wrote, "that we imprison ourselves in the ghetto before they drive us in there. When we will be crowded together, tightly cleaving to one another in the ghetto we will be able to exist and to live a reduced life, without honor and external radiance, but we will not be destroyed."[21] Yet Feigin also believed that the ghetto could function as a site for the Jews to rebuild a sense of national pride and even superiority, revivifying the biblical idea of divine election and the liturgical phrase recited by traditional Jews thrice daily, "You have chosen us." Practically speaking, the Jews should respond to the Polish ghetto benches with indifference, demonstrating to the Poles that they consider it no dishonor to sit among fellow Jews. Taking a less extreme position than Feigin, Tcherikower explained that the proponents of a "'return to the ghetto' do not mean by this to close themselves off from the world. Rather it is a feeling of coming back to oneself, of strengthening the national discipline."[22]

Those who opposed the phrase "return to the ghetto" represented a range of ideologies, but struck a few recurring notes. They rejected the idea that Jews, of their own will, had ever sought enclosure in ghettos. The acclaimed Yiddish poet H. Leyvik maintained, "We Jews have never freely accepted the ghetto. We were always *forced* therein, we were violently locked up, like in prisons." He argued, "We can't believe in God simply because it's not good without God."[23] The New York Yiddish novelist and short story writer Joseph Opatoshu, in an article titled "What Is Jewishness?," asserted that when Jewish life hangs in the balance, "it is laughable and harmful . . . to see our only salvation in the ghetto, between the four walls of the House of Study."[24] Even those who admitted to a feeling of loneliness and betrayal by the democracies, and who agreed that world Jewry needed to fortify its internal cultural and spiritual reserves, continued to insist that Jews were too entwined with the world to secede from it and could not capitulate in the fight against fascism. Leyvik, for one, hedged his opposition to the "return to the ghetto" mantra. If the slogan simply meant rooting ourselves in our folk history and culture— "that is, ghetto in the broadest sense of the term"—then Leyvik had no issue with it; this was a "ghetto" that Jews should never have left in the first place. But even if the world had abandoned the Jews, the Jews could not abandon the world by sequestering themselves in a ghetto.[25] The Yiddish writer Shmuel Niger took an even stronger line on the subject of the Jews' responsibility to the world. "We are a world-people," he wrote, "and will remain a world-people. We cannot help it. If we must improve the world, then we cannot take leave of it . . . our fate is bound up with the fate of humanity."[26] Believing that Judaism or *Yidishkayt* could not be reduced to a mere particularism, the Yiddish poet and publicist Dovid Eynhorn declared, "Jews have had a world-idea and have always sent messengers, emissaries into the world to preach this idea. . . . The tendency of Jewish history is going into the world, not 'ghetto.'"[27]

Strikingly, this "return to the ghetto" discourse remained almost exclusively limited to Yiddish writers living in either New York or Paris. There were some echoes of the controversy in the Yiddish press of Eastern Europe, but they were faint. Tcherikower acknowledged that "here [i.e. in Eastern Europe], where the question of a forced ghetto is not theoretical, but a pitilessly concrete political reality, there is no one, not even in the non-leftist press, who has stepped forward with a call to renounce the struggle, who has given up on Jewish rights to return to the ghetto of [his or her] free will."[28] Fewer than six months later, the Nazis would invade Poland, and the meaning of "ghetto"—which had never been the subject of as much discussion as it was from the early spring of 1938 to the early spring of 1939—would assume the "pitilessly concrete" dimensions Eastern European Jews had feared. The "return to the ghetto" debated in the newspapers and cafés would, throughout Nazi-occupied Eastern Europe, become a literal return to the ghetto.

Up until the Anschluss, the Nazis had taken various steps to degrade German Jews and set them apart. They had driven them from the civil service, stripped them of their German citizenship, and generally promoted their social and spiritual ostracism. They had not, however, segregated them residentially. Hitler is said to have told a small circle of party members in 1935 that he wished to drive the Jews "out of all the professions, into a ghetto, enclosed in a territory where they can behave as becomes their nature, while the German people look on as one looks at wild animals."[29] And a slide from a Hitler Youth educational presentation from the 1930s titled "Germany Overcomes Jewry" contains a picture of a Jew with the caption, "As a member of an alien race, the Jew in the Middle Ages had no rights of citizenship. He had to live in a separate quarter, the ghetto." But this fantasy was not acted on.

Therefore, it seems that before 1938 both the concept and indeed specter of "ghettoization"—as well as the word *ghetto* itself—were much more a part of an intra-Jewish discourse than of German policy or propaganda. Even Nazi uses of the term tended to be metaphorical. In February 1937, for example, Reinhard Heydrich, the head of both the Security Police and the SS Security Service, proposed in a letter to Rudolf

Nazi propaganda slide from a Hitler Youth educational presentation titled "Germany Overcomes Jewry," circa 1934–1937. The text reads, "As a member of an alien race, the Jew in the Middle Ages had no rights of citizenship. He had to live in a separate quarter, the ghetto."

Hess, the Deputy Führer and Minister without Portfolio, barring Jews from vacationing at all but segregated "Jewish" resorts. This, he suggested, would build on the Nuremberg Laws and serve as another means "to return the Jews to the ghetto."[30] Yet this usage of the term was clearly figurative; the "ghetto" for Heydrich was simply a metaphor for the separation of Jews from the community of German blood.

The Nazis began to entertain the forced enclosure of the Jews more seriously in 1938. In the wake of the Anschluss, the seeming stabilization of Jewish legal status post-Nuremberg collapsed, and a wave of anti-Jewish legislation, humiliation, and violence aimed at isolating and segregating Jews more fully—and encouraging the hundreds of thousands of Jews who remained in the Greater Reich to emigrate posthaste—began in earnest. Ghettoization was first deliberated at the highest level in the immediate aftermath of Kristallnacht (Night of the Broken Glass), the massive pogrom on November 9–10, 1938, throughout the Greater Reich that saw hundreds of Jews killed, thousands of synagogues and Jewish businesses destroyed, and tens of thousands of Jews arrested and sent to concentration camps. The setting was a November 12 meeting of members of the Nazi leadership convened by Hermann Göring, then plenipotentiary of the Four-Year Plan to prepare Germany for war and, in that capacity, deeply involved in the campaign to "Aryanize" Jewish-owned businesses; this meeting was charged with addressing the Jewish Question in a sweeping and comprehensive fashion. The subject of ghettos arose in discussing how to increase the pressure on Jews to emigrate and to dramatically intensify the isolation of those who remained. Heydrich proposed various measures, including the introduction of a special insignia Jews would have to wear that would facilitate their identification. Göring responded to Heydrich's proposals for marking the Jews and separating them from German economic life in a thoroughgoing manner by claiming that they would ultimately force the "creation of ghettos on a very large scale, in all the cities." Heydrich balked at this particular suggestion:

> As for the matter of ghettos, I would like to make my position clear right away. From a police point of view I think that a ghetto, in the form of a completely segregated district with only Jews, is not possible. We would have no control over a ghetto where the Jew gets together with the whole of his Jewish tribe. It would be a permanent hideout for criminals and first of all [a source] of epidemics and the like. The situation today is that the German population [which lives together with the Jews] forces the Jews to behave more carefully in the streets and the houses.[31]

Though he had been perfectly willing to speak of "return[ing] the Jews to the ghetto" a year earlier with respect to the establishment of Jewish resorts, Heydrich opposed the creation of actual ghettos unequivocally. This seeming turnabout may have stemmed from his discovery in the intervening period that the ghetto was not merely a historical phenomenon or a metaphor in the present for isolation and segregation, but a real, and very much contemporary, place. A 1938 book titled *Jewry in the Territory of Eastern Europe* by Peter-Heinz Seraphim, a leading practitioner of Nazi "academic" research into the Jewish Question,[32] used the term *ghetto* as a label for the voluntary Jewish ethnic neighborhoods and quarters found in virtually all the midsized and major Polish, Lithu-anian, and Latvian cities.[33] These enclaves were "a city within a city, the Jewish *ghetto*," Seraphim wrote. But where Louis Wirth and his Chicago School colleagues viewed the modern Jewish urban ghetto as a tempo-rary settlement where immigrants and newcomers began a process of as-similation that would ultimately weaken the centripetal force of com-munity, Seraphim saw the ghetto as a permanent, noxious feature of the East European urban landscape. The East European Jewish ghetto served as a bastion for the strengthening of Jewish national feeling where "the *Jewish essence* is molded in its particular form." Of greater concern, the ghetto, because of its "overpopulation" and "social misery," was a base for Jewish expansion that, left unchecked, threatened to colonize ever larger sections of the city. It thus appeared to be entirely at odds with the Nazi goal of removing Jews from the economic and cultural life of their host societies.[34]

Heydrich's position prevailed for the time being.[35] At the November 12 meeting, it was decided to further separate Jews from Aryans by concen-trating Jews in special "Jewish houses" instead of in a single quarter.[36] In April 1939, the "Law Concerning Tenant Relations with Jews" stripped Jewish tenants of their rights of occupancy and sanctioned the eviction of Jews from Aryan-owned buildings on the condition that housing could be found for them in Jewish-owned buildings. It also stipulated that from that point on Jews were to sign leases only with Jewish landlords. Aryans in turn were encouraged to move out of Jewish-owned buildings to "Jew free" houses—in many cases to vacancies newly created by emigrating or evicted Jewish families. Since there were nowhere near enough houses to accommodate the influx of Jews seeking refuge, multiple individuals were forced to share single apartments and even rooms. Living conditions be-came appallingly cramped and unsanitary. Eventually, these "Jewish houses" came to serve as collection points and holding centers for the de-portations of Jews from the Greater Reich to ghettos and camps that would emerge in 1941.

The creation of ghettos proper only began in the wake of the German invasion, defeat, and partition of Poland in September 1939. The largest and best known of the ghettos were located in the cities with the two largest Jewries in prewar independent Poland: the Łódź Ghetto, founded in February 1940, where more than 165,000 Jews were forced into an

Top: Łódź Ghetto Jews behind the wooden and barbed wire fence that separated the ghetto from the rest of the city, 1940–1941.

Bottom: Polish and Jewish laborers construct a section of the wall that separated the Warsaw Ghetto from the rest of the city, November 1940–June 1941.

area of 1.5 square miles, and the Warsaw Ghetto, created in October 1940, which initially incarcerated roughly 380,000 people in an area of 1.3 square miles.[37]

Yet, for all their size and importance, these ghettos were only two among more than one thousand that the Nazis would create, in different waves, between 1939 and 1944.[38] Formerly, Holocaust scholars generally construed the establishment of ghettos as a conscious prologue to genocide, and this view continues to inform popular understandings of Nazi ghettoization policy. Some interpreted the ghetto as a coherent strategy for interning Jews prior to their deportation to the death camps, others as an essential, if not necessarily premeditated, preparatory stage that laid the foundation for mass murder.[39] Advocates of this "intentionalist" narrative (the view that ghettoization was implemented with the "Final Solution" already in mind) tend to cite a directive issued by Heydrich, the head of the newly created Reich Main Security Office, on September 21, 1939, which established guidelines for addressing the Jewish Question in the newly occupied territories.[40] The memorandum made a distinction between the areas of western Poland that were to be directly annexed to the Reich—from which Jews were to be expelled as much as possible—and the occupied part of Poland that would become known as the *Generalgouvernement*. In the latter area, Heydrich called for the concentration of Jews in cities that were rail junctions or were at least located on railroad lines. He also called for the creation of a Council of Jewish Elders (a *Judenrat*) in each community that would be responsible for implementing German decrees, conducting a census, and facilitating the evacuation of the Jews under their oversight. Today, the Heydrich memo notwithstanding, most scholars reject the notion that ghettoization was a top-down initiative conceived as a preliminary step toward genocide. Heydrich called loosely for concentrating Jews in cities, not for the creation of involuntary and segregated ghettos.[41] Ghettos were almost universally created at the behest of local Nazi civilian, military, and SS leadership and not as a result of calculated central planning. While ghettos were established as early as the fall of 1939, most scholars today believe that the Nazis did not decide on a policy of genocide against the Jews—the Final Solution—before 1941. Focusing on the Łódź Ghetto and the Warsaw Ghetto, Christopher Browning has shown how, through 1942, Nazi officials were split over the purpose of ghettoization, between "attritionists" who believed the objective was to steadily decimate the Jews through impoverishment, starvation, and disease and more pragmatic "productionists" who saw the ghetto as a means of exploiting Jews as slave labor for the benefit of the Nazi war economy and had a stake in maintaining a rudimentary level of nourishment.[42]

There is growing recognition today of the diversity of Nazi ghettos and how the very concept of the ghetto evolved over the course of the war. Ghettos differed on the basis of a whole set of variables; for instance, on when and where they were created; on the degree to which they were "open" or "closed," set off from the surrounding area with a few poles or placards or physically enclosed by walls, fences, and barbed wire, like the iconic ghettos of Łódź and Warsaw; on the extent to which, by virtue of the location chosen for the ghetto or the preservation of a structure of Jewish communal leadership, there was some form of continuity with prewar Jewish life, or whether the ghetto was situated in an area with no prior Jewish connection and with an internal leadership created from scratch. Meanwhile, debate over how to understand the Nazi decision to create ghettos in the first place shows no sign of abating. Browning sees the formation of the first wave of ghettos (e.g., Łódź and Warsaw) as a response, above all, to frustrated hopes of a solution to the Jewish Question that would entail the deportation of the Jews of Nazi Europe either to a vast "reservation" in Nazi Poland (the so-called Lublin Reservation or Nisko Plan) or outside Europe altogether (the Madagascar Plan).[43] Dan Michman, conversely, underscores the perception, fostered by Peter-Heinz Seraphim's 1938 book, that the ghetto was the natural habitat of the despised and dangerous East European Jew. "Conceptually speaking," Michman argues, "the ghettos were not *established* as some new ex nihilo creation, because ... ghettos, as the Germans understood them, already existed and were the hallmark of Eastern European Jewry. The Germans merely *demarcated their boundaries* and forced those Jews who had moved elsewhere in the city to return 'home.'"[44] Others have sought to locate and understand ghettoization within the context of the larger German colonial project for "Germanification" and ethnic cleansing of Eastern Europe to create *Lebensraum* (living space), which prioritized the clearing of real estate for ethnic Germans and displaced Poles as well as Jews.[45]

Perhaps the single most important shift in the essential nature of the ghetto came after the German invasion of the Soviet Union in June 1941.

Up until that point, ghettos were certainly the site of Nazi plunder, violence, and killings, but they were not a cog in a planned annihilation. Ghettos in the conquered areas of the Soviet Union (including eastern Poland, the Baltic states, Belarus, and Ukraine), in contrast, were typically created both after and in the midst of mass shootings of Jews on the Eastern Front. It was only with the decision to exterminate the Jews of Europe that ghettos became holding centers for the Final Solution, even if some survived into 1943 and even 1944 as in essence slave labor camps.

While most of the Jewish ghettos of the Holocaust were created in Poland and the parts of the Soviet Union conquered by the Nazis, there were two major exceptions. The first was Theresienstadt. Established in November 1941 on the site of a dilapidated eighteenth-century Hapsburg fortress around sixty kilometers north of Prague, Theresienstadt (Terezin) functioned primarily as a holding center for Jews from the Protectorate of Bohemia and Moravia as well as from Germany and Austria. Many of the internees from the Altreich in particular were elderly, often decorated war veterans and their spouses, who had been cynically promised that they were being sent to a kind of "Reich old-age home" in "Theresienbad."[46] From the outset, Theresienstadt occupied a gray zone between "camp" and "ghetto." Unlike most ghettos, it was not created on the site of a traditional Jewish neighborhood; Jews were deported there by train or bus. Moreover, deportations from Theresienstadt to the "East"—whether to other ghettos, to the extermination camps of "Operation Reinhard," and eventually to Auschwitz, where virtually all those sent were gassed on arrival—began in January 1942 and continued through October 1944. It thus served as a transit camp for deportation similar to other such camps in Western Europe. At the same time, unlike most camps, Theresienstadt had an elaborate Jewish internal administration led by a Council of Elders, and except during deportations, the SS generally left the maintenance of order in the ghetto to the Jewish Order Guards. In the spring of 1944, the Nazis notoriously "beautified" Theresienstadt (in part by thinning out the population through deportation) for a June visit by the International Red Cross, all with the aim of presenting the camp as a "Jewish settlement" (not a "ghetto") that was a "paradise" for Jews. Their deception was mostly successful, and those who had contributed to the "beautification" efforts were subsequently deported. By the time the Soviets liberated Theresienstadt in May 1945, there were nearly 30,000 Jews living there, more than one-third of whom had arrived the month before amidst the vast shuffling of Jews between camps at the end of the war. From its creation to its dismantling, some 87,000 Jews were deported from Theresienstadt to the camps; only 3,600 of those deported survived.

The other major site of ghettoization outside of Poland and the Soviet Union was Hungary after the Nazi occupation of March 1944. Beginning that April, German and Hungarian officials initiated a crash ghettoization of Hungary's 800,000 Jews, starting with the more rural and provincial Jews in the northeastern parts of the country. With incredible speed, the Jews of a region were rounded up and concentrated either in poor, slum-like Jewish neighborhoods of towns or in the even more deplorable and unsanitary conditions of open brickyards or deserted mills or factories. These ghettos proved in the end to be simply way stations, where Jews, on average, spent three to five weeks before being deported to Auschwitz, beginning in mid-May.[47] The Germans and Hungarians moved systematically throughout Hungary to first ghettoize, then deport Hungarian Jewry. Only Budapest, where roughly one-third of the Hungarian Jewish population lived before the Nazi occupation, proved something of an exception to this pattern. For a variety of reasons, though mainly because the central authorities wished to avoid a prolonged process of population relocation for a ghettoization then understood as a mere prelude to a mass deportation that would soon be forthcoming, Budapest Jews, beginning in June 1944, were segregated at the apartment level—in nearly two thousand buildings marked by a yellow star—rather than in specific Jewish enclosures (of which seven were initially planned). This setup was much closer to the German model of "Jewish houses" than to the Polish model of segregated Jewish quarters. After the Hungarian regent Miklos Horthy suspended the deportations in July 1944, Budapest Jews were largely spared from being sent to Auschwitz, though tens of thousands were killed after the Arrow Cross coup d'état in October 1944. Late that November, under the Arrow Cross, the Jews of Budapest were forced to relocate to a walled ghetto established on the site of the old Jewish quarter in Pest. For nearly two months, until Budapest was liberated by the Soviets on January 17, 1945, the "non-protected Jews" who had avoided deportation under the new government to labor battalions and concentration camps lived in harsh conditions marked by hunger, overcrowding, disease, and squalor, along with the constant fear of execution in Arrow Cross raids.[48] The only Budapest Jews spared internment or deportation were the sizable minority who had obtained protective certificates by various neutral powers (most notably, the Swiss and the Swedish) and lived in yellow-star houses in the so-called International Ghetto.[49]

In light of all the evidence of the variety of Jewish ghettos during the Holocaust and of their conceptual and functional change over time, it is increasingly difficult to speak of the "Nazi ghetto" as a uniform phenomenon. What is clear, however, is that the Nazi ghetto bore little in common with the early modern ghetto beside the name. The Nazis in some areas sought to bar the use of the word *ghetto,* most notably in Warsaw, where they insisted that the ghetto be officially referred to as the Jewish Living District; names employed elsewhere included Jewish Living Area and Jewish Settlement. The goal was to present the all-Jewish area as a kind of natural region or habitat rather than the coercive enclosure that it was. The Nazis thus sought disingenuously to avoid the pejorative connotations of the word *ghetto,* but even before the Nazi ghettos turned deliberately genocidal, they were intended to segregate, marginalize, control, and exploit Jews well in excess of anything the founders of the early modern ghetto could have envisioned. From a functionalist perspective, the early modern ghetto and Nazi ghetto were clearly divergent institutions, whatever superficial similarities they may have shared.

But this gulf between past and present would only become clear to the Jews forced to live in ghettos in the course of time. "Most ghetto inmates," Debórah Dwork and Robert Jan van Pelt have written, "whatever their personality traits, tried to understand their existence by viewing it within a continuum of Jewish history. . . . The concept of the ghetto had a past in Jewish memory and the ghettos themselves had a Jewish past. It was logical that, at least initially, there was hope for a Jewish future."[50]

The Nazi creation of ghettos was usually preceded by a period of extreme and seemingly arbitrary persecution. In the case of the ghettos established on the Eastern Front after the invasion of the Soviet Union in the summer of 1941, this took the form of mass shootings by mobile killing squads *(Einsatzgruppen)* in front of open graves, but even in the two years beforehand—in both the part of Poland annexed by Germany (the Warthegau) and the Generalgouvernement—ghettoization came on the heels of both official and informal humiliation and violence. Mass arrests and the grabbing of men and women off the streets to perform forced labor, surprise visits at night by a Gestapo officer or *Volksdeutsche* (ethnic German) to extort money and valuables, even—in the case of Łódź—the slaughter of Jewish intellectuals and representatives of the Jewish community and the peremptory expulsion of thousands over the border into Nazi-occupied Poland—all these became part of the daily experience of Jews in the initial months of living under Nazi rule. Before ghettoization, Jews were physically marked in a way that, intentionally or not, suggested a "return" to the Middle Ages. The prescribed badge differed by region—a yellow star on the chest and back shoulder in Łódź, an armband with the Star of David in Warsaw—but the upshot was to make a racial definition of Jewishness legible and the inferior status of Jews visible. Not that all Jews allowed themselves to experience their branding as a mortification. On November 30, 1939, the Warsaw diarist Chaim Aron Kaplan, a Zionist, contrasted the demeaning "yellow badge" of the "Middle Ages" imposed on Łódź Jews with the "national colors, which are our pride" represented by the blue and white armband with the Star of David.[51] The thirteen-year-old Vilna diarist Yitskhok Rudashevski chronicled his memory, from early July 1941, of the introduction of the "yellow circle and inside it the letter J." At first, he recoiled from it: "The large piece of yellow material . . . seemed to be burning me and for a long time I could not put on the badge. I felt a hump, as thought I had two frogs on me." Yet by the time he wrote about it, he had ceased to feel embarrassed. "Let those be ashamed," he declared, "who have hung them on us. Let them serve as a searing brand to every conscious German who attempts to think about the future of his people."[52] Whatever response it engendered, the "badge" had come to be symbolically linked to the "ghetto" in the popular image of pre-emancipated Judaism. Its implementation may not have been a premeditated step in the direction of ghettoization on the part of the Nazis, but one can see why the later and even contemporary perception of the two as part of a conceptual package could have taken shape.

Because of the constant terror and disorientation the Nazis instilled in the Jewish populace, and because the ground had already been laid for segregation via the badge and other discriminatory measures, the ghetto appeared to some Jews, at least initially, as a relief of sorts. This feeling was far from universal, but for many the ghetto seemed to promise an end to the random violence or the threat of total expulsion. Some even saw ghettoization as a kind of "ingathering" that would bring Jews together and provide security in numbers. Mark Dworzecki recalled an easing of tension and even hope for the future on the first night of confinement in the Vilna Ghetto in September 1941. "It is hard to believe," he later recounted, "but it was nevertheless so." People greeted each other not plaintively, but with a smile and with a degree of optimism. Even if they would be poor and hungry, the thinking went, in the ghetto they would at least be free to breathe. The snatchings off the street and from people's homes would end (in the near term, an entirely vain hope as it turned out), and the Jews would be able to wait for better times in seclusion, among their own.[53] The Vilna Jewish intellectual Zelig Hirsch Kalmanovich, the first acquaintance Dworzecki remembered running into in the ghetto, captured this mood by repeating the phrase "as long as we are among Jews."[54] The writer Isaiah Spiegel, who survived the Łódź Ghetto, sounded a similar, if more socially acerbic, sentiment of "among Jews" in a story he wrote in early March 1940, by which point the herding of Łódź Jews into the site of the ghetto, the old Jewish slum neighborhood of Bałuty, was mostly complete. Later published in edited form as "The Family Lipschitz Goes Into the Ghetto," the story portrays the migration into the ghetto of an upper-middle-class Jewish family that, to that point, had held its poor relatives still living in Bałuty at arm's length. They are consequently surprised when they are received with such warmth and solicitude by Uncle Yankl and his two daughters, who scurry to move all the possessions the Lipschitz family was able to carry into their small and rundown apartment. Fending off the protests of their formerly well-off relatives, Uncle Yankl responds, "Are we strangers? All Jews are today a family . . . a misfortune has struck us."[55] In the weeks leading up to the establishment of a formal ghetto in Warsaw, the Zionist Kaplan consistently viewed the creation of any segregated quarter, let alone a sealed one like that in Łódź, as a catastrophe for the four hundred thousand Jews of the city, yet read carefully, his diary indicates that some of those uprooted were more hopeful. "Those who come to seek refuge in the ghetto," he wrote on October 2, 1940, "imagine they can save themselves and their property and come to 'rest'; perhaps only in one room, but at least they will be able to dwell there in peace." They failed to see, Kaplan claimed, that the ghetto would remain vulnerable to Nazi depredations of all kinds.[56]

If the ghetto was viewed as a return, albeit involuntary, to a Jewish neighborhood that could potentially serve as a buffer and would, one might hope, represent the point at which Nazi persecution would peak, it was also seen by many as a reversion to the Jewish past, in a way that was jarring but could also provide some inkling of precedent and familiarity. On November 8, 1940—one week before the closure of the Warsaw Ghetto—the historian Emanuel Ringelblum wrote in his diary, "There's been the growth of a strong sense of historical consciousness recently. We tie in fact after fact from our daily experience with the events of history. We are returning to the Middle Ages."[57] In fact, this surge in historical consciousness had already been evident months earlier in the secret publication of the first book in Jewish Warsaw under Nazi occupation, released when the question of whether a closed and mandatory ghetto would be established in the city still appeared to hang in the balance. Issued in four hundred copies between July and August 1940 by the pioneering socialist Zionist youth movement Dror, *Suffering and Heroism in the Jewish Past in the Light of the Present* was an anthology of martyrologies, translated into Yiddish, stretching from the eleventh-century Hebrew Crusade chronicles to contemporary Hebrew poetry. The introduction, written by the leader of the movement Yitzhak Zuckerman, wavered between acknowledging the radical novelty of the current Jewish plight and seeking consolation and encouragement in the Jews' survival of previous spasms of persecution. "The darkest days of the new Middle Ages have come upon us," he wrote. All the "rotten nightmares of the Middle Ages" had returned: "hermetically sealed Jewish ghettos, the yellow badge in front and back, the distinguishing signs of special Jews—armbands on the sleeve and mass murder." In many ways, he conceded, "Our troubles of today exceed . . . those of the past." And yet, by familiarizing themselves with earlier trials that the Jewish people had suffered, Warsaw's Jews (and the pioneering youth in particular) could acquire the resolve to meet the present-day threat to the Jewish future. Without admitting any tension between his claims, the author stated that "in the course of our existence of three thousand years we have already endured countless difficult hours like these—*and perhaps even more difficult than these*—and we have continued to exist, to the anger and wrath of our enemies and oppressors."[58] For all the ambiguity of the introduction about how grave the current moment was relative to the past history of Jewish suffering, the implication was that this moment had a pedigree, a prototype. It was the latest chapter in the tragic yet heroic saga of Jewish martyrdom.

In the months after the closure of the Warsaw Ghetto on November 15, 1940, at least three articles in competing branches of the vast underground Jewish press, which was splintered along ideological lines, portrayed the Nazi ghetto as a revival of a medieval concept. In December 1940, the underground publication of the socialist Zionist Poale Zion (The Workers of Zion) Right party ran in its first (and only) volume a short historical overview of the ghetto from the Middle Ages to the present, written by an anonymous "Spectator." "The clouds of our Middle Ages have once again begun to establish themselves over our heads," the article opened. "All the evil decrees and oppressive measures that had grown moldy and been almost completely forgotten—of interest only to the professional historian—have floated back over the territory of our bleak daily lives and become a part of our bitter reality."[59] A month later, the underground monthly of Poale Zion Left printed a terser survey of the ghetto's lineage that was broadly similar to the earlier article in its periodization and details. Stressing the medieval origins of the ghetto, the anonymous author expressed disbelief that "in the twentieth century, the age of the telephone, the radio, and—by contrast—the 'Stuka' bombers, Warsaw, like a long string of cities beforehand, has had the merit to see within its borders a 'cultured' achievement like this: walls, fences, and guard posts, all with the aim of cutting off half a million people from the entire world because of their origin."[60] Finally, in April 1941, the secret organ of the pioneering left-wing Zionist movement Ha-Shomer ha-Tsa'ir (The Young Guard), published in Polish a piece titled "Between the Ghetto Walls," with the subtitle, "The Eternal Nightmare." "This ghetto," the author wrote, "is not the first in history. It already existed, in the Middle Ages; in the course of time it was annulled, and here it is again." Compared to the previous two articles, the essay stressed that the ghetto was symptomatic of an economic antisemitism that would endure so long as Jews did not live as farmers and workers on their own land. "The ghetto of our days," the author underscored, "is neither new nor exceptional. It is a direct result of the abnormal situation of the Jewish people." Only with the restoration of the Jewish people to its agrarian and pioneering origins in its homeland would there come "an end to the nightmare of the Jewish ghetto."[61]

All three of the clandestine articles provided a genealogy for the Nazi ghetto, implying that it was a historically familiar institution for Jews, even if the confinement it imposed was a complete novelty in the contemporary Jewish experience. There were analogies with prior episodes in Jewish history that could be made, antecedents that could serve as life rafts, preventing ghetto readers from feeling as if they had become wholly unmoored from the past. The German historical theorist Reinhart Koselleck's twin concepts of the "space of experience" and the "horizon of expectation" are helpful in making sense of this phenomenon. For Koselleck, the individual at every moment of her existence is always subject to two fundamental tugs: a backward tug toward the "space of experience," replete with historical and biographical archetypes, and a forward tug toward the "horizon of expectation," the realm of anticipation and projection that, to a greater or lesser degree, is informed by what the past has led the person living in the present to think likely or probable to happen in the future. Koselleck's central argument is that, in modernity, the "space of experience" gradually shrinks, as the perceived relevance of previous exemplars for the present diminishes, while the "horizon of expectation" continually expands, as the future becomes increasingly open-ended, no longer imagined as a repetition of the past. Bracketing this argument, we can view the three essays in the underground Warsaw press as efforts to assimilate the Nazi ghetto to the Jewish "space of experience," in a way that could sustain a "horizon of expectation" characterized by hopes of continuance and survival.[62]

Yet, even from the outset, not everyone believed that there were grounds for comparison between the Nazi ghetto and the premodern ghetto. Kaplan, who consistently equated the prospect of a closed ghetto to the creation of a "concentration camp," was especially skeptical. On November 28, 1940, just two weeks after the closure of the Warsaw Ghetto, Kaplan wrote of the unprecedented nature of the ghetto in its current form. Jews, he noted, had had a taste of the ghetto more than once in their history. Indeed, there were times the Jews themselves established the ghetto as an asylum from the mischief of the enemy. But even when it was forced on them, its goal was not to achieve their economic ruin. "The gates of the ghetto were open all day," Kaplan wrote, "and only closed at night. . . . During the hours of the day Jews exited the gates of the ghetto in order to trade and do business. Mutual commerce between Jewish ghetto dwellers and their gentile neighbors never ceased throughout the existence of the ghettos." The same could not be said for the ghettos the Nazis had created in Łódź and Warsaw and throughout Poland.[63] Meanwhile, it did not take long for Ringelblum to walk back his initial suggestion of a "return to the Middle Ages." As a result of the continued streaming into the ghetto of Jews expelled from provincial towns, coupled with the woefully insufficient caloric rations supplied by the Nazis, the Warsaw Ghetto was direly affected by homelessness, hunger, and disease by the early months of 1941. Corpses on the streets were already a commonplace. In a diary entry from March 1941, Emanuel Ringelblum describes an "interesting argument" among several leading ghetto intellectuals on the subject of the ghetto. From his later writings, it is clear this was a debate that stretched over several Saturday afternoons. "The participants in the discussion," Ringelblum noted, "stressed that it was impossible to compare the ghettos of old and today, since the ghetto in our days was a ghetto in name only. In truth it is a concentration camp."[64] Oskar Rosenfeld, a Central European Zionist intellectual, was among the wave of deportees from Prague to the Łódź Ghetto in November 1941, by which point the ghetto had already existed for more than a year and a half. He found a position in the ghetto's official "statistics department" set up by the "Eldest of the Jews," Mordechai Chaim Rumkowski and thus was saved from subsequent deportation to the death camps until the final dissolution of the ghetto in August 1944. Throughout his confinement, Rosenfeld kept a diary rich in both empirical description and philosophical reflection, which he hoped one day—should he survive the war—would be the basis for a cultural history of the ghetto. One of his chief concerns was language, specifically how the "transformations of forms of living" wrought by the ghetto had altered the lexicon, generating a situation where "new words had to be created" and "old ones had to be endowed with new meaning." Together with the head of the statistics department, his fellow Prague deportee Oskar Singer, he compiled in secret an *Encyclopedia of the Ghetto* that contained entries on everything from ghetto personalities to ghetto argot. In two of the earliest of his twenty-one notebooks, Rosenfeld mused on the significance of the word *ghetto,* claiming that it functioned "to mark Jews as a piece from the Middle Ages with a yellow star." Yet Rosenfeld quickly recognized that this was mere symbolism, not reality: "In contrast to the medieval ghettos," he wrote in another early notebook, "the present-day ghetto is 'closed' through a misunderstanding of the term on the part of the Eldest and the Ashkenes [Rosenfeld's codeword for the Germans]."[65]

Even with the growing sense of a chasm between past and present, the perception of the ghetto as a return to the Middle Ages proved tenacious. Though native to Warsaw, Stanisław Różycki was living in Lwów (Lviv) when the Nazis overran it in June 1941; that September he returned to Warsaw and began collaborating with Ringelblum's secret Oyneg Shabes group dedicated to amassing a clandestine archive that would record for posterity the history of the ghetto from the vantage of its victims.[66] Three months later Różycki wrote a report about daily life in the Warsaw Ghetto and the city's appearance titled "This Is the Ghetto! Reporting from the Inferno of the 20th Century." For Różycki, the war as a whole and the slaughter of innocents it had inspired were proof "that in 1941 we are regressing several centuries backwards, systematically and consistently." The ghetto, however, which Różycki observed with the unfathoming eyes of a newcomer, was the epitome of this winding back of the clock:

> No evidence is needed to prove that the ghetto fully and absolutely resembles the Middle Ages; it can be seen at a glance. The idea of creating separate districts sealed by walls—this is a repetition and a deliberate imitation of the Middle Ages. Not only the walls but the fate of the imprisoned resembles medieval times. The yellow badge, never mind whether it is a white-blue or a yellow band, whether it is worn on the right arm, in the front or in the back—the intention remains the same, to stigmatize with a symbol of disgrace.

In spite of presenting the ghetto as a picture of the Middle Ages in miniature, even Różycki conceded at the end of his piece that the Nazis had surpassed "all the persecutions of medieval and earlier times."[67] The analogy could only be taken so far.

Perhaps the most arresting example of the "return to the Middle Ages" motif in ghetto literature—one that moves in the direction of the perception of an absolute historical rupture—appears in Josef Zelkowicz's agonized depiction of the most traumatic period in the history of the Łódź Ghetto: the mass deportation of 20,000 Jews, including nearly all children ten and under and all adults sixty-five and older, in early September 1942 to the killing center at Chełmno. To prevent anyone from escaping the order, the Germans imposed house arrest for days, as they, with the assistance of the Jewish police, methodically proceeded building by building, inspecting all the residents and snatching young children, the elderly, and anyone who appeared too infirm as a result of the terrible undernourishment to contribute to the ghetto's economic productivity. Like Rosenfeld, Zelkowicz was employed in the statistics department and contributed to the semi-official archive's daily *Chronicle of the Łódź Ghetto,* which ran from January 1941 through July 1944. A trained rabbi, he also kept a Yiddish diary in which he reported, in brutally frank fashion, on how hunger, starvation, and disease were wreaking an utter breakdown in Jewish family relations, traditional bourgeois values, and religious life. "In Those Nightmarish Days," his fastidious day-by-day, blow-by-blow narration of the September 1942 deportations, is among the most significant accounts we have of this event.

In his entry for Sunday, September 6, 1942, after the roundups had begun in earnest and the house arrest was still in effect, Zelkowicz comments on the dreadful slowness of time's passage, such that mere hours seemed days and even longer:

> What time must it be? Only ten o'clock in the morning. How large can the ghetto be? All told, the size of a single stride. But how many days feel as if they've passed during those few early morning hours? Just days? Years! Centuries! How much time will it take for the ghetto to finish its return to the Middle Ages? Just a few days more, and maybe just a few hours![68]

The line about a "return to the Middle Ages" at first resembles a familiar reference to Nazi savagery and bloodthirstiness. But then the passage gives this idea an unanticipated twist. Zelkowicz explains how the curfew has effectively balkanized the ghetto into separate buildings and streets, "making them feel as if they're located on different continents." Thus, when rumors arrive from two buildings over, it is not only as if they have "come from over the sea": they seem to emanate from the distant past as well. "So you listen to these various stories as if they were chronicles from some ancient, bygone era. You listen to them as if they were legends read out from old, musty scrolls and end up shrugging your shoulders. 'Are these stories true or false? Where does the truth end and fantasy begin?'" The seeming "medievalism" of these reports ("chronicles from some ancient, bygone era") feeds doubt that they can in fact be true. Zelkowicz goes on to cite earlier massacres from Jewish history—the massacre of Jews in the Rhineland during the Crusades, the massacre of Jews in Ukraine by Bohdan Chmielnicki's Cossacks in 1648–1649—that later generations related to with a sense of disbelief. Even the reports of the cruel persecution of Jews in Germany in the 1930s before the war were met with skepticism. The remoteness of all these events from a familiar human reason and logic—from what the intellect was capable of grasping—meant that they ran into a "steel wall of doubt and disbelief." Zelkowicz goes so far as to suggest that the very ghetto inmates "who have seen with our own eyes and heard with our own ears the senseless actions and measures we've been subjected to"—if they are fortunate enough to survive the war—will one day relate to their own eyewitness memories with similar distrust. "A few years will be all it takes before we too begin to shake our heads doubtfully once again, and in just the same way." The "return to the Middle Ages" that once anchored the ghetto within a distinctively Jewish "vale of tears," and implied the existence of a continuum to Jewish historical suffering, transforms into a perception of the utter untranslatability of horror across time: "There exists no pen and no language with the vocabulary to convey every range of emotions that overtake a human being forced to see and hear all that has occurred in the last few days."[69]

This sense of wordlessness—and of the absence of any historical precedent for the current trial—became magnified in other ghettos as well during the period of mass deportations to the death camps. The Łódź Ghetto remained mostly in the dark about the annihilation of Polish Jewry in Operation Reinhard, starting with the deportation of the vast majority of the Jews of Lublin to Bełżec in March 1942. Yet news of the mass killing soon reached the Warsaw Ghetto and inaugurated a harrowing period of awaiting Jewish Warsaw's turn, coupled with continued disbelief on the part of many that the Nazis would ever expel, let alone destroy, a community of hundreds of thousands of Jews. Writing on June 3, 1942, seven weeks exactly before the beginning of the Great Deportation of Warsaw Jewry, Kaplan contrasted the Jewish expulsions of the medieval past with those of the present. In the Jewish imagination to that point, expulsion had represented the most severe punishment that the state could inflict on its Jews, but no longer:

> For these days are not like the days of old. Even the original expulsions were distinguished by their cruelty and by all the terrible troubles and awful misfortunes that were wrapped up in a sweeping decree like this; but the expelled remained alive. Every exile had the permission to go to wherever his feet led him. . . . It is not this way now: the exiles are transported like captives in closed and sealed cars under the watch of Nazi oppressors and are given over into the hands of the angels of destruction until they reach the site of the scaffold where their lives are taken.[70]

When the Great Deportation finally began on July 22, Kaplan—whose last entry was made on August 4 and who apparently was deported with his wife on that date to Treblinka—was so overcome by his personal fear and the scenes of unspeakable chaos and wickedness ("the ghetto has turned into hell," he wrote) that he struggled to find words that could describe the situation: "There are no words to express what has befallen us from the day the deportation was announced and the hour it began. Those whose notion of the subject of historical deportation comes from the pages of books know nothing. We, the children of the Warsaw Ghetto, are now tasting it."[71] The teacher Abraham Lewin, a contributor to Ringelblum's secret archive who survived the first deportation and kept a diary throughout, echoed Kaplan's insistence on the radical singularity of the present destruction. The ancient Roman war against the Judeans portrayed in Josephus and the Eastern European pogroms of 1905–1906 and 1918–1919: Lewin invokes them all only to reject the possibility of comparison. It was "a slaughter the like of which human history had not seen. Even in the legend of Pharaoh and his decree: every newborn boy will be thrown into the river."[72]

Of all the passages in ghetto literature on the ultimate irrelevance of the legacy of the Middle Ages or any historical past for making sense of the Nazi ghetto, arguably the most memorable is the most oft-quoted excerpt from Oskar Rosenfeld's Łódź Ghetto diary. It follows his description of the first wave of deportations of Western and Central European Jews in May 1942, who had arrived in the ghetto only around six months earlier ("the outsettlement of the insettled"):

> The tragedy is tremendous. Those in the ghetto cannot comprehend it. For it does not bring out any greatness as in the Middle Ages. This tragedy is devoid of heroes. And why tragedy? Because the pain does not reach out to something human, to a strange heart, but is something incomprehensible, colliding with the cosmos, a natural phenomenon like the creation of the world. Creation would have to start anew with *berajshit* [Hebr., "In the beginning," the first word in the Hebrew Bible.] In the beginning God created the ghetto.[73]

As with many of Rosenfeld's observations, this one resists a simple explanation. The claim that the tragedy of the ghetto "does not bring out any greatness as in the Middle Ages" may refer to the lack of opportunity for choosing death and saving the soul at the expense of the body. There is no place for martyrdom here, Rosenfeld implies.[74] The pain of the ghetto "is something incomprehensible"; it cannot be mitigated because it dwarfs the human capacity for imagination and understanding. It is instead akin to "a natural phenomenon like the creation of the world." The Nazi ghetto is such a radical novelty, such a rupture with "reality," as to demand a new cosmogony: "In the beginning God created the ghetto."

On April 20, 1943, a representative of the Polish underground cabled the Polish Government-in-Exile in London to report that the Germans had entered the Warsaw Ghetto the day before to liquidate it and deport its remaining population—and the ghetto had fought back. "The Jews are defending themselves; we can hear shots and grenade explosions," the cable noted. "The Germans have used bombs and armored cars. They have losses."[75] Thus began a series of messages—some penned by delegates of the Jewish Fighting Organization (ŻOB)—that would be cabled to London in the days and weeks that followed and, through regular coverage in the international and Jewish press, brought the "battle of

Warsaw's Jews" to the attention of the world. A Jewish vanguard with little formal military training and scarce ammunition held out against the tanks and artillery of the Germans for nearly four weeks. By May 16, when the SS commander of the suppression of the uprising declared that "the Jewish residential quarter of Warsaw is no more," virtually the entire ghetto had been burnt to the ground.[76] Of the 40,000 Jews who had still been living in the ghetto on the eve of the German *Aktion,* only a small number managed to survive the demolition by escaping to the "Aryan" side.

Even as the war still raged and the destruction of European Jewry continued apace, the commemoration of the ghetto uprising and the shaping of its collective memory began in earnest. Before the full dimensions of the catastrophe were known, before the "Holocaust" even existed as a concept, the Warsaw revolt had emerged as the prime symbol of Jewish heroism and martyrdom during World War II. The consensus that quickly formed around the uprising's iconic status was accompanied from the start by ideological conflict over its meaning and the most exemplary fighters of the revolt.[77] The ŻOB had briefly brought together movements that were otherwise steadfast opponents; it was a coalition of a consortium of left-wing Zionist parties with the anti-Zionist and socialist Bund. In the aftermath, members of these streams offered different accounts of the battle and of its true heroes. What would prove most consequential for the subsequent history of the word *ghetto* was the widely shared view of the Warsaw Ghetto Uprising as a paradigm of resistance.

This perception was evident in a name for the revolt coined in the first year after the revolt, only to vanish from the collective memory soon afterward: "Ghettograd." It first appeared in a June 1943 report sent by the surviving members of the Jewish Labor Underground in Poland, which reached the Bund in the United States through London channels. "What was going on in April and May," the report stated, "that Jewish-German war . . . named the Battle of Ghettograd—this really does surpass any analogy from the history, either of our own or of any other nation."[78] Shortly before the first anniversary of the uprising in April 1944, the Chicago Jewish newspaper *The Sentinel* published a page-long article about the revolt titled "The Battle of Ghettograd." According to the editor, the Nazis themselves had been the first to dub the resistance the "Battle of Ghettograd or Jewgrad, remembering their bitter retreat at Stalingrad."[79] Later that year, the U.S. representation of the Bund in New York published a volume, *Ghetto in Flames,* that labeled "Ghettograd" the "new symbol" that had inspired Jews living "under Hitler's yoke" to rebel in ghettos like Białystok and Częstochowa and in camps including Treblinka and Trawniki. "Ghettograd," the first chapter concluded, "possesses far more than transient value. It gives a new content and meaning to life, for when it is dark all around, when the heart writhes in pain because of the great misfortune, and the world is rolling around in a burning shame— there is a warm and radiant point, to which one can raise one's eyes: that is *Ghettograd.*"[80]

The date of the outbreak of the uprising, April 19—starting with the very first anniversary in 1944—regularly became the occasion of commemorative events and moments of silence, first in the United States, Palestine, and the United Kingdom and eventually in liberated Europe and Jewish communities around the globe.

The World Jewish Congress—and in particular the head of its Organization Department, Ignacy Schwarzbart, a Polish Zionist who had survived the war as one of two Jewish members of the Polish Parliament-in-Exile in London—pressured its various branches to organize memorials each anniversary and collected reports about events held from Latin America to India.[81] By the tenth anniversary of the revolt in 1953, so much had already been written about the Warsaw Ghetto, in multiple languages, that the pioneering Holocaust historian Philip Friedman claimed to have amassed a bibliography of some 740 works on the subject.[82] For that anniversary, Schwarzbart authored and the World Jewish Congress published a special pamphlet titled *The Story of the Warsaw Ghetto Uprising: Its Meaning and Message.* Schwarzbart asked,

> Will this uprising become an eternal source of national pride in our history? I think it will. But the eternal meaning and purpose of the Warsaw Ghetto Uprising will be realized only if the Jewish people, and particularly the coming generations, feel and understand that the spirit which animated the fighters of the Warsaw Ghetto Uprising is an integral, inseparable part of the eternal spirit which keeps our people alive and active, creative and optimistic despite all disillusionment and ever recurring suffering.[83]

For the ghetto inmates, as we have seen, the daily experience of starvation, disease, corpses on the streets, and eventually the deportations—

Poster created by the Congress for Jewish Culture, in Yiddish and English, encouraging the lighting of six candles in memory of the six million martyrs on the eighth anniversary of the outbreak of the Warsaw Ghetto Uprising.

together with the spreading awareness that deportation meant annihilation—had appeared to vitiate the possibility of bringing the Nazi ghetto under the rubric of any antecedent in the history of Jewish persecution. The Warsaw Ghetto Uprising, in contrast, made Jewish history relevant again. The "deeper meaning of the revolt," Schwarzbart stressed, "is part and parcel of the spirit of the Maccabees, of the fighters of Massada, of the generations who died in the Middle Ages for the sake of our faith and religion, as well as centuries later for true humanity and morality in the relations between men and nations."[84] Because they had chosen to die in battle, the ghetto fighters had reclaimed, it was implied, the mantle of true martyrdom. The singling out of the Warsaw Ghetto as the prism par excellence through which the murder of the six million was remembered—especially in the early decades of Holocaust commemoration—may have been driven at least in part by a desire to find a counterpoint to what appeared otherwise (however dubiously) as a history of Jewish passivity.[85] Its appropriateness as a symbol of the scale of the destruction (especially once that scale was known) was questionable from the start. Yet the ramifications of this decision for the connotations of the word *ghetto* were profound. Speaking at the eighth Ghetto Uprising anniversary commemoration in New York in 1951, Israel Goldstein, an American Conservative rabbi and Zionist who was then chairman of the Western Hemisphere Executive of the World Jewish Congress, evoked this change:

We are meeting on a day which elicits historic and tragic memories. It is the anniversary of the battle of the Warsaw Ghetto, a battle fought by those who knew it was hopeless but sacrificed their lives to demonstrate that the Jewish courage to die "al Kiddush Hashem" is not dead, that Jews will not let themselves be led like sheep to the slaughter, that the barbarity of the Nazi beast in human form must not be cheaply perpetrated.

Thus a new and proud connotation was given to the word "ghetto," a connotation not of humiliation and passive submission, but of dignity and active resistance.[86]

The ghetto itself had yielded a foil to the "ghetto Jew" in the form of the fighting martyr, whose bravery was so remarkable as to transform the very meaning of *ghetto*. When the word would be mentioned going forward, it would conjure not only thoughts of weakness, domination, capitulation, and genocide. It would also function as a symbol of resistance.

The ghetto thus could serve as a symbol of the legacy of Christian maltreatment of the Jews and of the perceived insularity and backwardness of Old World Judaism wherever it was found, an emblem of darkness, narrowness, and physical and mental closure. The ghetto could also represent an authentic, holistic, autonomous Jewishness buffeted by the universalizing and corrosive forces of modernity. While this discourse continued in the years of persecution leading up to World War II and the Holocaust, the Nazi ghetto ultimately could not be fit into this framework, for the simple reason that for anyone sane it could not be the object of nostalgia. In a tribute to "The Spirit in the Ghetto" he wrote but was never to deliver for the second anniversary of the Vilna Ghetto in September 1943 (he was deported to a labor camp in Estonia first, where he ultimately died in 1944), Zelig Hirsh Kalmanovitch conceded, "The only wish that united all the inhabitants of the ghetto, from the first to the last, is that the ghetto should soon disappear."[87] At most the confined population could pride itself on maintaining a society with children's homes, a library and reading hall, a theater, and youth clubs against all the odds; "that," Kalmanovitch concluded, "is clearly a victory of spirit over matter."[88] Eventually, in the wake of the Warsaw Ghetto Uprising, the Nazi ghetto would come to evoke images of armed resistance. But none of this could change the fact that the primary associations of the Nazi ghetto were overwhelmingly pejorative. The old ambivalence, at least as applied to this latest iteration of the concept, was gone.

Right around the time the Nazis were transforming the significance of the word *ghetto* in Europe, American blacks were increasingly appropriating the term to represent their own segregation and exclusion. In the postwar period, Jews would have to reckon not only with the new baggage that "ghetto" bore as a result of the Holocaust. They would also have to respond to its assimilation into the experience and jargon of another people—a people, moreover, with whom they were ensconced in a relationship that was growing more and more fraught. The final major migration in the odyssey of the word *ghetto* was its migration from Jews to blacks.

5

THE GHETTO
IN POSTWAR AMERICA

IN 1928, LOUIS WIRTH introduced the immigrant ghetto to urban sociology as a site that was deeply anchored in the Jewish historical experience, yet for all that was broadly similar to a whole range of minority
neighborhoods that dotted the modern metropolitan city. "While the
ghetto is, strictly speaking, a Jewish institution," he wrote in *The Ghetto*,
"there are forms of ghettos that concern not merely Jews. There are Little
Sicilies, Little Polands, Chinatowns, and Black belts in our large cities,
and there are segregated areas, such as vice areas, that bear a close resemblance to the Jewish ghetto." His mentor Robert Park concurred,
noting in his foreword to Wirth's book that within the city "every people
and every cultural group may be said to create and maintain its own
ghetto."[1] The original Jewish referent for the term remained intact, but
properly understood the ghetto was a multicultural phenomenon, to the
point that the word had a universal reach and significance.

Fast forward forty years, and we find that what Wirth presented as one
among several analogies to the Jewish case—the "Black belt"—had come
to eclipse them all and even became the putative prototype in exempli-
fying the word *ghetto*. In the spring of 1968, the National Advisory Commission on Civil Disorders (known as the Kerner Commission after its
chairman, Otto Kerner, then governor of Illinois), convened by President
Lyndon B. Johnson roughly six months earlier to investigate and recommend solutions to the rash of urban race riots in the "long, hot summer"

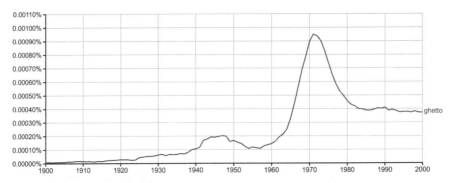

Results of a Google Ngram search for the word "ghetto" in English-language books published between 1900 and 2000. The y-axis indicates the frequency of occurrence of that word among all words in the corpus.

of 1967, released its long-awaited report. "This is our basic conclusion," the report famously stated: "Our Nation is moving toward two societies, one black, one white—separate and unequal." The main symptom of this division was the setting for the violence—the ghetto—responsibility for which was laid directly at the feet of the white majority:

> Segregation and poverty have created in the racial ghetto a destructive environment totally unknown to most white Americans.
> What white Americans have never fully understood—but what the Negro cannot forget—is that white society is deeply implicated in the ghetto. White institutions created it, white institutions maintain it, and white society condones it.[2]

Nowhere in the document did the word *ghetto* appear in quotation marks, as if to suggest any tentativeness to the label or its appropriation from another cultural lexicon. In the American context of the sixties at least, it was implied, there was no longer a diversity of ethnic ghettos in the plural. There was only "white society" and "black society," and the sole ghetto of note was the black one. The Jewish history of the term appeared quite literally to have been whited out.

The story of the ghetto's migration from Jewish to black enclaves concerns more than the shifting nuance of a particular word. Arguments about the usage, application, and even ownership of "ghetto" served as a stage on which were played out fundamental debates over everything

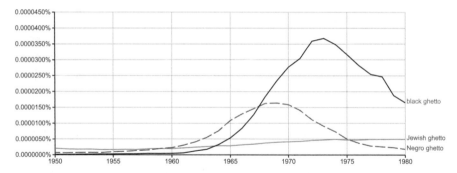

Results of a Google Ngram search for the phrases "Jewish ghetto," "Negro ghetto," and "black ghetto" in English-language books between 1950 and 1980. The y-axis indicates the frequency of occurrence of each phrase among all two-word phrases in the corpus.

from the meaning of integration and segregation, to the uniqueness of the black and Jewish experiences, to the ethics of metaphor and comparison. What is clear, is that the conversion of the word *ghetto* into a term more popularly associated with blacks than Jews was not a matter of indifference for Jews. This was so not only because it was frequently Jewish neighborhoods that were changing or because Jews remained a presence in these neighborhoods, whether as landlords, small businesspeople, teachers, social workers, or, in decreasing numbers, residents. It was so because the word itself, *ghetto,* however fraught, had become so closely bound up with images of what it meant to be Jewish.[3]

The conversion of "ghetto" into a term more commonly associated with blacks than with Jews began in the 1960s. Digital history resources allow us to plot trends in the usage of a word with an exactitude that years ago would be unthinkable. There was a general surge in the use of *ghetto* in the 1960s, cresting in the early 1970s. From 1960 to 1965, phrases like "Negro ghetto" or "black ghetto" began to surpass "Jewish ghetto" in popular usage (though "Negro ghetto" plateaued and then decreased below "Jewish ghetto" in the mid-1970s as the term "Negro" came to be regarded as offensive and unfashionable).

The sharp rise in references to the "black ghetto" from the mid-1960s onward was so dramatic that it seemed to many as if the contemporary black referent was a complete novelty. "Is there actually such a thing as an American 'ghetto,'" an August 1967 column in *U.S. News and World Report* asked. The column continued: "A few years ago somebody conceived the idea of applying the word 'ghetto' to Negro neighborhoods in the United States. Used in this way, the word gives an impression of an oppressed people, restricted by law, compelled to live in a certain area. A look at the facts, however, shows that the Negro neighborhoods of today do not have the true characteristics of a ghetto."[4] *U.S. News and World Report* was the most conservative of the three major American news weeklies, and its skepticism was echoed by several other right-wing outlets and op-ed columnists, who opposed what was seen as an attempt to besmirch the United States' reputation by identifying it with a word and concept as allegedly un-American as the ghetto.[5] Yet if the right-wing's resistance to the term *ghetto* reflected a particular (albeit growing) segment of public opinion, its perception that there was something new and even unsettling about its application to black neighborhoods seems to have been broadly shared. In the same month as the *U.S. News* article appeared, August 1967, the black magazine *Ebony* ran a piece titled "I'll Never Escape the Ghetto" by Stanley Sanders, a black Rhodes scholar and native of Watts in Los Angeles. Sanders recalled how different things had been eight years earlier when he left home for Whittier College and thought that fleeing Watts was both possible and desirable: "Negro college youth during those undergraduate years had none of its present mood. . . . Good grades, athletics, popularity—these were the things that mattered. The word 'ghetto' had not even entered the lexicon of race relations. People were not conscious of the ghetto as a separate phenomenon."[6] An African American character in a science-fiction short story from the late sixties, "Calliope and Gherkin and the Yankee Doodle Thing," is similarly struck by the novelty of the black referent for "ghetto": "When I was a boy, people used the word ghetto to mean a place where Jews lived. . . . They even talked about a 'Gilded Ghetto' where rich Jews lived. How did it get to mean a black slum all of a sudden?"[7]

In fact, uses of the word *ghetto* with reference to the segregation of black Americans reached back much earlier than the 1960s. Indeed, they antedated Wirth's assertion of an analogy between the "Black belt" and the Jewish ghetto in 1928. To find the first appropriations of "ghetto" in the African American public sphere, one has to go back to the early twentieth century. In 1910, Baltimore became the first city to pass a municipal zoning ordinance that divided every street into black and white blocks. The ordinance forbade the sale of a home to a black on a block in which the majority of residents were white, and vice versa. Its example was soon copied by other cities throughout the South and Midwest, including Richmond, Atlanta, New Orleans, Oklahoma City, St. Louis, and Louisville.[8] The growing trend of residential segregation by law galvanized African American newspapers throughout the United States, from the *Chicago Defender* to the *Washington Bee,* and stopping it became the overriding mission of the newly founded National Association for the Advancement of Colored People (NAACP).

It was in the context of the struggle against the gathering movement to extend "Jim Crow" to city neighborhoods that the word *ghetto* began to appear with growing frequency in African American newspapers and periodicals. "Do you really want a Negro ghetto established here in the Capital of the Nation?" asked a November 1913 letter in the *Washington Bee,* appealing for support for the NAACP: "a ghetto like that already established a few miles away in Baltimore?—a ghetto where the law and courts of 'justice' compel you and your families to live herded together and apart from the rest of humanity as though your color were the plague?"[9] On occasion, uses of *ghetto* in this period prefigured how charged the term would later become in black-Jewish relations, as in this March 1917 letter that appeared in the radical St. Paul–based black newspaper *The Appeal.* It lambasted Joel Spingarn, then chairman of the NAACP, for supporting a military training camp for blacks: "Spingarn the Jew, is classed as a white man in the United States. There is no Jewish problem here. Now that he is out of Russia, from whence he came, leaving the ghetto behind, he is willing to put the colored man in the ghetto here."[10] The most noteworthy and repeated example of the use of *ghetto* in the early twentieth-century black press could be found in the pages of the *Crisis,* the official journal of the NAACP, founded and edited (and, in the early years, largely written) by W. E. B. Du Bois. Starting in December 1910, in the second issue of the first volume, a column titled "The Ghetto," written almost certainly by Du Bois in spite of the anonymous authorship, appeared in most editions of the *Crisis.* Significantly, in his 1899 book *The Philadelphia Negro: A Social Study,* a pioneering investigation of a black urban community, Du Bois had never once used the word *ghetto* to describe his object of analysis, though he certainly addressed the factors that contributed to black Philadelphia's isolation.[11] This suggested that the term only became a part of his frame of reference in the first decade of the twentieth century. Most of the news included in "The Ghetto" simply reported on the latest developments around the nation concerning segregation (not simply residential), and indeed December 1910, when the column debuted, was the month the Baltimore ordinance was passed. The opening column offered a pointed critique of the ghetto concept. For Du Bois the ultimate threat of the "color line" was its culmination in "the extreme Ghetto idea":

> In America by the accident of color it is possible roughly to separate much ignorance and bad manners by drawing the color line. But it is a barbarous and unjust and unwise expedient, and it leads to the extreme Ghetto idea. The half-trained white Baltimore tradesman reasons logically: If I can push black men out of my way in train and street car, in theatre and art gallery, in church and park, why can I not segregate them in a Ghetto? The Atlanta "cracker," newborn to good wages and political power, is jealous of ambitious black folk. If he can take a black man's vote away why can he not take his home and force him back to the alley, whence he came?[12]

In 1917, the Supreme Court found Baltimore-style residential ordinances unconstitutional in *Buchanan v. Warley*, curbing (though not ending) the effort to introduce blatantly government-mandated ghettos in American cities while doing little to stem the hemming in of African Americans in practice.[13] In the following decades, as racially restrictive covenants, realtor steering, and redlining (not to mention physical violence) only hardened the "color line" in housing, the word *ghetto* became an increasingly central term in the black lexicon for describing residential segregation by race.[14] In the 1920s and 1930s, the phrase "Negro Ghetto" might have sounded discordant in the mainstream press, but it would have been familiar to readers of the black press and in particular to black intellectuals.[15] In an unpublished paper from the mid-1970s, the anthropologist St. Clair Drake revealed that, in 1930s Chicago (where he "became conscious for the first time of what life in a northern Black ghetto really meant"), both the black leadership class of the city "and the small coterie of Black graduate students around the University of Chicago used the term 'ghetto' to describe" urban "concentrations" of blacks in hemmed-in quarters. It was, Drake noted, a "quite obvious analogy to the kinds of communities that had been associated with Jewish life," and some deemed it too "Jewish-specific."[16] *Black Metropolis,* Drake and Horace Cayton's magisterial 1945 history and ethnography of African American life on the South Side of Chicago, illustrated the growing prominence of the term in the black community. Notably, Drake and Cayton used different nomenclature in their study to signify the opposing aspects of the neighborhood concentration of blacks. As a cramped, largely dilapidated enclave that African Americans found almost impossible to escape even if they wanted to, the "Black Metropolis" was a "Black Ghetto." As a vibrant, internally diverse community rich in institutions and culture and crackling with energy, the "Black Metropolis" was "Bronzeville."[17]

By the end of World War II, the term *ghetto* was clearly part of a vocabulary used by African Americans to denote their ongoing struggle against segregated neighborhoods and housing, even as the concept continued to be primarily associated with Jews. In the aftermath of the war, U.S. black and Jewish organizations jointly waged a mostly successful legal fight against one of the chief pillars of residential segregation, racially restrictive covenants, and the word *ghetto,* with all its recent Nazi overtones, was a crucial part of their arsenal. "Homes for Aryans Only" was the title of the first of a series of articles against covenants in *Commentary* magazine in the late 1940s; its author, the Polish-born American Jewish housing expert Charles Abrams, warned, "The involuntary ghetto may soon be an unalterable American institution."[18] In 1948, the National Committee on Segregation in the Nation's Capital issued a ninety-one-page report, *Segregation in Washington,* that included a chapter on housing segregation titled "Ghettos in the Capital." "Ghetto is an ugly word," the chapter began. "To a Dane it is ugly. To any Nazi victim. To anyone who saw how Hitler placed a yellow mark on Jews so they could be made to live apart, suffer apart, die apart. To an American it is ugly." Nevertheless, the report went on: "In the capital of the Nation live a quarter of a million people, one-fourth of the city, who need no mark sewed on their clothing. . . . let there be any color in the skin identifiable as Negro, half Negro, or one-eighth Negro, and the possessor of that skin has lost his

American right to live anywhere in town."[19] Robert Weaver, a Washington native who was one of the organizers of the committee that issued *Segregation in Washington,* published that same year a book *The Negro Ghetto* that was a detailed history of residential segregation in the North and the first to feature the word *ghetto* with a black referent in its title.[20] The book appeared at roughly the same time that the Supreme Court, in *Shelley v. Kraemer* (1948), banned judicial enforcement of restrictive covenants. Four American Jewish organizations filed a joint amicus brief in the case, arguing that the Court should find such covenants unconstitutional. Acknowledging that "Negroes have suffered most from the widespread use of restrictive covenants," the brief cited a recent case in a Washington suburb involving a covenant against Jews, in which a group of homeowners had asked a Maryland court to order the non-Jewish wife to "oust" her Jewish husband from their home. "The organizations sponsoring this brief," it continued, "are peculiarly alert to the dangers to democracy arising from racial or religious residential segregation. Jewish experience under European despotism gave rise to the word 'ghetto.' The threat of revival of that institution—implicit in the mushroom growth in almost every major American city of racial restrictive covenants—demands intercession in these cases."[21]

The battle against restrictive covenants brought blacks and Jews together, but already by 1948, blacks frequently perceived the ghetto—the black ghetto—largely as an arena of conflict, not commonality, with Jews. The main irritant was the fact that what had emerged as black ghettos had in many cases previously been largely Jewish ethnic enclaves, and even though the number of Jewish residents had fallen drastically, Jews remained visible in the neighborhood as small businesspeople, merchants, landlords, social workers, and schoolteachers. Fairly or not, they came to be seen as the face of white dominance, exploitation, and control. To this brew of hostility were added classic antisemitic tropes about Jewish greed and wiliness. In *Black Metropolis,* Drake and Cayton briefly discussed a major organized antisemitic campaign that erupted in Bronzeville in 1938, at a time when "about three-fourths of the merchants in Bronzeville were Jewish." This was one of the periodic "anti-Semitic waves that sometimes sweep through Bronzeville," the authors conceded, because "as the most highly visible and most immediately available white persons in the community, Jewish merchants tend to become the symbol of the

Negroes' verbal attack on all white businessmen."[22] In 1948—the very year that witnessed successful black and Jewish collaboration to challenge restrictive covenants in the courts—*Commentary* magazine published a young James Baldwin's "The Harlem Ghetto: Winter 1948," with its brutally honest and jaded account of "the Negro's ambivalent relation to the Jew." In the first two decades of the twentieth century, Harlem had been a largely Jewish neighborhood comprised of both poor and affluent Jews. As of 1917, when its Jewish population peaked at roughly 175,000, it was home to the second-largest Jewish community in the United States after the Lower East Side.[23] By 1930, however, most Jews in the neighborhood had abandoned the deteriorating housing stock of Harlem and decamped for areas such as Brooklyn, the Bronx, Washington Heights, and the Upper West Side—and African Americans had in the main replaced them, to the point that Harlem came to house about 72 per cent of Manhattan's black population.[24] For Baldwin, the continued presence in Harlem of Jewish merchants was only one (albeit major) aggravator of a deeply charged and complex relationship. Part of the problem was the intensity of the black identification with "the image of the wandering, exiled Jew" transmitted in the churches of all kinds and sizes that filled the streets of Harlem. "The more devout Negro," Baldwin wrote, "considers that he is a Jew, in bondage to a hard taskmaster and waiting for a Moses to lead him out of Egypt." But the closeness of this kinship with the figural Jew only made the encounter with the Jew in the flesh that much more contemptuous: "This same identification, which Negroes, since slavery, have accepted with their mothers' milk, serves, in contemporary actuality, to implement an involved and specific bitterness. Jews in Harlem are small tradesmen, rent collectors, real estate agents, and pawnbrokers; they operate in accordance with the American business tradition of exploiting Negroes, and they are therefore identified with oppression and are hated for it." The blacks of Harlem, so goes the logic, saw themselves as heirs to biblical Israel, and modern-day Jews in the role of the Egyptian taskmasters. Baldwin proceeds to further nuance his account of Negro antisemitism and Jewish racism. In both cases, he argued, a despised minority was motivated to seek cultural acceptance by adopting the prejudicial attitudes of the majority. Moreover, just as Drake and Cayton had argued, Jews present in the ghetto proved convenient targets for Harlem blacks' rage against white society. "The Negro," Baldwin concluded, "facing the Jew, hates, at bottom, not his Jewishness but the color of skin. It is not the Jewish tradition by which he has been betrayed, but the tradition of his native land. But just as a society must have a scapegoat, so hatred must have a symbol. Georgia has the Negro and Harlem has the Jew."[25] Antisemitism had originally served as motivation for concentrating Jews in ghettos; now, it was increasingly a spur for driving them out.

The battle against restrictive covenants appears in hindsight to have been a crucial landmark in the transference of the ghetto concept. To be sure, blacks were the main target of such covenants from their inception, and even before the judiciary washed its hands of them, the suburbanization of the Jews had begun in earnest. Still, in 1948 it was at least possible for American Jews to invoke the word *ghetto* to convey a shared, if less significant, experience of housing discrimination in the present. For blacks, the ban on legally enforceable covenants remained mostly impotent in the face of the physical violence, systematic redlining, and the simple refusal to sell to blacks, which continued to restrict their residential options.[26] For Jews, however, the demise of those covenants lifted the main surviving structural obstacle to moving into leafy neighborhoods that were previously off-limits to them.

Between 1945 and 1965, one out of every three Jews left the city for the suburbs, a rate higher than that for most Americans.[27] This mass exodus was often construed as an "emptying out of the old Ghettos," as a 1949 study of the Jews of Trenton, New Jersey, put it.[28] Writing ambivalently in *Commentary* in 1954 of his generation's and his own flight to suburbia, Harry Gersh, a writer as well as Jewish professional in community relations, claimed that the Jewish neighborhoods they had abandoned "*were* ghettos, no matter how well concealed." The "nameless" green stretches of "broad acres, half-acres, quarter-acres" that were their new homes bore no resemblance to the second-generation ethnic enclaves thickly populated with fellow Jews, not to mention synagogues and kosher butchers, bakeries, and delicatessens, that they had once inhabited.[29] A Jewishness that formerly had been experienced as something natural and organic now required the creation of new forms of affiliation to be sustained. "In the compacted Jewish neighborhoods of the cities," historian Edward Shapiro writes, "Jewish identity was absorbed through osmosis. In suburbia it had to be nurtured."[30] Synagogue memberships soared with the move to suburbia, as Jews who previously felt no pressure to belong to what Rabbi Simon Glustrom referred to as "the synagogue around the corner" felt compelled to join so as to maintain a connection with "Jewish community life."[31] In 1959, on the occasion of the republication of Wirth's The Ghetto, the then-young Israeli sociologist Amitai Etzioni published a critique of one of the book's core arguments. Wirth, hewing to Chicago School orthodoxy and the teachings of his mentor Robert Park in particular, had posited a one-to-one relationship between geographical distance from the original West Side Ghetto and the degree of assimilation; "not only does the Ghetto tend to disappear," Wirth had argued, "but the race tends to disappear with it." From the vantage of three decades later, Etzioni countered that the evidence belied the thesis that concentration in one area was a prerequisite of survival of the cultural group. The "ecological approach" embodied by Wirth and Park failed to appreciate that "members of the third (and later) generations of an ethnic minority may maintain a particular subculture and not lose their identity, although they are neither isolated nor concentrated in specific ecological areas."[32] While observers might debate the vitality and authenticity of a Judaism that lacked an "ecological basis," the resilience of communal ties in the form of synagogue and club affiliations vitiated the notion that Judaism could not outlive the "ghetto."

To be sure, there were limits to this exodus. Not all Jews were on the move in this period. The ability and desire to relocate were, among other things, a function of age and class. Jo Sinclair's 1955 novel The Changelings portrayed the anxieties of a Midwestern residential street of mostly Jewish working-class and small-time businessmen, alarmed at the prospect of a penetration of their neighborhood by the Schwartzes (or "Black Ones") that they might not be able to flee.[33] Meanwhile, the writers and sociologists who minutely dissected the experience of those who did leave for the suburbs often questioned how much, in fact, they had left the ghetto behind.[34] De facto prejudice in housing against Jews endured, as did the Jewish preference for living in close proximity with other Jews. The Minneapolis rabbi Albert I. Gordon, in his pioneering 1959 study

Jews in Suburbia, quoted an anonymous Jewish woman who resorted to the ghetto metaphor to convey the continued social divide between Jews and non-Jews in the suburbs:

> Our husbands do business with them. We see them in the town's shopping area. It's always a very pleasant, 'Hello, how are you?' kind of superficial conversation. We may even meet at a meeting some afternoon or even perhaps at a PTA school affair, but it is seldom more than that. It is a kind of "9 to 5" arrangement. The ghetto gates, real or imagined, close at 5:00 p.m. "Five o'clock shadow" sets in at sundown.[35]

In 1962, the Reform rabbis Eugene Lipman and Albert Vorspan warned that the social separation and lack of genuine interreligious dialogue among American Catholics, Protestants, and Jews were sufficiently pronounced to cause "some ground for fear that America is becoming not a triple melting pot but rather a triple ghetto."[36] Though each of the religions contributed to the problem, the Jewish propensity for self-segregation loomed large: "Among American Jews," they argued, "there appears a distinct tendency to seek 'Jewish' neighborhoods, to find comfort among Jewish friends, and to belong principally to Jewish organizations." As a result of the settlement patterns of the three religions, "millions of Americans—Protestant, Catholic, and Jewish—are living in homogenized white neighborhoods and sending their children to schools where everybody is the same racial, economic, and—increasingly—religious grouping. Our communities are not preparing Americans for leadership of a changing and plural world."[37]

The term "gilded ghetto," which had originated in the early twentieth century to refer to new Jewish urban neighborhoods like the Upper West Side, accompanied them in their move to the suburbs as well. In Philip Roth's 1993 *Operation Shylock,* one character cynically yet aptly describes Roth's rendering of the suburbanization of the Jews in his 1959 fictional debut *Goodbye, Columbus* as a "pastoralization of the ghetto."[38] Perhaps the most forceful, if over-the-top critique of Jewish suburbia came in psychiatrist Bruno Bettelheim's controversial 1962 essay "Freedom from Ghetto Thinking."[39] While the piece was largely a condemnation of European Jews for an allegedly deep-rooted streak of passivity and provincialism that prevented them from responding adequately to the threat of annihilation, Bettelheim made clear in spoken versions of his thesis that what he labeled "ghetto thinking" continued to plague U.S. Jewry. "Among the Jews of America," he stated in a 1963 lecture, "there exists a paradox which gives evidence of the continuation of the 'spirit of the ghetto.' It seems that Jewish desires in regard to housing are downright contradictory. They definitely wish to reside in unsegregated communities. Yet they prefer and feel comfortable only when living in close association with other Jews."[40] Still, as in the case of Judith R. Kramer and Seymour Leventman's 1961 *Children of the Gilded Ghetto*, which combined sociological analysis with a strong dose of snark, references to "gilded ghettos" or "ghetto thinking" were most common among intellectuals hostile to suburban Judaism.[41] They do not appear to have been terms of everyday usage. "Jewish children of today don't even understand the meaning of the word 'ghetto' unless it has been explained in a particular historical setting," Rabbi Simon Glustrom explained in his 1961 book *Living with Your Teenager: A Guide for Jewish Parents*.[42] Six years later in the periodical *Judaism*, Richard Fein suggested that the "children of today" probably would understand the word *ghetto*, but only in an altogether different setting. "How ironic," he mused, "that that word, *ghetto*, from Italian, for centuries a word coined for where we would live, and now for *them*, is slipping past the moorings of our immediate consciousness and instant concern. There must be a new generation of American Jews growing up to whom the word *ghetto* is instinctively connected with Negro, not Jew."[43]

By the 1950s, it appeared that the ghetto was in decline not only as a framework for Jewish life in the present. As a signifier for the Jewish past writ large, it also had begun to recede. Previously, writers had commonly used "ghetto" to refer to the Ashkenazic "Old World" of Jewish Eastern Europe, notwithstanding that most Jews of this region did not live in technical ghettos. But now there was a newly anglicized and globalized designation for this real and imagined Jewish space: *shtetl* or "little town" in Yiddish. In the wake of Mark Zborowski and Elizabeth Herzog's popular 1952 book *Life Is with People: The Jewish Little Town of Eastern Europe*, the first major anthropological study of Eastern European Jewish culture in English, "shtetl" emerged as a postwar Jewish keyword.[44] As had been the case with *ghetto*, *shtetl* came to be applied in a diffuse manner that glossed over the considerable diversity of Eastern European Jewish locales; it muddled the difference between the rural village (dorf) thinly populated by Jews and a larger city with a substantial or even majority Jewish presence. In the minutes for the working group that produced *Life Is with People* under anthropologist Margaret Mead's supervision, Zborowski admitted that his hometown had 60,000 people and was referred to by people as a *shtot*, or city. But size, Zborowski claimed, was an irrelevant factor in determining what constituted a shtetl. Echoing Wirth on the ghetto almost word for word, he said of the shtetl, "It's not a place; it's a state of mind."[45] The "esprit was shtetl," Zborowski explained of the city of his birth. And that esprit was the mentality of a "culture island, sharply differentiated from . . . the surrounding community."[46] With the word *ghetto* now compromised by its association with the Holocaust and increasingly with black Americans, the shtetl became the locus of Jewishness par excellence, the de rigueur shorthand for the vibrant culture of a lost world that lived on only on the page and in memory. Here was another resonance to the theme of Jews leaving the ghetto behind at mid-century.

Zborowski and Herzog's romanticized portrait of the shtetl offered readers a picture of what was, in essence, an "antisuburb."[47] The nostalgia for a world of piety, simplicity, and heightened community that it tapped—a nostalgia that would reach its apotheosis in the wildly successful 1964 musical *Fiddler on the Roof*—also bathed the immigrant ghettos Jews had tried so hard to escape in a soft and appealing light.[48] In September 1966, the Jewish Museum of New York opened a ballyhooed exhibition titled "The Lower East Side: Portal to American Life (1870–1924)" to rave reviews and huge crowds. "Any New Yorker," the *New York Times* asserted, "who can trace his lineage back to Ellis Island, not quite so far back, perhaps, as the pedigree of his poodle, should take his children to the museum to show them the land of their fathers."[49] The accompanying volume, edited by the curator and assistant director of the museum Allon Schoener, placed the Lower East Side within the pantheon of American landing places ("Plymouth, Jamestown, New Amsterdam, Philadelphia") while also conveying a sense of loss. In the preface, Schoener admitted that he was "born and raised in Cleveland" and only first encountered the Lower East Side in college. "When I came to New York on weekends from New Haven, I found myself roaming around

Delancey Street and Second Avenue eating food that my mother had never cooked and trying to find the world of my father's youth. By the time I started to look, it was gone."[50] Writing for *Harper's*, Alfred Kazin commented on "great crowds of prosperous, well-dressed, extremely sophisticated people—the usual museum crowd—standing in front of enormously blown-up pictures of their parents and grandparents." On one hand, it was implied, there was a pride in the distance they had traveled, in the "prosperous, well-dressed, extremely sophisticated people" they had become. But there was also a sense of returning to try to find an identity and a place that had vanished. "They have come to these photographs looking for their ancestors, their old selves, their hidden selves. The city is no longer their frontier, and usually they are afraid of it as well as ashamed of it."[51]

This disenchantment with the city had various sources, but one of them was the sense that the old Jewish neighborhoods had become home to dangerous slums of a different racial and ethnic character.[52] Could these present-day "ghettos" be fruitfully compared to the immigrant "ghettos" from earlier in the twentieth century, the ones most Jews had abandoned and were returning to visit in 1966, only in pictures, in the Jewish Museum's posh Upper East Side home? Or were the contemporary "ghettos" of a fundamentally different character, with far less porous boundaries and few hopes for dissolution? These were questions that Jewish and black intellectuals were debating in the 1960s, between each other and among themselves.

The widening in the postwar years of what was already, in 1948, a substantial social and economic divide between Jews and blacks changed the tenor of the ghetto analogy. American Jewish activists and organizations, however, still drew on the ghetto experience to mobilize Jewish commitment to civil rights and forge common ground with blacks. In September 1963, only a few weeks after his memorable speech at the March on Washington, the Newark Reform rabbi and president of the American Jewish Congress Joachim Prinz reminded American Jews that "the word 'ghetto,' often used to describe segregated Negro neighborhoods, is a part of Jewish history."[53] The key word here was history, history that was both centuries old and incredibly recent, so recent that the line between past and present was frequently blurred, not least for the refugees and survivors themselves. Still, even appeals that drew on this present past to generate support for civil rights could not escape the fact that, for the ghetto to serve as a bridge between peoples, it also had to be a bridge across time.

Time, in fact, was at the heart of what made the transference of the word *ghetto* so charged. The debate over whether the term was a good fit for the geography of black America centered on an interpretation not only of the spatiality of the ghetto but also of its temporality. "Underlying practically all of the controversies about the American city," Irving Kristol wrote in the *New York Times* in 1966, "there lies the question: can the Negro be expected to follow the path of previous immigrant groups or is his a special 'pathological' case?"[54] The word *ghetto* had, for a time, been pressed into service to forge a connection between the experiences of previous migrant groups and the expectations for future ones. Even after the Holocaust, this resonance endured. In *The Uprooted* (1951), Oscar Handlin, an American Jew who would become the dean of immigration historians, depicted settlement in "The Ghettos" quite literally as a chapter in the generic immigrant narrative.[55] This was a period of wrenching adaptation, as "ways long taken for granted in the village adjusted slowly and painfully to density of population in the cities, to disorder in the towns, and to distance on the farms. That adjustment was the means of creating the new communities within which these people would live."[56] In the late 1950s and 1960s, Handlin became one of the foremost spokesmen of those who believed that the latest "newcomers" to the American metropolis—the Negroes and Puerto Ricans—were following in the footsteps of their foreign-born precursors and that the problems of their segregated enclaves differed in degree, but not in kind from those of yesteryear. Drawing on the same logic of ethnic "succession" that had animated the Chicago School, Handlin held that the Afro Americans of the urban North had largely clustered together of their own accord—just like the Irish, Germans, and Italians before them—in order to "best satisfy their social and cultural needs."[57] Handlin conceded that the "newcomers" faced more stubborn obstacles than their forerunners to escaping the ghetto, but on the whole, his assessment was that "the Negroes and Puerto Ricans have followed the general outline of experience of earlier immigrants. . . . Their adjustment, difficult as it is, is but the most recent of a long series. These newest arrivals have thus but assumed the role formerly played by European immigrants."[58] According to this logic, the Negro ghetto could legitimately be compared to the ethnic ghetto of the immigrant; they were analogous social and spatial forms. The demise of the former might be prolonged and protracted, but with time it too would pass. This was an argument against the radical uniqueness of the black experience of migration to the city.

By the sixties, however, "ghetto" had more or less ceased to convey a phase common to all, signifying instead a prison imposed on one. It was not the beginning or middle of a migration story, but seemingly its end.[59] Pushback against the immigrant analogy had in fact begun with Drake and Cayton's *Black Metropolis* in the 1940s. The "Black Ghetto" they described was a hard "color line," not a pit stop on the road to a more integrated setting. "The impecunious immigrant, once he gets on his feet, may . . . move into an area of second settlement. Even the vice-lord or gangster, after he makes his pile, may lose himself in a respectable neighborhood. Negroes, regardless of their affluence or respectability, wear the badge of color. They are expected to stay in the Black Belt." Yet Drake and Cayton's "Black Ghetto" also had its "Bronzeville" side: the more homey, neighborhood-like face of black residential segregation. "Bronzeville's people," Drake and Cayton wrote, "have never let poverty, disease, and discrimination 'get them down.' The vigor with which they enjoy life seems to belie the gloomy observations of statisticians and civic leaders who know the facts about the Black Ghetto."[60]

By the early 1960s, this more pleasant gloss on ghettoization appeared to many to have vanished. The late Arnold Hirsch famously coined the phrase the "second ghetto" to refer to the newly distinctive conditions of ghettoization in the period from roughly 1940 to the 1960s. These included a major increase in the black population in northern and western cities as a result of a resurgence of migration out of the South (e.g., the black population of Chicago went from 277,731 in 1940 to 812,687 in 1960, a jump from 8.2 to 22.9 percent of the total population); they also included a much greater degree of government involvement, through housing and other policies (e.g., the encouragement of redlining, the building of official or de facto segregated public housing, the support for urban renewal projects, the creation of the interstate highway system) that typically increased the size and scale of the black ghetto. As Hirsch writes,

"The most distinguishing feature of post–World War II ghetto expansion is that it was carried out with government sanction and support."[61]

Against this backdrop, authors increasingly perceived the relationship between the immigrant ghettos of the past, not to mention their white ethnic neighborhood successors, and the black ghettos of the present as one of stark antithesis. The socialist intellectual Michael Harrington's 1962 *The Other America: Poverty in the United States,* which proved hugely popular, placed this opposition at the center of its analysis. In a chapter titled "Old Slums, New Slums," Harrington drew a sharp contrast between the camaraderie of the old ethnic slum and the dysfunction of the new slum of "internal migrants." "There once was a slum in American society," Harrington reminisced, "that was a melting pot, a way station, a goad to talent. . . . The neighborhoods were dense and the housing was inadequate, yet the people were not defeated by their environment. There was community; there was aspiration."[62] Harrington even recalled moving into "a Jewish slum on the Lower East Side" in the early fifties and how, on his first day there, the man behind the counter of a nearby store already knew his street number. Whereas the "old slum" was remembered as a "self-enclosed" community where everyone knew everyone and a "culture of aspiration" prevailed, the "new slum" was synonymous only with "social disintegration," "hopelessness," and a "culture of poverty." "Culture of poverty" was, at the time Harrington wrote, a pet phrase of left-liberal intellectuals who sought to convey both the spiritual and strictly economic reality of impoverishment.

In his 1964 *Crisis in Black and White,* the Jewish author and journalist Charles E. Silberman challenged Handlin's thesis head-on. "The plain fact," he stated, "is that the Negro faces a problem different in kind, and far more complex, than that faced by any of his European predecessors." Blacks had migrated to northern industrial centers at a time of decreasing need for unskilled and semiskilled labor, resulting in mass unemployment. Moreover, it was harder for Negroes to bear their poverty in part because the surrounding society had become so very affluent. But the main problem with the Handlin approach was that it "diverts attention from what is surely the central fact. The Negro is unlike any other immigrant group in one crucial regard: he is colored. And that makes all the difference." The Negro did not have the same ability to conceal his identity and "lose himself in the crowd." Barring a radical transformation in American society, there was little hope that Negroes might move into "the main stream of American life" anytime soon. After all, "the mere presence of a Negro in a white residential neighborhood unleashes fears and hatreds of the most elemental sort, and leads almost without exception to an exodus of the white residents." As a result, residential segregation of blacks had become worse in recent decades, notwithstanding the general improvement in their economic status "in sharp contrast with the experience of European immigrant groups—or with the current experience of Puerto Rican immigrants." The Negro, in short, could not get out of the ghetto. And the more blacks experienced "a sense of rejection by American society," the greater and more violent became their rage against the entirety of the white world. For Silberman, as for Harrington, there was no reasonable analogy to be made between the immigrant and the black histories. The Negro experience of residential segregation was unique and, in the history of the United States, unprecedented.[63]

This emphasis on singularity received further reinforcement from Kenneth Clark's 1965 *Dark Ghetto,* which did more than any other individual work to connect "ghetto" and "black" in the mainstream media.[64] Clark was an African American psychologist whose research on the effects of segregation on children had proved pivotal to the 1954 *Brown v. Board of Education* de jure desegregation of schools. He was among the founders of Harlem Youth Opportunities Unlimited (HARYOU), an organization devoted to enhancing the education and job prospects of Harlem's youth, and many of his findings in the studies he carried out for HARYOU would be incorporated into *Dark Ghetto.* In the book, Clark effectively substituted a new logic of "succession" for that of Handlin, who saw the Negro "newcomers" as the successors to the earlier wave of immigrants and their urban enclaves as heir to the ethnic ghettos of old. On the contrary, Clark introduced the contemporary "dark ghetto" as the successor to the mandatory Jewish quarter of sixteenth-century Venice and to other sections of cities where Jews had been forcibly confined. What America had "contributed to the concept of the ghetto," he famously argued, was "the restriction of persons to a certain area and the limiting of their freedom of choice on the basis of skin color," a far cry from the earlier view of the American ghetto as a site where alienation gradually gave way to acculturation.[65] The title of Clark's book was, perhaps unwittingly, doubly appropriate. For the darkness of the "dark ghetto" was evident not only in the skin color of its inhabitants but also in the fact that it was an unremittingly bleak, desperate place, devoid of faith in a better future and awash in self-destructive behavior and social vices. Using language that would later make his work the object of criticism, Clark made no attempt to mitigate what he saw as the ghetto's inherent "pathologies":

> The dark ghetto is institutionalized pathology: it is chronic, self-perpetuating pathology; and it is the futile attempt by those with power to confine that pathology so as to prevent the spread of its contagion to the 'larger community'. . . .

> Not only is the pathology of the ghetto self-perpetuating, but one kind of pathology breeds another. The child born in the ghetto is more likely to come into a world of broken homes and illegitimacy; and this family and social instability is conducive to delinquency, drug addiction, and criminal violence. Neither instability nor crime can be controlled by police vigilance or by reliance on the alleged deterring forces of legal punishment, for the individual crimes are to be understood more as symptoms of the contagious sickness of the community itself than as the result of inherent criminal or deliberate viciousness.[66]

This "institutionalized pathology"—reflected in the higher rates of broken homes, juvenile delinquency, drug addiction, and violent crime—ultimately had its roots not, as white conservatives were wont to say, in stubborn character defects within black society that made them responsible for their own condition. Any group living in a ghetto, trapped in a vicious cycle of rundown and inadequate schools and homes and poor job prospects, would act out similarly. If fault were to be assigned, it was to the white majority's complicity in the existence of the ghetto in the first place. "The dark ghetto's invisible walls," Clark wrote, "have been erected by the white society, by those who have power, both to confine those who have *no* power and to perpetuate their powerlessness." Like Silberman, Clark argued that the rage of the ghetto inmates derived in part from their consciousness, via mass media, that their plight was not the norm. "Those who are required to live in congested and rat-infested homes," Clark noted, "are aware that others are not so dehumanized." For Clark, it was obvious that the immigrant experience bore no relevance for the Negro. While the second generation of European immigrants often felt compunction about their desire to escape the Old World language and folkways of their parents, they had the ability to move into the middle class or upper class and break with their origins, severing the knot that linked them to those left behind. "But in a society where wealth, aristocratic bearing, and talent are insufficient to overcome the stigma of the color of one's skin, there is no escape for any generation." Clark believed that, in the short term, efforts to cure the social malaise of the ghetto should focus on "ego and 'culture-building'" programs like HARYOU, rather than on attempts to solve the various pathologies in isolation. "Until all ghettos prove unnecessary," Clark opined, "the nation's Harlems should be made literally so attractive and beautiful that they would affirm the highest human aspirations." But the whole thrust of *Dark Ghetto* was that the ultimate solution to the crisis of "the nation's Harlems" lay not in a "gilding" of the ghetto, but in an abolition of the ghetto altogether. Implicitly rejecting the Chicago School's (and Handlin's) understanding of the voluntary origins of the modern urban ghetto, Clark insisted, "The victims of segregation do not initially desire to be segregated, they do not 'prefer to be with their own people,' in spite of the fact that this belief is commonly stated by those who are not themselves segregated. . . . The fact remains that exclusion, rejection, and a stigmatized status are not desired and are not voluntary states. Segregation is neither sought nor imposed by healthy or potentially healthy human beings."[67]

Clark's sociological argument about the involuntary nature of black ghettoization dovetailed with a wave of historical studies about the formation of specific ghettos that began to appear in the mid-sixties. They included Gilbert Osofsky's *Harlem: The Making of a Ghetto* (1963) and Allan Spear's *Black Chicago: The Making of a Negro Ghetto, 1890–1920* (1967) and continued in the 1970s with David Katzman's *Before the Ghetto: Black Detroit in the Nineteenth Century* (1973), Kenneth Kusmer's *A Ghetto Takes Shape: Black Cleveland, 1870–1930* (1976), and Thomas Philpott's *The Slum and the Ghetto: Neighborhood Deterioration and Middle-Class Reform, Chicago, 1880–1930* (1978). Perhaps it was sheer coincidence, but several of the pioneers in this area happened to be Jewish, and Osofsky was actually the author of an earlier study of the Hebrew Emigrant Aid Society in the beginning years of mass Eastern European immigration to the United States.[68] These works tended to trace the emergence of a black ghetto far back in time, to the very nucleus of an African American population in the city in question and well before the first major wave of migration from the South (the "Great Migration") from 1914–1920. In a 1968 article titled "The Enduring Ghetto," Osofsky stressed that for all the ostensible changes in the black urban experience "between the Jacksonian era and the America of Watts, Newark, and Detroit," appearances were deceptive: "There has been an unending and tragic sameness about Negro life in the metropolis over the two centuries."[69] The books underscored that, contrary to the Chicago School's conventional wisdom, African Americans were the only migrant group to be subject to true ghettoization in the U.S. metropolis. Like Clark harking back to the premodern Jewish experience for antecedents, Spear concluded, "From its inception, the Negro ghetto was unique among the city's ethnic enclaves. It grew in response to an implacable white hostility that has not changed. . . . Like Jewries of medieval Europe, Black Chicago has offered no escape."[70]

For all these efforts to divorce the two groups, the notion that white ethnics (including Jews) and blacks nevertheless "shared" a history of ghettoization in America continued to resonate among the former. In a January 1965 article, the civil rights activist Bayard Rustin described a debate he had recently held with the chairman of Parents and Taxpayers (PAT), a group of New York City citizens, almost all of them white, that had been founded in 1963 to oppose the Board of Education's experimental program for reducing de facto school segregation through busing.[71] According to Rustin, the chairman, who was Jewish, told him, "Well you know, Mr. Rustin, the problem is I was born in a ghetto; I got out of it, I now own a Cadillac, I have my three children in college." The implication was that the Negro failure to break out of the ghetto—the same ghetto, more or less, that the chairman had "got out of" decades earlier—could be chalked up to innate shortcomings and certainly should not be made the responsibility of others. Rustin, not surprisingly, rejected the analogy entirely. "Now here is something that Jews must understand," he explained, "namely, that they never faced a closed ghetto such as the

Negro faces. First of all, they could change their name—and they could escape. The Negro has never had such avenues of escape. Hence for Jews to compare the closed ghetto with the ghetto they faced is a distorting oversimplification."[72]

The same year that Clark's *Dark Ghetto* appeared saw the publication of the notorious *The Negro Family: The Case for National Action*, better known as the Moynihan Report. Its author, Daniel Patrick Moynihan, was then Assistant Secretary of Labor in charge of the Office of Policy Planning and Research in the Johnson administration. Borrowing language from Clark's book, Moynihan wrote of a "tangle of pathology" in the black ghettos rooted above all in the prevalence of broken homes that lacked a male breadwinner and were mired in welfare dependency. To explain this phenomenon, Moynihan reached back to the experience of slavery and Jim Crow in the South and one of its alleged main outcomes (and obsessions): the emasculation of the black male. Without spelling out specific policy proposals, the report was intended as a "call to action" for the federal government to assume the responsibility of taking measures to strengthen the Negro family. This was to be the next major step in the campaign for civil rights for blacks; a shift from a focus on the lifting of legal barriers to the lifting of blacks out of poverty. "The policy of the United States," Moynihan concluded, "is to bring the Negro American to full and equal sharing in the responsibilities and rewards of citizenship. To this end the programs of the federal government bearing on this objective shall be designed to have the effect, directly or indirectly, of enhancing the stability and resources of the Negro American family."[73] On its release, the Moynihan Report provoked a firestorm among many in the civil rights movement and in academic social science circles. The chief objection was that Moynihan was scapegoating the Negro family for the problems of black society, rather than confronting the more blatant patterns of discrimination in American life responsible for impeding black advancement. Others protested the application of "pathologizing" rhetoric to the Negro family; they claimed that the implication that the often matriarchal structure of the family was by definition defective ignored a history of black adaptations to their lower-class existence and presumed that black success could only result from conformity to white middle-class norms. Writing in *The Nation* in November, the psychologist William Ryan, who would eventually coin the phrase "blaming the victim" to describe the Moynihan Report, indicted the report's author for unwittingly propagating "a new form of subtle racism."[74]

The Moynihan Report galvanized a backlash against the whole premise that black society was damaged or maladjusted and that its big-city enclaves lacked the communal character of the old immigrant neighborhoods.[75] With this criticism came a rejection, by some black intellectuals, of the very word *ghetto* that others contended in America at least was appropriate only in reference to the black experience. In a 1965 interview, Ralph Ellison, who lived near Harlem, described the portrayal of Harlem as a ghetto as "one of the most damaging misuses of a concept that has ever come about in the United States."[76] Ellison opposed the use of the word for two main reasons. He was averse to sociological analyses of Negro life in general, which he felt sapped the Harlems of America of their vitality and multidimensionality. Speaking of the responsibility of the Negro writer soon after the appearance of the Moynihan Report, Ellison claimed that "if he accepts the clichés to the effect that the Negro family is usually a broken family, that it is matriarchal in form and that the mother dominates and castrates the males, if he believes that Negro males are having all of these alleged troubles with their sexuality, or that Harlem is a 'Negro ghetto'—which means, to paraphrase one of our writers, 'piss in the halls and blood on the stairs'—he'll never see the people of whom he wishes to write."[77] Ellison also believed that the word *ghetto* implied a fallacious distance between Negro culture and American culture. On the contrary, while blacks were keeping alive the nineteenth-century tradition of high oratory in their churches, they were also enriching American English as well as song and dance:

> The music, the dances that Americans do are greatly determined by Negro American style, by a Negro American sense of elegance, by an American Negro sense of what the American experience should be, by what Negroes feel about how an American should move, should express himself. The ghetto concept obscures this. It's much better to say you have slums. It's an old term and it doesn't cause as much confusion. It's economic, not cultural.[78]

For Ellison, then, the effort of sociologists like Cayton and Drake or Clark to apply the word *ghetto* to Negro neighborhoods was nothing less than an attempt to impose onto them a cultural estrangement that was perhaps characteristic of the European Jewish experience, or even of the Jewish immigrant experience on the Lower East Side (where the language barrier was far more profound), but was completely unrepresentative of the Negro experience. Another fierce critic of the rhetorical ghettoizing of black residential areas was Ellison's friend and fellow African American writer and Harlem denizen, Albert Murray. Murray shared Ellison's abhorrence of social science formulas and argued that the "glib pseudo-terminological use of such clichés as the ghetto, minority group, middle class Negro, and so on . . . can never do justice to the facts of life." He lambasted Clark's *Dark Ghetto* as a "good example of how a book by a black writer may represent a point of view toward black experience which is essentially white." Its portrait of Harlem as "an urban pit writhing with derelicts" made a more emphatic case for "black wretchedness" than the writing of *"white racists to justify segregation."* For Murray, as for Ellison, what were needed were more broadly humanistic writers who could depict the black experience in all its pride, messiness, and complexity and fewer social science experts "who confuse metaphorical ghettos with real ones." Regardless, there was no ground for

> confusing segregated housing in the U.S. with the way Jewish life was separated from the gentile world in the days of the old ghettos. . . . The term ghetto does not apply to Harlem, if indeed it applies to any segregated housing area in the United States. Perhaps it applies to this or that Chinatown. It does not and never has applied to segregated areas where U.S. Negroes live. . . . Harlem contains a vast network of slum areas which are an ambitious social worker's absolute delight, but Harlem is no ghetto at all. No matter how rotten with racial bigotry the New York housing situation is, it is grossly misleading to imply in any way that the daily involvements, interests, and aspirations of Negroes are thereby restricted to the so-called black community.

As was the case for Ellison, "ghetto" for Murray meant not only "physical segregation" but also "profound differences in religion, language, food customs, and . . . even . . . a different calendar" that he alleged were simply not to be found in black life.[79] Their repudiation of "ghetto" as a label for black America may have indicated an exaggerated notion of just how much cultural distance the old Jewish ghettos of Europe had engendered. Still, what is clear is that Ellison and Murray saw no basis for comparison between the European or immigrant Jewish and the American black experiences—and for that very reason they recoiled at the appropriation of the word *ghetto* from the one to characterize the other.

There was another resonance to the term *ghetto* in the postwar period, and it was the most recent of them all. Perhaps the first effort of note to contemplate the relevance of the Holocaust ghetto to the black experience was W. E. B. Du Bois in his address, "The Negro and the Warsaw Ghetto," which he delivered at a 1952 commemoration of the Warsaw Ghetto Uprising and later published in the communist periodical *Jewish Life*. The specifics of both the Holocaust in general and the Ghetto Uprising in particular were basically immaterial to Du Bois's lecture. His main concern was to explain how he came to be aware that the problem of the "color line" in the United States was not sui generis, but was part of a much more global dynamic of discrimination and persecution on the basis of some inherited or ascribed factor. The author had acquired this awareness through three previous sojourns abroad in Europe (including a time in Hitler's Germany), culminating in a trip to Warsaw in 1949, where he saw the ruins of the ghetto and the memorial that had recently been erected on the spot. "The result of these three visits," Du Bois explained, "and particularly of my view of the Warsaw ghetto, was not so much a clearer understanding of the Jewish problem in the world as it was a real and more complete understanding of the Negro problem." By expanding his mental horizon to include the Warsaw Ghetto, Du Bois had come to see that the race problem in which he was interested

> cut across lines of color and physique and belief and status and was a matter of cultural patterns, perverted teaching and human hate and prejudice, which reached all sorts of people and caused endless evil to all men. So that the ghetto of Warsaw helped me to emerge from a certain social provincialism into a broader conception of what the fight against race segregation, religious discrimination, and the oppression by wealth had to become if civilization was going to triumph and broaden in the world.[80]

Du Bois's speech made no reference to the phenomenon of black residential areas in the United States, so that the question of the relationship of the Negro "ghetto" (and we have seen that Du Bois used the term to signify the segregation of African Americans as early as 1910) to the Warsaw Ghetto never arose. Still, his speech was a brief for the possibility of analogy, which appeared to mobilize memory of the Warsaw Ghetto on behalf of the victims of antisemitism and antiblack racism alike.[81]

Some twelve years later, the Jewish writer Marie Syrkin reacted to anything smacking of a "sharing" of the word *ghetto* with considerable pique.[82] Syrkin, the coeditor of the Labor Zionist *Jewish Frontier* and an English professor at Brandeis, published an article in the September 1964 edition of the journal on the subject of segregation. Significantly, she was the author of the 1947 *Blessed Is the Match: The Story of Jewish Resistance,* which was one of the first books to deal with the subject of armed resistance during the Holocaust in a comprehensive fashion; it included a long chapter on the Warsaw Ghetto Uprising.[83] In September 1964, amid the first of the New York public school crises that would roil the city in the sixties, Syrkin advocated the need to restore a distinction between legal and de facto segregation that she saw as being fudged by the civil rights movement. According to Syrkin, while a minority was within its rights to oppose the former, it overstepped its bounds in seeking to make "complete integration a goal." The issue of the word *ghetto* arose amid a discussion of the supposed parallels between the Jewish and Negro experiences, with Syrkin keen on dispelling the notion that American blacks were the quintessential "suffering minority." "The term 'ghetto,'" Syrkin pointed out, "now often prefixed with the adjective 'black,' has a specific Jewish origin: it means literally a quarter to which Jews were restricted by law." Recognizing, moreover, that "any point of view which runs counter in any significant respect to the current Negro civil rights program is bound to be suspect," she claimed to be writing "not as a white liberal, though I believe the label fits, but as a member of a minority which knows more about systematic discrimination and violent persecution than any group in history." Syrkin then added, "In the immediate as well as historic experience of the Jews a ghetto is not a metaphor; it is a concrete entity with walls, stormtroopers and no exit save the gas chamber."[84] For Syrkin, the "ceding" of the word *ghetto* to Negroes was plainly a distortion of both Jewish history and the black present.

Syrkin's blind eye to the profound differences between the American Jewish and American black experiences of residential and school concentration was roundly criticized. Her coeditor and fellow Brandeis professor Ben Halpern—who shared Syrkin's Zionist-influenced hostility to Jewish assimilation, even if avoiding it required some measure of de facto segregation—nevertheless scolded Syrkin for viewing the situation only through Jewish eyes and for papering over the historical fact of Jewish mobility. "Our concern to preserve our collective identity," Halpern wrote, "never led us to insist that Jews stay in the immigrant, first settlement slum, with its crime, vice, and corruption. We were able to lift ourselves by our bootstraps effectively because, in spite of discrimination, it was entirely possible for Jews to get out of the slum ghetto and move to better neighborhoods, even if to other ghettos."[85] The writer and Jewish communal professional Judd Teller was even more scathing. Implicitly, he rejected Syrkin's attempt to associate the word *ghetto* exclusively with the "stormtroopers" and "gas chamber" of the Holocaust, calling the "Hitler era" an "almost 'extra-historical' event." More categorically, he refuted any comparison between the "Jewish gilded ghetto today and the Negro ghetto" while insisting that the racism blacks encountered in the North was more or less akin to legal segregation. "The difference between the Southern Negro ghetto and the Harlems of the North," Teller asserted, "is that between the medieval Jewish ghetto and the Pale in Czarist Russia. Jews resented both types of segregation, and opposed them. The Harlem type of de facto segregation makes a mockery of de jure desegregation."[86]

Still, Syrkin was not alone in feeling that the phrase "Negro ghetto" problematically conjured the specter of the Holocaust. In a 1968 article on the "urban crisis," then executive vice president of the American Jewish Committee Bertram H. Gold made a less polemical case for shunning the term. Gold quoted a May 1968 letter to the editor of the *New York Times* by the British conservative journalist Malcolm Muggeridge, who called the application of the word *ghetto* to downtrodden Negro areas "a perfect example of . . . the falsification of words to make them serve political ends. By equating Negro slums with a ghetto . . . white racialism—in itself bad enough in all conscience—is associated with the additional horrors of Nazi anti-Semitism." Nevertheless, Gold conceded that his principled avoidance of the term was unlikely to move minds: "If you want to read Negro 'ghetto' where I say Negro slum or some alternative phrase, you have my permission to do so."[87]

Starting in 1964, as violent uprisings in black ghettos became a recurring summer phenomenon, certain black intellectuals began to posit an analogy between the contemporary protesters and the fighters of the Warsaw Ghetto revolt. In 1965, Bayard Rustin invoked the Warsaw Ghetto in the context of an attempt to explain "the incident near the Brooklyn Yeshiva," probably a reference to an attack on students and teachers from a Lubavitcher Yeshiva in Bedford-Stuyvesant that had taken place in April of the previous year.[88] Rustin attributed the violence to the desperation of the area's Negroes. "I," he claimed, "a pacifist who was opposed to all war and violence, have often publicly stated that I have nothing but complete respect for Jews who in the Warsaw ghetto rose up in arms. Why? Because in spite of my pacifism I have empathy enough to understand that men who have been forced into desperation must behave desperately." Rustin was careful to qualify the implied comparison, adding that "I do not mean to suggest that the Negro youth in Brooklyn had anything other than this in common with the fight in the Warsaw Ghetto."[89] Two years later, James Baldwin would not include the same caveats. In his blistering 1967 *New York Times* essay "Negroes Are Anti-Semitic Because They Are Anti-White," Baldwin fingered the dismissal of comparisons between Watts and Harlem and the Warsaw Ghetto by Jews and whites (or, for Baldwin, Jews *as* whites) as a factor in black antisemitism. "The uprising in the Warsaw ghetto was not described as a riot," he complained, "nor were the participants maligned as hoodlums: the boys and girls in Watts and Harlem are thoroughly aware of this, and it certainly contributes to their attitude toward the Jews." Baldwin acknowledged that his "comparison of Watts and Harlem with the Warsaw Ghetto will immediately be dismissed as outrageous." But while allowing that "there are many reasons for this," he emphasized that "one of them is that while white America loves white heroes, armed to the teeth, it cannot abide bad niggers."[90]

By the late 1960s, there were a growing number of Jewish leftists determined to prove Baldwin wrong: not for including Warsaw and Watts in the same conversation, but for thinking that all Jews would object to this. These radicals sought to vindicate the semantic shift that had taken place in America with respect to the word *ghetto,* an acknowledgment of the current uniqueness of the black plight that was intended, nevertheless, to conserve solidarity between Jews and blacks. "During the lifetime of many of us the word ghetto has changed its meaning," the formerly blacklisted screenwriter Albert Maltz was quoted in the far-left *Jewish Currents* in 1969 as saying. "Once, of course, it meant that part of a city in which Jews were confined by law or by anti-Semitic devices and pressures. Today in our country there are no ghettos for Jews but there *are* for black citizens—areas in which they are confined by poverty and by the varied pressures and devices of white racism." Any Jew, he went on to say, who did not commit himself wholeheartedly to combating the racism that had created these ghettos "automatically spits on the past struggles and sufferings of his own people" and is "kin to the SS guards at Auschwitz."[91] Perhaps the most striking example of a ratification of the transference of the word *ghetto* from Jewish to black, and of the new notion of succession it entailed, was the 1969 Freedom Seder ("Passover in the Ghetto," the *Village Voice* reported) organized by the Washington, DC-based Jews for Urban Justice.[92] The haggadah for the occasion, written by a young Arthur Waskow and steeped in the language of the antiwar movement and black militancy, spun from the ritual of spilling the wine a whole chain of tradition of violent revolts in the struggle for freedom, with excerpts from Emanuel Ringelblum's *Notes from the Warsaw Ghetto* followed almost immediately by a selection from the *"shofet"* ("judge") and Black Panther leader Eldridge Cleaver's 1968 collection of essays *Soul on Ice.*[93]

The issue of comparison was thus beset from the beginning by an array of difficulties and complications. Any "transference" of the word *ghetto* from Jews to blacks raised the question of which prior application of the term was intended. Was it the involuntary Jewish ghetto of late medieval and early modern times? The voluntary immigrant ghetto? The Holocaust ghetto? Was Venice, the Lower East Side, or Warsaw the frame of reference? The effort to portray the contemporary black enclave as a physical and spiritual successor to the immigrant ghetto was, by the 1960s, generally condemned for blindness to the intractable nature of the segregation of blacks and to the "pathologies" that plagued the modern ghetto; yet this singling out of the nation's Harlems as uniquely troubled increasingly faced blowback from blacks and white liberals determined to defend the neighborhood qualities of African American residential areas. The suggestion that Harlem or the South Side was a Venetian-style ghetto ran into skepticism from literalists who cited a lack of statutory restriction for the black ghetto in America; yet such literalism ignored a whole range of state actions—from the enforcement of restrictive covenants before 1948 to the denial of home insurance for blacks in the suburbs to the building of public housing in already segregated districts—that made black residential concentration far more than purely a case of de facto segregation.[94] The implication, by some blacks, that Watts and Harlem were heir to the Warsaw Ghetto was clearly inflammatory; yet the attempt to limit the ghetto's gamut of meanings to the Holocaust (the ghetto as "a concrete entity with walls, stormtroopers, and no exit save the gas chamber") was likewise an aggressive rhetorical move. The issue, it seemed, was not whether analogies for the black ghetto per se were legitimate, but which ones.

With the passing of time, what Jewish resistance there was to the changing application of the word *ghetto* ebbed. But not entirely, especially when memory of the Holocaust was at stake. In April 1993, on the eve of the gala opening of the U.S. Holocaust Memorial Museum in Washington, DC, the American Jewish author Melvin Jules Bukiet published an editorial in the *Washington Post* titled "The Museum vs. Memory: The Taming of the Holocaust." Bukiet was bitingly critical of the museum, which he judged a well-intentioned but insidious attempt to absorb the Holocaust melting-pot style into a vocabulary of American politics and culture and sap it of its Jewish specificity. "Something similar," Bukiet wrote,

> has also begun to happen with other elements of the Jewish tradition. Take the word "ghetto," which is commonly used as a synonym for slum. A ghetto is an enclosed, preferably walled-in, domain within a city, and despite the invisible walls around Harlem, there is no barbed wire across 125th Street and there are no guard towers. The second part of the historical definition of the word 'ghetto' is that its residents must be Jews. There's an iconography to Jewish history that encourages others covetous of its passion to try to appropriate its imagery.[95]

Bukiet's target is obviously the notion of the ghetto as "black," not "Jewish," but it is also striking how his definition of "ghetto" deviates from the one Abraham Cahan offered almost a hundred years ago, before the rise of Holocaust ghettos and black ghettos. Cahan declared in 1925, as emphatically as Bukiet did decades later, that "every American understands the meaning of the word ghetto. He knows that it is not the part of the city in which Jews are compelled to live; that kind of ghetto does not exist. It is merely the neighborhood in which large numbers of Jews have settled."[96] We seem to be back at the question that Cahan's editor at the *New York Sun* posed in the 1880s, the one Cahan dismissed as ignorant, but in hindsight appears anything but: What *is* a ghetto?

CONCLUSION

IN THE EARLY 2000s, the affluent New Jersey town of Tenafly, a suburb of New York, became embroiled in a bitter three-year legal battle over the proposed construction of an eruv to accommodate Orthodox Jewish families. The controversy was haunted by the specter of the ghetto. "The word 'ghetto' came up so frequently in the discussions about the eruv," one scholar writes, "that it would be impossible to avoid the conclusion that this was a central issue."[1] In many ways, the controversy pitted Jew against Jew. The secular Jewish residents of Tenafly expressed the "there goes the neighborhood" fear, projecting that the bedroom community would be overrun by Orthodox Jewish families and by synagogues, restaurants, groceries, and other establishments designed to cater to that particular group. A letter sent to the (Jewish) mayor by a Mrs. Bernard Golden Sr. stated,

> [The eruv] will . . . be the beginning of many more demands the orthodox people will impose on the town of Tenafly and its non-orthodox residents. Once this wire is put up on public property, that will be the signal for many more orthodox people to move into Tenafly and the value of property in Tenafly will go down and welfare will go up. This will be the making of a ghetto, and, Mayor, I don't think you want this to happen on your watch.[2]

Others expressed concerns about the creation of a "community within a community" just like the enclaves "the Jews of Europe were forced to live in." What is clear is that, when threatened with the prospect of their neighborhood becoming more Orthodox, liberal and secular Jews in Tenafly demonstrated the degree to which anxiety about the creation of a Jewish "ghetto" in suburbia—and a perceived step back in time in American Jewish life—remained potent. The word remains a keyword for American Jews, one that carries a special ideological charge and is capable of evoking images and associations that exceed any dictionary definition of the term.

Yet, at least outside Israel, such Jewish resonances of the word *ghetto* have mostly become the property of Jews themselves. The "ghetto" today is almost universally identified first and foremost with the experience of black Americans. Since the 1970s, there have been two primary developments with respect to the biography of the word and the genealogy of the concept. First, as William Julius Wilson among others has shown, the overlapping of race and class in the profile of the American ghetto has become more thoroughgoing.[3] If earlier measures such as restrictive covenants and the simple refusal to sell or rent to blacks kept them hemmed into racial ghettos independent of their economic means, the passage of legislation aimed at outlawing housing discrimination (starting with the Fair Housing Act of 1968) gradually made it possible for middle- and upper-class blacks to move out of the ghetto. This created an outflow of the class that had basically sustained the institutional fabric of the ghetto. Simultaneously, the hollowing out of the urban manufacturing sector as a result of the larger trend of deindustrialization exacerbated the already existing problem of high unemployment and yielded the phenomenon of the "jobless" ghetto. This in turn led to the further social deterioration of ghetto neighborhoods and the escalation of violent crime and drug- and gang-related deaths. It also yielded an increasing depopulation of the American ghetto, creating the street scenes of boarded-up buildings and vacant lots that came to characterize the landscape of what photographer Camilo José Vergara has called the "New American Ghetto."[4] Side by side with these material changes, the "ghetto" came to loom large in the emergent hip-hop culture that evolved from an alternative art form in the late 1970s to the mainstream music industry and global idiom that it is today.[5] The images of the "ghetto" (or "hood") generated by rappers vary considerably. They can be unsparing in their depiction of the dangers and dilapidation of the streets.[6] They can also occasionally be surprisingly nostalgic for the urban terrains that formed the artist.[7] Above all, the "ghetto" is linked to a rhetoric of the "real" in hip-hop: however much the ghetto may be a place the rapper wants or wanted to get out of, the fact that he or she is a product of it and can recall it in such precise detail can serve as a symbol not only of authenticity but also of pride. Meanwhile, the past two decades have seen a virtual explosion in hip-hop variants of the term that has reverberated in American culture more generally. The *Random House Historical Dictionary of American Slang* of 1994—which was never completed, let alone revised—contains three entries with the word "ghetto," though two of the three receive only a cross-reference to the one term that had broken into the larger vocabulary by that time, namely "ghetto-blaster," the large, portable radio-cassette players that had become a fad starting in the late seventies.[8] By contrast, the now online *Green's Dictionary of Slang* contains ten entries, from the word "ghetto" alone to "ghettofabulous." Both of these slang terms offer evidence of how "ghetto" today can serve not only as a racialized slur, a means of stigmatizing someone or something, but also as an at least partially reclaimed slur, somewhat like the term "queer." The *Green Dictionary*'s definition of "ghetto" is a picture of contrasts: the first meaning is "second-rate, old-fashioned, inferior, badly made," while the second is "superior, first-rate." The adjective "ghettofabulous" (or "ghetto fabulous") was coined in the late nineties as a term for "anything flashy and impressive in black culture," especially in fashion.[9] All the slang expressions, however, have an African American template, even if some—like the ubiquitous and, to many, offensive and derogatory "that's so ghetto" to describe something cheap and tawdry—have come to be widely used by millennials of all races. The proliferation of ghetto slang, coupled with the internationalization of hip-hop, contributes to an erasure of the ghetto concept's Jewish origins. If the black appropriation of the term *ghetto* was once a source of tension and controversy, it now elicits little if any blowback.

There is one country where the Jewish associations of *ghetto* remain salient. In Israel today, the ghetto metaphor figures prominently in the ever starker conflict between left and right. The shared premise is that Israel was meant from the outset to be an antithesis to the ghetto; what divides the two sides is the belief that the other threatens to turn the state into a modern ghetto. On the liberal Zionist left, the argument runs that Israel, by creating and expanding settlements on the West Bank and pursuing an inward-looking politics oblivious to international opinion, is reviving the ghetto. As Amos Oz told columnist Roger Cohen in 2014, "There is a growing sense that Israel is becoming an isolated ghetto, which is exactly what the founding fathers and mothers hoped to leave behind them forever when they created the state of Israel."[10] In an editorial in Israel's flagship liberal newspaper *Ha'aretz* in September 2017, Carolina Landsmann castigates the right-wing Benjamin (Bibi) Netanyahu government's obsession with advancing a vision of a more homogeneously Jewish Israel by closing ranks against all African refugees. "Zionism," she writes, "sought to effect a political and societal revolution, not to create a ghetto with nuclear bombs."[11] For the left, the transformation of Israel into a metaphorical ghetto is based on its presumed embrace of the status of a "nation that dwells alone" in its rhetoric and politics. On the right, the fear of Israel's evolution into a ghetto has long been connected to the size of the territory it controls. With the increasing resort to Holocaust imagery starting under the first Likud prime minister, Menachem Begin, in the late 1970s to describe the threats Israel confronts, the ground was laid for comparison of proposed territorial concessions with the return of Israel to the ghetto. In 2013, the right-wing news outlet *Arutz Sheva* ran an opinion piece titled "Israel's Ghetto Mentality." The author discerned the signs of this state of mind not in isolationist or xenophobic politics, but in the alleged readiness of Israel's government, during the last major round of negotiations with the Palestinians, to withdraw from most of the West Bank. "It is . . . ghetto-like thinking," the author wrote, "that leads Israel's government ministers to seriously advocate uprooting Jewish homes and villages in the Jews' ancestral homeland; that they speak of exiling thousands of Jews in order to curry favor with Arab potentates' and US coteries; that they make pacts with unrepentant terrorists whose anti-Semitism matches anything in the pages of *Der Stürmer*." He predicted that the upshot of any two-state solution "will be a squeezed, narrow and urban Jewish ghetto with Muslim neighbors pressing from the eastern highlands, those which have been abandoned by the Jewish army."[12] The present-day incarnation of the "ghetto Jew," according to the right, is the "Jew who is endlessly obsessed with how the rest of the world sees Israel" and "has reduced the reborn Jewish state to another ghetto, forever in peril and unable to escape from it, dependent on the goodwill of its masters outside the ghetto."[13] Thus, the argument essentially hinges on dichotomous assessments of the value of concern for Israel's public image; the left judges the lack of it and the right the presence of it as evidence of ghetto thinking.

What further complicates the complexion of the ghetto metaphor in Israel is its appropriation by the Palestinians and their advocates, as well by Arab citizens of Israel, to designate their own experience of segregation at the hands of Israelis. The appropriation carries with it an accusation that the former ghettoized people par excellence have become the ghettoizers. Gaza, whose areas have some of the highest population densities in the world and which the Palestinian population is not free to leave or enter as a result of Israeli and Egyptian border closures and the Israeli sea and air blockade, has long been pictured in the Palestinian imagination as a "ghetto."[14] The ethics of analogy has figured prominently there, as well as in the battle over prototypes for Gaza. In particular during the fighting between Hamas-led Gaza and the Israelis in 2009 and 2014, some Palestinians and their supporters sought to compare Gaza with the Warsaw Ghetto, an equivalence that papers over the gaping differences between the two and is designed more to provoke than to enlighten.[15] Still, the allegation of ghettoization extends from the Palestinians of the territories to the Palestinians of Israel. In a 2017 op-ed about Israeli plans to build the first non-Jewish town in the history of the state, one that will be "one-and-a-half times more densely populated than badly crowded Tel Aviv," the author, Israeli Arab Odeh Bisharat, drew attention to the "terrible irony" of the government's preference for containing the Arab population in its own villages, towns, and cities: "Europe enclosed the Jews in ghettos and today, the Jews enclose the Arabs in ghettos."[16]

In 2017, the Lebanese writer Elias Khoury published his latest novel, *Children of the Ghetto: My Name Is Adam,* offering a new perspective on the Palestinian Nakba ("Catastrophe") of 1948. The "ghetto" in his title refers to the mandatory enclosures surrounded by barbed wire and guarded by Israeli soldiers in which Palestinians who remained in places like Lod (the focus of the novel), Ramle, and Jaffa conquered by Israel in the 1948 War were confined during and in the immediate aftermath of the conflict. This is where and when the word *ghetto* entered the Palestinian lexicon, and it remains to this date an unofficial name for the Arab neighborhoods of these mixed cities. Yet what is particularly striking about the book's title is its perhaps unwitting plagiarism of Israel Zangwill's 1892 classic of the same name. The mantle of "children of the ghetto" in the novel is worn both by the survivors of the Holocaust and by the Palestinians restricted to the enclosures under their watch. The victims have become victimizers; the Palestinians, in the novel's logic, are the "Jews of the Jews." Khoury dramatizes this shared history of the word *ghetto* in the person of the protagonist, Adam Dannoun, an Arab citizen of Israel in his fifties living and working as a cook in a falafel restaurant in New York as he writes about his childhood memories in order to forget them. His parentage is unclear, and his identity as an Arab Israeli has proved, throughout his life, to be fluid and uncertain. What he knows is that he is a child of the ghetto—the ghetto created by the Israelis in Lod in July 1948 after their conquest of the city and expulsion of most of the Arab residents. He was a newborn in the newly established ghetto, and much of the book is devoted to recounting the story of the horrific suffering inflicted on the ghetto's inhabitants after the conquest, which he has pieced together from the memories and testimonies of others. Yet Adam recalls that when he began studying Hebrew literature at the University of Haifa and, when asked where he was from, responded simply, "the ghetto," "his comrades regarded him with compassion and took him for the son of a survivor of the Warsaw Ghetto."[17] Indeed, at an early age after he had left "home," he invented a parallel "Jewish" narrative for himself in which he was the son of a survivor of the Warsaw Ghetto killed in the 1948 War. The doubling of Warsaw and Lod functions as a recurring motif in the novel. There is thus a triangular structure to the ghetto metaphor in contemporary Israel/Palestine, where the term serves not only as fodder in the ongoing conflict between the Israeli left and right but also as a rhetorical arrow in the Palestinian quiver against Israel.

In 2016, Venice commemorated the five-hundredth anniversary of the establishment of the ghetto in a year-long sequence of events and festivities. By all accounts, this was a first; there is no evidence of similar efforts to mark earlier major anniversaries of the founding of the Venetian

Ghetto. Perhaps a certain measure of distance from the phenomenon was necessary to recommend the idea of a grand gesture of collective remembrance. The planning of the year's series of events was a joint effort of the Jewish community of Venice and the municipality that had confined the former to the Ghetto Nuovo five centuries earlier. The opening ceremony was held on the date of the anniversary—March 29, 2016—at La Fenice Opera House with a keynote lecture by historian Simon Schama, followed by the playing of Gustav Mahler's Symphony No. 1 in C Major by the Fenice symphony orchestra. From June to November, a lavish exhibition titled "Venice, the Jews, and Europe" was held in the majestic setting of the Ducal Palace, whence the 1516 decree restricting Venice's Jews to the area of the ghetto had originated. For six days at the end of July, Shakespeare's *The Merchant of Venice* was performed on the main square of the Ghetto Nuovo, setting the play in what would have been Shylock's home, though the ghetto is not so much as mentioned in Shakespeare's text. Several other events were held with reference to the play, including a mock appeal by Shylock presided over by none other than RBG herself, Justice Ruth Bader Ginsburg. In a letter appended to the beginning of the exhibition's catalog, the president of the Jewish community, Paolo Gnignati, underscored that "the spirit that inspires us to commemorate this milestone in the history of the Jewish presence in Venice is devoid of even the slightest hint of any celebrative intentions." But this sobriety proved difficult to sustain. The year's events were, in the end, something of a celebration, not only of the Venice Ghetto's tenacity and flourishing over its 281 years of existence but also, as the president of the Fondazione Musei Civici di Venezia put it, of the "cultural diversity existing in the cosmopolitan Venice of the early sixteenth century."[18]

The word *ghetto* has traveled a long distance to this moment of remembrance and reflection. It would be fair to say that it only truly emerged as a pan-European signifier at the very instant that it came to serve in nineteenth-century ghetto literature as a *lieux de mémoire,* a site of memory. As a literary and imagined space the "ghetto" has been laced with recollections of times past from its inception. Yet the word has undergone numerous resurrections, each time seemingly in defiance of the assumed course of modernity out of the ghetto. The demise of the Venetian Ghetto, like that of all the other early modern ghettos, was only the beginning of a semantic odyssey that continues into the present. Today, when the term *ghetto* has been universalized and its formerly dominant Jewish associations muted, there is value in retracing the sinuous road the word has voyaged to get to this point. Only by understanding the winding journey of the word *ghetto* within the Jewish experience can we begin to understand the complications that have attended its journey beyond it.

NOTES

ACKNOWLEDGMENTS

ILLUSTRATION CREDITS

INDEX

NOTES

Introduction

1. Friedrich Nietzsche, *On the Genealogy of Morals and Ecce Homo* (New York: Random House, 1989), 80.

2. *Oxford English Dictionary,* s.v. "ghetto," accessed June 18, 2018, http://www.oed.com.proxygw.wrlc.org/view/Entry/78056?rskey=mKYih2&result=1#eid.

3. Benjamin Ravid, "All Ghettos Were Jewish Quarters, but Not All Jewish Quarters Were Ghettos," in *The Frankfurt Judengasse: Jewish Life in an Early Modern City,* ed. Fritz Backhaus et al. (London: Valentine Mitchell, 2010), 5–24.

4. Geoffrey Megargee and Martin Dean, eds., *The United States Holocaust Memorial Museum Encyclopedia of Camps and Ghettos,* vol. II, *Ghettos in German-Occupied Eastern Europe* (Bloomington: Indiana University Press, 2012), xliii.

5. Paul Jargowsky and Mary Jo Bane, "Ghetto Poverty in the United States, 1970–1980," in *The Urban Underclass,* ed. Christopher Jencks and Paul E. Peterson (Washington, DC: Brookings, 1991), 235–273; William J. Wilson, *The Truly Disadvantaged: The Inner City, the Underclass, and Public Policy* (Chicago: University of Chicago Press, 1990); Loïc Wacquant, "A Janus-Faced Institution of Ethnoracial Closure: A Sociological Specification of the Ghetto," in *The Ghetto: Contemporary Global Issues and Controversies,* ed. Ray Hutchinson and Bruce D. Haynes (Boulder, CO: Westview Press, 2012), 1–32; Mitchell Duneier, *Ghetto: The Invention of a Place, the History of an Idea* (New York: Farrar, Straus & Giroux, 2016); Mario Small, "Four Reasons to Abandon the Idea of the 'Ghetto,'" *City and Community* 7, no. 4 (December 2008): 389–398.

6. Michael Meng, "Layered Pasts: The *Judengasse* in Frankfurt and Narrating German-Jewish History," in *Space and Spatiality in Modern German-Jewish History,* ed. Simone Lässig and Miriam Rürup (New York: Berghahn Books, 2017), 115.

7. Raymond Williams, *Keywords: Vocabulary of Culture and Society,* rev. ed. (New York: Oxford University Press, 1983), 15, 14. Indeed, there is some irony in the fact that the last keyword profiled in Williams's book is "Work," since it is precisely one of the hallmarks of the keyword that it is in many ways *overworked.*

8. Katz's "ghetto" is a kind of conceptual metaphor that is meant to denote "premodern" Judaism. See Katz, *Out of the Ghetto: The Social Background of Jewish Emancipation, 1770–1870* (Cambridge, MA: Harvard University Press, 1973), 9–27.

9. Ari Shavit, *My Promised Land: The Triumph and Tragedy of Israel* (New York: Spiegel & Grau, 2013), 5.

10. See Robert Bonfil, *Jewish Life in Renaissance Italy,* trans. Anthony Oldcorn (Berkeley: University of California Press, 1994); David B. Ruderman, "The Cultural Significance of the Ghetto in Jewish History," in *From Ghetto to Emancipation: Historical and Contemporary Reconsiderations of the Jewish Community,* ed. David N. Myers and William V. Rowe (Scranton, PA: University of Scranton Press, 1997), 1–16; Roni Weinstein, "'Mevudadim 'Akh Lo Dehuyim': Ha-yehudim ba-hevrah ha-'italkit bi-tekufat ha-reformatsyah ha-katolit,'" in *Mi'utim, Zarim ve-Shonim: Kevutsot shulayim ba-historyah,* ed. Shulamit Volkov (Jerusalem: Zalman Shazar Center, 2000), 93–132; Stefanie Siegmund, *The Medici State and the Ghetto of Florence: The Construction of an Early Modern Jewish Community* (Palo Alto, CA: Stanford University Press, 2005).

11. Gershon David Hundert, *Jews in Poland-Lithuania in the Eighteenth Century: A Genealogy of Modernity* (Berkeley: University of California Press, 2004); Eliyahu Stern, *The Genius: Elijah of Vilna and the Making of Modern Judaism* (New Haven: Yale University Press, 2013).

12. Dipesh Chakrabarty, *Habitations of Modernity: Essays in the Wake of Subaltern Studies* (Chicago: University of Chicago Press, 2002), xix.

13. Carl H. Nightingale, "A Tale of Three Global Ghettos: How Arnold Hirsch Helps Us Internationalize U.S. Urban History," *Journal of Urban History* 29, no. 3 (March 2003): 257.

14. Duneier, *Ghetto.*

15. Cynthia Baker, *Jew* (New Brunswick, NJ: Rutgers University Press, 2017).

1. The Early History of the Ghetto

1. William Shakespeare, *Romeo and Juliet,* ed. Joseph Pearce (San Francisco: Ignatius Press, 2011), 45.

2. Tom Kington, "Venice Jews Work to Preserve the World's First Ghetto as 500th Anniversary Nears," *Los Angeles Times,* March 7, 2016.

3. Benjamin Ravid, "All Ghettos Were Jewish Quarters, but Not All Jewish Quarters Were Ghettos," in *The Frankfurt Judengasse: Jewish Life in an Early Modern City,* ed. Fritz Backhaus et al. (London: Valentine Mitchell, 2010), 13.

4. Joachim Prinz, *Das Leben im Ghetto* (Berlin: Löwe, 1937), 18.

5. Louis Wirth, *The Ghetto* [1928] (New Brunswick, NJ: Transaction Publishers, 1998), 18.

6. Salo W. Baron, "Ghetto and Emancipation" [1928], in *The Menorah Treasury: Harvest of Half a Century,* ed. Leo W. Schwarz (Philadelphia: Jewish Publication Society, 1964), 56.

7. See Agnes Vince, "Le quartier juif: comparaisons européennes," *La société juive en travers l'histoire* 2 (1992): 509, which includes a map demonstrating that the French city of Orléans in the twelfth century had a church in the midst of the *juiverie* or Jewish quarter.

8. M. Brann and A. Freimann, eds., *Germania Judaica,* vol. 1 (Frankfurt a. M.: J. Kauffmann, 1917), 71; Adolf Kober, *Cologne,* trans. Solomon Grayzel (Philadelphia: Jewish Publication Society, 1940), 83–84. The *Bürgerhaus* is first mentioned between 1135 and 1159.

9. Benjamin Ravid, "On the Diffusion of the Word 'Ghetto' and Its Ambiguous Usages, and a Suggested Definition," in *Frühneuzeitliche Ghettos in Europa im Vergleich,* ed. Fritz Backhaus et al. (Berlin: Trafo, 2012), 15–38.

10. Philo, "Flaccus *(In Flaccum),*" *The Works of Philo: New Updated Edition,* trans. C. D. Yonge (Peabody, MA: Hendrickson Publishers, 1993), 729.

11. Philo, "On the Embassy to Gaius: The First Part of the Treatise on Virtues," *The Works of Philo: New Updated Edition,* 768.

12. Pieter Willem van der Horst, ed., *Philo's Flaccus: The First Pogrom* (Leiden: Brill, 2003).

13. E. M. Smallwood, *The Jews under Roman Rule: From Pompey to Diocletian* (Leiden: Brill, 1976), 240.

14. Julius Aronius, ed., *Regesten zur Geschichte der Juden im Fränkischen und Deutschen Reiche bis zum Jahre 1273* (Berlin: Leonard Simion, 1902), Number 168. Qtd. in Wirth, *The Ghetto,* 21–22.

15. For examples of such perspectives, see Markus J. Wenninger, "Grenzen in der Stadt? Zu Lage und Abgrenzung mittelalterlicher deutscher Judenviertel," *Aschkenas—Zeitschrift für Geschichte und Kultur der Juden* 14 (2004), 9 f3.

16. This points to a criterion—stigma—that appears to be missing in Ravid's definition of the pre-emancipation ghetto. If, in fact, the Speyer enclave were compulsory, segregated, and enclosed, the rhetoric justifying its creation would still appear to distinguish it from later ghettos where the motivation was at least partly to keep a despised minority in its "place." Venice and Rome did not boast in their edicts creating Jewish ghettos that they were thereby contributing to the glory of the city. On the importance of "stigma" as a constituent element of a sociological definition of the ghetto, see Loïc Wacquant, "A Janus-Faced Institution of Ethnoracial Closure: A Sociological Specification of the Ghetto," in *The Ghetto: Contemporary Global Issues and Controversies,* ed. Ray Hutchinson and Bruce D. Haynes (New York: Routledge, 2011), 1–32.

17. Carl Nightingale, *Segregation: A Global History of Divided Cities* (Chicago: University of Chicago Press, 2013), 27–39.

18. Aronius, *Regesten*, Number 724, 301f.; qtd. and trans. in Baron, *Social and Religious History of the Jews*, vol. 9 (New York: Columbia University Press, 1965), 32.

19. Johannes Heil, for example, regards the given explanation for imposing residential segregation on the Jews as improbable, because Christianity was not in fact so new to Poland. See Heil, "Die propagandistische Vorbereitung des Ghettos—Diskussionen um Judenquartiere," in *Frühneuzeitliche Ghettos in Europa im Vergleich*, 151–159.

20. The Council of Basel (1431–1449), which took place amidst intense internal division in the church between reformers and the papacy, came out, in 1434, in favor of creating separate Jewish quarters that were as far removed from churches as possible. See Heil, "Die propagandistische Vorbereitung des Ghettos," 159, 158.

21. Ariel Toaff, *Love, Work, and Death: Jewish Life in Medieval Umbria*, trans. Judith Landry (London: Littman Library of Jewish Civilization, 1996), 187.

22. This brief account of the politics of ghettoization in Frankfurt am Main is based on Fritz Backhaus, "Die Einrichtung eines Ghettos für die Frankfurter Juden im Jahre 1462," *Hessisches Jahrbuch für Landesgeschichte* 39 (1989): 59–86.

23. Haim Beinart cites as an example of this trend toward a more rigid separation between Jews and Muslims and Christians in the fourteenth century the Catalonian city of Cervera. In 1369 the Infante Juan issued orders with respect to Cervera prohibiting Christians from renting property to Jews outside the Jewish quarter and obligating all Christians to block all doors, windows, and roof passages in their homes that abutted the Jewish quarter. See Beinart, "Megore ha-yehudim be-me'ah ha-tet"vav u-gezerat ha-hafradah," *Zion* 51, no. 1 (1986): 63.

24. Beinart, "Megore ha-yehudim," 63–68; David Nirenberg, "Conversion, Sex, and Segregation: Jews and Christians in Medieval Spain," *American Historical Review* 107, no. 4 (October 2002): 1065–1093.

25. Nirenberg, "Conversion, Sex, and Segregation," 1083.

26. Translated in Elias Hiam Lindo, *The History of the Jews of Spain and Portugal* (London: Longman, Brown, Green, & Longmans, 1848), 196.

27. Haim Beinart, *The Expulsion of the Jews from Spain*, trans. Jeffrey M. Green (Oxford: Littman Library of Jewish Civilization, 2002), 10, 4–18, 15.

28. Qtd. in Beinart, *The Expulsion of the Jews from Spain*, 49–51.

29. Toaff, *Love, Work, and Death*, 188.

30. See Fritz Backhaus, "The Population Explosion in the Frankfurt *Judengasse* in the Sixteenth Century," in *The Frankfurt Judengasse: Jewish Life in an Early Modern German City*, 23.

31. The most comprehensive account of the history of the area that would become known as the *Ghetto* or *Geto* before its emergence as the mandatory and exclusive

Jewish quarter of Venice in 1516 can be found in Ennio Concina, "Parva Jerusalem," in *La Città degli Ebrei*, ed. Ennio Concina, Ugo Camerino, and Donatella Calabi (Venice: Albrizzi Editore, 1991), 10–24. Much of the account that follows is a highly condensed version of the chronology that Concina traces.

32. Erika Timm and Gustav Adolf Beckmann, *Etymologische Studien zum Jiddischen* (Hamburg: Helmut Buske Verlag, 2006), 3–5.

33. Ariel Toaff has argued that the word *ghetto* derives not from the Venetian version of the Latin verb *jactare* (to throw), but from the verb *ghettare*, referring to the production of slag *(ghetta)* through the refining of ore. See Toaff, "Getto-Ghetto," *American Sephardi* 6 (1973): 71–77.

34. The testimonies, recorded in Latin, were published for the first time in Tommaso Temanza's *Antica pianta dell'inclita città di Venezia* (Ancient Map of the Noble City of Venice) (Venice: Palese, 1781), 70–73.

35. Temanza, *Antica pianta dell'inclita città di Venezia*, 72. My thanks to James Redfield for his assistance in translating the original Latin for me.

36. The text in question comes from Marcantonio Coccio Sabellico's 1494 *De situ urbis Venetae* and is quoted in Timm and Beckmann, *Etymologische Studien zum Jiddischen*, 8–9.

37. E. Teza, "Intorno alla voce Ghetto: Dubbi da togliere e da risvegliare," *Atti del Reale Istituto Veneto di Scienze, Lettere ed Arti* 43 (1903–1904): 1277–1278.

38. Francesco Sansovino, *Venetia, città nobilissima, et singolare* (Venice: Altobello Salicato, 1604), 256a–b.

39. Sandra Debenedetti Stow, "The Etymology of 'Ghetto': New Evidence from Rome," *Jewish History* 6 (1992): 83.

40. J. B. Sermoneta, "'Al mekorah shel ha-milah 'ghetto,'" *Tarbits* 32 (1962–1963): 195–206.

41. A selective bibliography would include Cecil Roth, *Venice* (Philadelphia: Jewish Publication Society, 1930); the many articles of Benjamin Ravid on the subject, most notably Ravid, "The Religious, Economic, and Social Background and Context of the Establishment of the Ghetti in Venice," in *Gli Ebrei e Venezia*, ed. Gaetano Cozzi (Milan: Edizioni Comunità, 1987), 211–259; Riccardo Calimani, *The Ghetto of Venice*, trans. Katherine Silberblatt Wolfthal (Milan: M. Evans, 1988); Ennio Concina, "Parva Jerusalem," in *La Città degli Ebrei: Il Ghetto di Venezia: Architettura e Urbanistica*, 10–49; Richard Sennett, "Fear of Touching: The Jewish Ghetto in Renaissance Venice," in *Flesh and Stone: The Body and the City in Western Civilization* (New York: W. W. Norton, 1994), 212–251; and, most recently, Donatella Calabi, *Venice, the Jews, and Europe 1516–2016* (New York: Marsilio, 2016).

42. In 1385, Venice, for the first time, granted Jews from its mainland territories and overseas possessions a ten-year charter recognizing their right to settle in the city and to lend at predetermined rates of interest. For various reasons, including

dissatisfaction with the degree to which the newcomers were lending to the poor and broad-based popular hostility, the Senate soon came to regret this invitation and refused to renew the charter when it ended, requiring the Jews who had settled in Venice to leave. On this, see Ravid, "The Legal Status of the Jews in Venice to 1509," *Proceedings of the American Academy for Jewish Research* 54 (1987): 169–202.

43. Ravid, "Religious, Economic, and Social Background," 213.

44. Elisabeth Crouzet-Pavan, "Venice between Jerusalem, Byzantium, and Divine Retribution: The Origins of the Ghetto," *Mediterranean Historical Review* 6, no. 2 (1991): 164.

45. Qtd. in Ravid, "Religious, Economic, and Social Background," 215.

46. Qtd. in Ravid, "Religious, Economic, and Social Background," 215. Giudecca is an island in the Venetian lagoon that forms part of the city. It was once thought that the name *Giudecca* was derived from the Latin "Judaica" and that it had served as the original Jewish quarter of Venice centuries earlier. Yet there is no evidence that Jews ever lived in Giudecca, nor is there a history of the name "Giudecca" ever being used to label a Jewish quarter in northern Italy.

47. Qtd. in Ravid, "Religious, Economic, and Social Background," 215.

48. Robert Finlay, "The Foundation of the Ghetto: Venice, the Jews, and the War of the League of Cambrai," *Proceedings of the American Philosophical Society* 126, no. 2 (1982): 140–154.

49. David Chambers and Brian Pullan, eds., *Venice: A Documentary History, 1450–1630* (Oxford: Blackwell, 1992), 338–339. The edict was translated by Brian Pullan.

50. Qtd. in Brian Pullan, *Rich and Poor in Renaissance Venice: The Social Institutions of a Catholic State, to 1620* (Cambridge, MA: Harvard University Press, 1971), 490.

51. Benjamin Ravid, "On Sufferance and Not as of Right: The Status of the Jewish Communities in Early-Modern Venice," in *The Lion Shall Roar: Leon Modena and his World*, ed. D. Malkiel (Jerusalem: Magnes Press-Ben-Zvi Institute, 2003), 17–61.

52. Ravid, "Religious, Economic, and Social Background," 228–230, 231–234.

53. See Robert Bonfil, *Jewish Life in Renaissance Italy* (Berkeley: University of California Press, 1994), 70–71.

54. Qtd. and trans. in Kenneth R. Stow, *Catholic Thought and Papal Jewry Policy, 1555–1593* (New York: Jewish Theological Seminary, 1977), 294–295.

55. Stow, *Catholic Thought and Papal Jewry Policy*, 295.

56. Kenneth R. Stow, *Alienated Minority: The Jews of Latin Christian Europe* (Cambridge, MA: Harvard University Press, 1992), 304–308.

57. *Vocabolario degli accademici della Crusca*, 3rd edition, *s.v.* "ghetto," accessed June 6, 2018, http://www.lessicografia.it/Controller?E=182;199754340;&c1=350;-7;3;-21159276;212722725;&c2=129;-39;3;40;69;1;130;32;5;40;66;1;129;-39;65;-3

1;69;4;130;1025;5;40;75;13;130;27;3;1646876352;1545561153;&qi=&q1
=ghetto&q2=&q3=&q4=&qr=null&num=20&o=115;-38489505;
-1185594668;&idV=695299;-10;7;-1563780446;-304690787;&TDE
=ghetto;&TDNE=.

58. Benjamin Ravid, "From Geographical Realia to Historiographical Symbol: The Odyssey of the Word *Ghetto,*" in *Essential Papers on Jewish Culture in Renaissance and Baroque Italy,* ed. David B. Ruderman (New York: NYU Press, 1992), 378; Daniel Carpi, *Pinkas Va'ad Kahal Kadosh Padovah, 1577–1603* (Jerusalem: Israel Academy of Sciences, 1973).

59. Stefanie B. Siegmund, *The Medici State and the Ghetto of Florence: The Construction of an Early Modern Jewish Community* (Palo Alto, CA: Stanford University Press, 2005).

60. Sansovino, *Venetia, città nobilissima, et singolare,* 256b.

61. Qtd. in Ravid, "Religious, Economic, and Social Background," 234.

62. Donatella Calabi, "The City of the Jews," in *The Jews of Early Modern Venice,* ed. Robert C. Davis and Benjamin Ravid (Baltimore: Johns Hopkins Press, 2001), 45.

63. Strikingly, the most famous sixteenth-century depiction of Jewish Venice by a foreigner, albeit one who never visited—Shakespeare's *The Merchant of Venice*—contains no mention whatsoever of the ghetto.

64. Thomas Coryat's account of the Venetian ghetto is found in *Coryat's Crudities* (London, 1611), 230–237. Qtd. in Benjamin Ravid, "Christian Travelers in the Ghetto of Venice: Some Preliminary Observations," in *Between History and Literature: Studies in Honor of Isaac Barzilay,* ed. Stanley Nash (B'nei B'rak: Hakibbutz Hameuhad, 1997), 121–122.

65. Bonfil, *Jewish Life in Renaissance Italy,* 246.

66. Nicolas Audeber, *Le voyage et observations de plusieurs choses diverses qui se peuvent remarquer en Italie* (1656), 127–128; qtd. and trans. in Don Harrán's introduction to Sarra Copia Sulam, *Jewish Poet and Intellectual in Seventeenth-Century Venice,* ed. and trans. Don Harrán (Chicago: University of Chicago Press, 2009), 9. The "secret reason" mentioned by Auderber may have its source in myths about menstruating Jewish men.

67. See the entry for "ghetto" in the fifth edition (1863–1923) of the *Vocabolario* of the *Accademia della Crusca,* accessed June 6, 2018, http://www.lessicografia.it /pagina.jsp?ediz=5&vol=7&pag=178&tipo=3.

68. Qtd. in Kenneth R. Stow, "Was the Ghetto Cleaner?" in *Rome, Pollution, and Propriety: Dirt, Disease, and Hygiene in the Eternal City from Antiquity to Modernity,* ed. Mark Bradley and Kenneth R. Stow (Cambridge: Cambridge University Press, 2012), 170.

69. Francesco Alberti di Villanuova, *Dizionario universale critico enciclopedico della lingua italiana,* vol. 3 (Lucca: Domenico Marescandoli, 1798), 170.

70. Gio. Battista Fagioli, *Rime Piacevoli*, vol. 6 (Lucca, 1729), 19.

71. Ruth Hacohen, *The Music Libel against the Jews* (New Haven: Yale University Press, 2012).

72. Qtd. in Ravid, "Christian Travelers," 120–121.

73. Bonfil, *Jewish Life in Renaissance Italy*, 239.

74. Qtd. in Kenneth Stow, *Jewish Dogs: An Image and Its Interpreters* (Palo Alto, CA: Stanford University Press, 2006), 31.

75. Shlomo Simonsohn, "Ha-Geto be-Italyah u-mishtaro," in S. Ettinger et al., eds., *Sefer Yovel le-Yitzhak Baer* (Jerusalem: Hevra ha-historit ha-yisraelit, 1960), 272–273.

76. Qtd. in Kenneth R. Stow, "The Consciousness of Closure: Roman Jewry and Its *Ghet*," in *Essential Papers on Jewish Culture in Renaissance and Baroque Italy*, 386.

77. The original Hebrew title of the grammar was *Livyat hen*. Reproduced in I. Sonne, *Mi-Pavolo ha-Revi'i 'ad Pius ha-Hamishi* (Jerusalem, 1954), 113.

78. Gedalyah ibn Yahya, *Shalshelet ha-Kabbalah* (Venice, 1587), 117; Joseph Ha-Kohen, *Sefer 'Emek ha-Bakha*, ed. M. Letteris (Krakow: Faust, 1895), 134.

79. Ha-Kohen, *Sefer 'Emek ha-Bakha*, 134.

80. Stow, "The Consciousness of Closure," 386–400.

81. Sandra Debenedetti Stow, "The Etymology of 'Ghetto,'" 83.

82. I. Sonne, "'Avne Binyan: Le-Toldot ha-yehudim be-Verona," *Zion* 3, no. 2 (1938): 131, 137; Simonsohn, "Ha-Geto be-Italyah u-mishtaro," 278f34.

83. Isaac Cantarini, *Pahad Yitzhak* (Amsterdam: David de Castro Tartas, 1685), 11.

84. Ottavio Ferrari, *Origines linguae italicae* (Padua: Petri Mariae Frambotti Bibliopolae, 1676), 157; Gilles Menage, *Le origini della lingua italiana* (Geneva: Giovanni Antonio Chouët, 1685), 250.

85. Paolo Minucci, "Note al Malmantile," in Lorenzo Lippi, *Malmantile Racquisato* (Florence, 1688), 242.

86. Timm and Beckmann, "Ghetto," in *Etymologische Studien zum Jiddischen*, 18–19.

87. Kenneth R. Stow, "Sanctity and the Construction of Space: The Roman Ghetto," in *Luoghi sacri e spazi della santità*, ed. Sofia Boesch Gajano and Lucetta Scaraffia (Turin: Rosenberg and Sellier, 1990), 597.

88. Cecil Roth, "La fête de l'institution du ghetto: une célébration particulière à Vérone," *Revue des Études Juives* 79 (1924): 168.

89. See Sonne, "'Avne Binyan," 126–129; Yosef Hayim Yerushalmi, *From Spanish Court to Italian Ghetto: Isaac Cardoso: A Study in Seventeenth-Century Marranism and Jewish Apologetics* (New York: Columbia University Press, 1971), 388 f85.

90. Qtd. in Boaz Hutterer and Adam Mintz, "Ben ha-geto le-'ir: 'al eruv hatserot be-Italyah be-me'ot ha-sheva 'esreh ve-ha-shemonah 'esreh," *Pe'amim* 154–155 (2018): 34. Of course, the very fact that the upshot of the forced residential concentration in this responsum was to permit carrying on the Sabbath throughout the entire city should qualify our view of the degree to which the creation of the ghetto really did constitute a "divorce" between the Jews and the rest of the city.

91. Bonfil, *Jewish Life in Renaissance Italy*, 72.

92. This emphasis on the ghetto as an ambivalent, paradoxical space can be found not only in Bonfil but also in scholars like David B. Ruderman and Roni Weinstein. See Ruderman, "The Cultural Significance of the Ghetto in Jewish History," in *From Ghetto to Emancipation: Historical and Contemporary Reconsiderations of the Jewish Community*, ed. David N. Myers and William V. Rowe (Scranton, PA: University of Scranton Press, 1997), 1–16; Weinstein, "'Mevudadim 'Akh Lo De-huyim': Ha-yehudim ba-hevrah ha-'italkit bi-tekufat ha-reformatsyah ha-katolit,'" in *Mi'utim, Zarim ve-Shonim: Kevutsot shulayim ba-historyah*, ed. Shulamit Volkov (Jerusalem: Zalman Shazar Center, 2000), 93–132.

93. Leon Modena, *The Autobiography of a Seventeenth-Century Venetian Rabbi: Leon Modena's* Life of Judah, trans. and ed. Mark R. Cohen (Princeton: Princeton University Press, 1988).

94. Luzzatto, *Discorso circa il stato de gl'Hebrei et in particular dimoranti nell'inclita citta di Venezia* (Venice: Gioanne Calleoni, 1638), 30a. Emphasis mine.

2. The Nineteenth-Century Transformation of the Ghetto

1. Pier Gian Maria de Ferrari, the head of the Third Battalion of the Second Bucchia Brigade, penned this account of the demolition of the Ghetto of Venice on the evening of July 12, 1797. His description was included in a collection of documents related to the emancipation of Venice's Jews, titled *Raccolta di rapporti, decreti, processi verbali, e discorsi concernenti li cittadini ebrei di Venezia dopo la loro felice rigenerazione* (Venice, 1797), 16–25. The translation, by Benjamin Ravid, is taken from Paul-Mendes Flohr and Jehuda Reinharz, eds., *The Jew in the Modern World: A Documentary History*, 3rd ed. (New York: Oxford University Press, 2011), 146–147.

2. The figure for the city's Jewish population (1,626 to be exact in 1797) is taken from a table in Gadi Luzzatto Voghera, "Gli ebrei," in *Storia di Venezia. L'ottocento e il novecento*, ed. Mario Isnenghi and Stuart Woolf (Rome: Istituto della Enciclopedia Italiana, 2002), 623.

3. Adolfo Ottolenghi, "Il governo democratico di Venezia e l'abolizione del ghetto," *La Rassegna Mensile di Israel* 2 (1930): 104.

4. On the historical unfolding of the Napoleonic liberations of the ghettos, see Cecil Roth, *The History of the Jews of Italy* (Philadelphia: Jewish Publication Society, 1946), 421–445; Attilio Milano, *Storia degli ebrei in Italia* (Turin: G. Einaudi, 1963), 338–351.

5. On the symbolism of the revolutionaries' highly scripted dismantling of the spatial forms of the confessional state, see Mona Ozouf, *Festivals and the French Revolution,* trans. Alan Sheridan (Cambridge, MA: Harvard University Press, 1991).

6. See L. Scott Lerner, "Narrating over the Ghetto of Rome," *Jewish Social Studies* 8, nos. 2–3 (2002): 1–38; Cathleen Giustino, *Tearing down Prague's Jewish Town: Ghetto Clearance and the Legacy of Middle-Class Ethnic Politics around 1900* (New York: Columbia University Press, 2003).

7. Raymond Williams, *Keywords: A Vocabulary of Culture and Society,* rev. ed. (New York: Oxford University Press, 1985), 15.

8. On the "invention" of the expression *Ancien Régime* in or around 1789 as a foil to the French Revolution and the evolution of the phrase into the nineteenth century, see Olivier Christin, "*Ancien Régime.* Pour une approche comparatiste du vocabulaire historiographique," *Mots. Let langages du politique* 87 (2008): 13–26.

9. As Jacob Toury showed, the phrase "Jewish Question" *(Judenfrage)* was only coined in the middle of the nineteenth century to designate gentile doubts and anxieties surrounding the possibility of Jewish emancipation and assimilation (and eventually as a euphemism for antisemitism). Following in the footsteps of many other writers, I have opted to use the term anachronistically here, on the presumption that the roots of this discourse, if not the phrase itself, do in fact lie in the Enlightenment era. See Jacob Toury, "The 'Jewish Question': A Semantic Approach," *Leo Baeck Institute Year Book* 11 (1966): 85–106.

10. On the ghetto as a protective measure aimed at containing the threat of Jewish pollution, see Richard Sennett, "Fear of Touching: The Jewish Ghetto in Renaissance Venice," in *Flesh and Stone: The Body and the City in Western Civilization* (New York: W.W. Norton, 1994), 212–254.

11. This is the main argument of Kenneth Stow's landmark study, *Catholic Thought and Papal Policy, 1555–1593* (New York: Jewish Theological Seminary Press, 1977) and is reiterated in his *Alienated Minority: The Jews of Medieval Latin Europe* (Cambridge, MA: Harvard University Press, 1992), 304–307.

12. Christian Wilhelm von Dohm, *Über die bürgerliche Verbesserung der Juden* (Berlin: Friedrich Nicolai, 1781).

13. The translation of excerpts of Dohm's treatise comes from *The Jew in the Modern World,* 3rd ed., 27–34.

14. Dohm, *Über die bürgerliche Verbesserung der Juden,* 115–116; *The Jew in the Modern World,* 31.

15. M. Grégoire, *Essai sur la régéneration physique, morale, et politique des Juifs* (Metz: Claude Lamort, 1789). Quotations in the text are taken from the two-volume English translation, *An Essay on the Physical, Moral, and Political Reformation of the Jews* (London: C. Forster, 1791).

16. Grégoire, *Essay,* vol. 1, 184.

17. Dohm, *Über die bürgerliche Verbesserung der Juden,* 116; *Jew in the Modern World,* 31.

18. Grégoire, *Essai sur la regeneration,* 185.

19. On the beginnings of this discussion in Italy, see Renzo de Felice, "Per una storia del problema ebraico in Italia alla fine del XVIII secolo e all'inizio del XIX," *Movimento operaio. Rivista di storia e bibliografia* 7 (1955): 681–727.

20. Giovanni Battista Gherardo D'Arco, *Della Influenza del Ghetto nello Stato* (Venice: Arnaldo Forni, 1782). On this work and the rejoinder to it by the Italian Jewish enlightener Benedetto Frizzi (discussed later), see Paolo Bernardini, *La sfida dell'uguaglianza: Gli ebrei a Mantova nell'età della rivoluzione francese* (Rome: Bulzoni Editore, 1996), 67–80; Gadi Luzzatto Voghera, *Il prezzo dell'egualglianza: Il dibattito sull'emancipazione degli ebrei in Italia (1781–1848)* (Milan: FrancoAngeli, 1998), 40–50.

21. Joseph II, "Edict of Tolerance," trans. Paul Mendes-Flohr, in *Jew in the Modern World,* 42.

22. For an excellent study of a case in which ghettoization was rescinded before the French Revolution and the Napoleonic Wars, see Lois Dubin, *The Port Jews of Habsburg Trieste: Absolutist Politics and Enlightenment Culture* (Palo Alto, CA: Stanford University Press, 1998), 139–148. In Trieste, the formal lifting of restrictions on Jewish residence took place in 1785, in the era of Josephinan reforms, although the moving of Jews outside the ghetto had begun well before that.

23. D'Arco, *Della Influenza del Ghetto nello Stato,* 63–64, 68.

24. This kind of metonymic slippage from the space or place associated with the Jews to the Jews collectively is found in other languages in addition to Italian (e.g. the English "Jewry," the French "Juiverie").

25. *Dizionario universale critico, enciclopedico della lingua Italiana dell'abate D'Alberti di Villanuova,* vol. 3 (F–I), (Lucca, 1798), s.v. "ghetto."

26. On Frizzi, see, most recently, Lois Dubin, "Medicine as Enlightenment Cure: Benedetto Frizzi, Physician to Eighteenth-Century Italian Jewish Society," *Jewish History* 26 (May 2012): 201–221.

27. *Difesa contro gli attachi fatti alla nazione ebraia nel libro intitolato dell'influenza del Ghetto nello Stato* (Pavia: R. I. Monistero di S. Salvatore, 1784), 3, 4.

28. Undated entry of 1822, in F. Halévy *Journal inédit* (BN NAF 14349). The section of the journal describing the visit to the ghetto has been published in Olivier Bara, "*La Juive* de Scribe et Halévy: Un Opera Juif?" *Romanticisme* 125 (2004):

75–89. All quotations from the diary come from this article. In addition to Bara's article, Halévy's discovery of the Roman Ghetto is also discussed in Eric C. Hansen, *Ludovic Halévy: A Study of Frivolity and Fatalism in Nineteenth Century France* (Lanham, MD: University Press of America, 1987), 7; Ruth Jordan, *Fromenthal Halévy: His Life and Music, 1799–1862* (New York: Limelight Editions, 1996), 23–4; and Diana R. Hallman, *Opera, Liberalism, and Anti-Semitism in Nineteenth-Century France: The Politics of Halévy's* La Juive (Cambridge: Cambridge University Press, 2007), 89–92, 176–177.

29. Bara, "*La Juive* de Scribe et Halévy," 86.

30. Bara, "*La Juive* de Scribe et Halévy," 89, 88.

31. Robert Bonfil, *Jewish Life in Renaissance Italy,* trans. Anthony Oldcorn (Berkeley: University of California Press, 1994), 69. On the general decline of interest in the Venetian Ghetto among nineteenth-century writers after it ceased to be a site of mandatory enclosure of Jews, see Dana Katz, *The Jewish Ghetto and the Visual Imagination of Early Modern Venice* (Cambridge: Cambridge University Press, 2017), 113–114.

32. Attilio Milano, *Il Ghetto di Roma. Illustrazioni storiche* (Rome: Staderni, 1964), 110.

33. Milano, *Il Ghetto di Roma*, 94; Kenneth Stow, *Anna and Tranquillo: Catholic Anxiety and Jewish Protest in the Age of Revolutions* (New Haven: Yale University Press, 2016), 71.

34. For a translation and careful scrutiny of the language and composition of Anna's diary recounting her two-week confinement in the Casa dei Catecumeni, together with a history of the papacy's evolving policy vis-à-vis the Jews in the eighteenth and nineteenth centuries, see Stow, *Anna and Tranquillo.*

35. Charles-Marguerite-Jean-Baptiste Mercier Dupaty, *Lettres sur l'Italie en 1785,* 3rd ed. (Paris, 1796), 339–40.

36. Joseph Gorani, *Mémoires secrets et critiques des cours, des gouvernements, et des moeurs des principaux États d'Italie,* vol. 2 (Paris, 1793), 386–387.

37. On this assault, see Enzo Sereni, "L'assedio del Ghetto di Roma nel 1793 nelle memorie di un contemporaneo," *Rassegna Mensile d'Israel* 10 (1935): 100–125.

38. Renzo de Felice, "Gli ebrei nella repubblica romana del 1798–9," *Rassegna storica del Risorgimento* 40 (1953): 338.

39. Qtd in de Felice, "Gli ebrei nella repubblica romana," 388.

40. Aram Matteoli, "Das Ghetto der „ewigen Stadt" im Urteil deutschsprachiger Publizisten (1846–1870), in *Zwischen Selbstbehauptung und Verfolgung. Deutsch-jüdische Zeitungen und Zeitschriften von der Aufklärung bis zum Nationalsozialismus,* ed. Michael Nagel (Hildesheim: Olms, 2002), 163.

41. Milano, *Storia degli Ebrei in Italia,* 352–353.

42. Massimo d'Azeglio, *Dell'emancipazione civile degl'Israeliti* (Florence: Felice le Monnier, 1848), 24–25.

43. Ferdinand Gregorovius, *The Ghetto and the Jews of Rome,* trans. Moses Hadas (New York: Schocken, 1948), 85–86.

44. On the growing Western and Central European Jewish preoccupation with the plight of Roman Jewry in the middle decades of the nineteenth century, see Ari Joskowicz, *The Modernity of Others: Jewish Anti-Catholicism in Germany and France* (Palo Alto, CA: Stanford University Press, 2013), 169ff.

45. Qtd. in Matteoli, "Das Ghetto der „ewigen Stadt," 180–181.

46. Heinrich Graetz, *Geschichte der Juden von den ältesten Zeiten bis auf die Gegenwart,* vol. 11 [1870] (Leipzig, 1900), 303f, 534.

47. Theodor Mannheimer, "Das Ghetto in Rom," *Kalender und Jahrbuch für Israeliten auf das Jahr (1847) 5607 5* (1846): 111–112.

48. Gregorovius, *The Ghetto and the Jews of Rome,* 19.

49. Abraham Berliner, *Aus den letzten Tagen des römischen Ghetto: Ein historischer Rückblick* (Berlin: Rosenstein & Hildesheimer, 1886), 2.

50. See, for instance, Nicoló di Castelli and Philipp Jakob Flathe, *Nuovo Dizionario Italiano-Tedesco e Tedesco-Italiano,* vol. 1 (1782), s.v. "ghetto"; Annibale Antonini, *Dizionario Italiano, Latino, e Francese,* vol. 1 (1770), s.v. "ghetto."

51. Benjamin Ravid, "'All Ghettos Were Jewish Quarters but Not All Jewish Quarters Were Ghettos,'" *Jewish Culture and History,* 10, nos. 2–3 (2008): 5–24.

52. *Dictionnaire de la langue française* (1873), s.v. "ghetto," http://littre.reverso.net/dictionnaire-francais/definition/ghetto.

53. *Grand dictionnaire du XIX siècle* (1872), s.v. "ghetto," https://archive.org/stream/LarousGrdictionnXIX08bnf#page/n1243/mode/1up.

54. James Augustus Henry Murray, ed., *A New English Dictionary on Historical Principles,* vol. 4 (Oxford, 1900), s.v. "ghetto."

55. F. Bösigkeit, "Ghetto," in *Allgemeine Encyklopädie der Wissenschaften und Künste. Erste Section, A–G. Sechundsechzigster Theil (Gewicht-Gidom),* ed. J. S. Ersch and J. G. Gruber (Leipzig: F. A. Brockhaus, 1857), 299–300.

56. Overviews of the history of etymologies proposed for the word *ghetto* include Cecil Roth, "The Origin of Ghetto: A Final Word," *Romania* 60 (1934): 67–76; Ariel Toaff, "Getto-Ghetto," *American Sephardi* 6 (1973): 70–77; Erika Timm and Gustav Adolf Beckmann, "Ghetto," *Etymologsiche Studien zum Jiddischen* (Hamburg: Helmut Buske Verlag, 2006), 1–32.

57. "Über die Abstammung des Wortes Ghetto," *Die Gegenwart: Organ für die Interessen des Judenthums* II, no. 8 (April 15, 1869): 78.

58. On Auerbach's reception of Spinoza specifically, see Daniel B. Schwartz, *The First Modern Jew: Spinoza and the History of an Image* (Princeton: Princeton

University Press, 2012), 55–79; Sven-Erik Rose, *Jewish Philosophical Politics in Germany, 1789–1848* (Waltham, MA: Brandeis University Press, 2014), 200–240.

59. As of 1837, the word *ghetto* had yet to appear in the Brockhaus *Conversations—Lexicon*. As mentioned earlier, it would first be included in the 1857 edition of the encyclopedia.

60. Berthold Auerbach, "Das Ghetto," in *Spinoza, ein historischer Roman* (Stuttgart: Scheible, 1837), III, VII.

61. While the first edition of Auerbach's Spinoza novel in 1837 found few readers, in 1854—by which point Auerbach was an internationally renowned author—he produced a revised edition that was translated into multiple languages (including Hebrew and Yiddish) and went through several print runs. See Auerbach, *Spinoza: Ein Denkersleben* (Mannheim: Bassermann, 1854).

62. Kenneth Ober discusses precursors and contemporaries of Kompert, such as Meir Goldschmidt and Aaron David Bernstein. See Ober, *Die Ghettogeschichte: Entstehung und Entwicklung einer Gattung* (Göttingen: Wallstein, 2001), 29–37, 45–46.

63. Leopold Kompert, "Judith der Zweite," in *Aus dem Ghetto: Geschichten* (Leipzig: Grunow, 1850), 8–9.

64. The passage comes from the English translation of this story. See Leopold Kompert, *Scenes from the Ghetto: Studies of Jewish Life* (London: Kessinger, 1882), 77.

65. Hillel Kieval, *Languages of Community: The Jewish Experience in the Czech Lands* (Berkeley: University of California Press, 2000), 21–22.

66. Leopold Kompert, "Im Jahre 1850," in *Aus dem Ghetto: Geschichten* (Leipzig, 1850), xii–xiii.

67. Leopold Kompert, "Draußen vor dem Ghetto," in *Aus dem Ghetto: Geschichten* (Leipzig, 1850), ix–x.

68. Leopold Kompert, "Der Dorfgeher," *Böhmische Juden* (Vienna: Jasper, Hügel, & Manz, 1851), 1–82. An English translation of the novella, by Jonathan M. Hess, can now be found in Jonathan M. Hess, Maurice Samuels, and Nadia Valman, eds., *Nineteenth-Century Jewish Literature: A Reader* (Palo Alto, CA: Stanford University Press, 2013), 25–63. All future quotations of the story come from this translation.

69. Kompert, "The Peddler," 38.

70. "Kompert, "The Peddler," 38 50–51.

71. Kompert, "The Peddler," 63.

72. Kompert, "Im Jahre 1850," xiii.

73. On this duality of repugnance and wistful reminiscence in attitudes toward the "ghetto" on the part of nineteenth-century acculturated Jews, see Steven E. Aschheim, *Brothers and Strangers: The East European Jew in German and German-Jewish Consciousness* (Madison: University of Wisconsin Press, 1982), 3–31; and Richard I.

Cohen, "Nostalgia and 'Return to the Ghetto': A Cultural Phenomenon in Western and Central Europe," in *Assimilation and Community: The Jews in Nineteenth-Century Europe,* ed. Jonathan Frankel and Steven J. Zipperstein (Cambridge: Cambridge University Press, 1992), 130–155.

74. Reinhart Koselleck and Karl Martin Grass, "Emanzipation," in *Geschichtliche Grundbegriffe: Historisches Lexicon zur politisch-sozialen Sprache in Deutschland,* vol. 2, ed. Otto Brunner, Werner Conze, and Reinhart Koselleck (Stuttgart: Klett-Cotta, 1979), 153–197; Koselleck, "The Limits of Emancipation: A Conceptual-Historical Sketch," in *The Practice of Conceptual History: Timing History, Spacing Concepts,* trans. Todd Presner (Palo Alto, CA: Stanford University Press, 2002), 248–264.

75. Koselleck, "The Historical-Political Semantics of Asymmetric Counterconcepts," in *Futures Past: On the Semantics of Historical Time,* trans. Kenneth Tribe (New York: Columbia University Press, 2004), 155–191.

76. On the shtetl in history and memory, see the various essays in Antony Polonsky, ed., *Polin,* vol. 17: *The Shtetl: Myth and Reality* (Oxford: Littman Library, 2004) and Steven T. Katz, ed., *The Shtetl: New Evaluations* (New York: NYU Press, 2007).

77. See, in particular, Israel Bartal, "Imagined Geography: The Shtetl, Myth and Reality," in *The Shtetl: New Evaluations,* 179–192.

78. Karl Franzos, *The Jews of Barnow,* trans. M. W. Macdowell (New York, 1883), 260.

79. The following biographical precis is lifted from Franzos's own autobiographical foreword to arguably his greatest novel, *Der Pojaz: Eine Geschichte aus dem Osten* (The Clown: A Story from the East) (Stuttgart: J. G. Cotta'sche, 1905), 5–14.

80. Franzos, *Der Pojaz,* 6.

81. Karl Franzos, *Aus Halb-Asien: Culturbilder aus Galizien, der Bukowina, Südrussland, und Rumanien* (Leipzig: Duncker & Humblot, 1876), 1: iii, 143.

82. Franzos, *The Jews of Barnow,* 30.

83. Wilhelm Goldbaum, "Das Ghetto und seine Poeten," in *Das Jüdische Literaturblatt. Wissenschaftliche Beilage zur 'Israelitschen Wochenschrift'* 7 (1878): 157. Reprinted in Wilhelm Goldbaum, *Literarische Physiognomieen* (Vienna: K. f. Hofbuchhandlung Karl Prochaska, 1884), 163–216.

84. Leopold Ritter von Sacher-Masoch, "Moses Goldfarb und sein Haus," in *Judengeschichten* (Leipzig: Johann Friedrich Hartknoch, 1878), 29.

85. Louis Wirth, *The Ghetto* [1928] (New Brunswick, NJ: Transaction Publishers, 1998), 8. I discuss Wirth's role in the elaboration of the ghetto concept in detail in Chapter 3.

86. "Bastille und Ghetto," *Die Neuzeit: Wochenschrift für politische, religiöse und Cultur=Interessen,* July 19, 1889, 1.

87. David Philipson, *Old European Jewries* (Philadelphia: Jewish Publication Society, 1894), 20, 32, 34.

88. Philipson, *Old European Jewries*, 177–178.

89. Theodor Herzl, *Das neue Ghetto: Schauspiel in 4 Acten* (Vienna: "Industrie," 1903), 29–30.

90. Herzl, *Das neue Ghetto*, 100.

91. The original title, in the handwritten draft of the play kept in Herzl's archive in the Central Zionist Archives, was simply *Das Ghetto*.

92. On the place of *Das neue Ghetto* in Herzl's intellectual and ideological development, see Jacques Kornberg, *Theodor Herzl: From Assimilation to Zionism* (Bloomington: Indiana University Press, 1993), 130–158.

93. On Nordau's Zionism, see Michael Stanislawski, *Zionism and the Fin-de-Siècle: Cosmopolitanism and Nationalism from Nordau to Jabotinsky* (Berkeley: University of California Press, 2001), 74–97.

94. Max Nordau, *Zionistische Schriften* (Cologne: Jüdischer Verlag, 1909), 379–380; trans. in *Jew in the Modern World*, 616–617.

95. Nordau, *Zionistische Schriften*, 48; trans. in Arthur Hertzberg, ed., *The Zionist Idea: A Historical Analysis and Reader* (Philadelphia: Jewish Publication Society, 1997), 237, 239.

3. The Ghetto Comes to America

1. Abraham Cahan, *The Education of Abraham Cahan*, trans. Leon Stein, Abraham P. Conan, and Lynn Davison (Philadelphia: Jewish Publication Society, 1969), 355.

2. Cahan, *The Education of Abraham Cahan*, 355.

3. On Cahan and the labeling of New York's Lower East Side as a "ghetto," see Moses Rischin, "Toward the Onomastics of the Great New York Ghetto: How the Lower East Side Got Its Name," in *Remembering the Lower East Side: American Jewish Reflections*, ed. Hasia Diner, Jeffrey Shandler, and Beth S. Wenger (Bloomington: University of Indiana Press, 2000), 13–27.

4. Hasia R. Diner, *The Jews of the United States, 1654–2000* (Berkeley: University of California Press, 2004), 71–111.

5. See Moshe Shulvass, *From East to West: The Westward Migration of Jews from Eastern Europe in the Seventeenth and Eighteenth Centuries* (Detroit: Wayne State University Press, 1971).

6. Lloyd Gartner, "The Great Jewish Migration 1881–1914: Myths and Realities," *Shofar* 4, no. 2 (Winter 1986): 16.

7. On the history of Jewish settlement in Vienna from the Middle Ages to the latter decades of Habsburg rule, see Ignaz Schwarz, *Das Wiener Ghetto: Seine Häuser und*

seine Bewohner (Vienna: Braumüller, 1909); Hans Rottter and Adolf Schmieger, *Das Ghetto in der Wiener Leopoldstadt* (Vienna: Burgverlag Wien, 1926); Marsha L. Rozenblit, *The Jews of Vienna, 1867–1914: Assimilation and Identity* (Albany: SUNY Press, 1983).

8. Rozenblit, *The Jews of Vienna,* 77, 78.

9. In *Juden in Wanderschaft (The Wandering Jew),* a book of essays on the plight of the "Eastern Jew" following World War I, Joseph Roth devoted a chapter to Vienna as one of the "ghettos of the West." See Joseph Roth, *The Wandering Jew* [1937], trans. Michael Hoffman (New York: W. W. Norton, 2001), 55–67.

10. On the history of this *juiverie* in the Middle Ages, see the classic article by Robert Anchel, "The Early History of the Jewish Quarters of Paris," *Jewish Social Studies* 2, no. 1 (January 1940): 45–60.

11. Paula Hyman, *From Dreyfus to Vichy: The Remaking of French Jewry, 1906–1939* (New York: Columbia University Press, 1979), 69, 64, 68.

12. Qtd. in Hyman, *From Dreyfus to Vichy,* 72.

13. Iwan Goll, "Abend in Pariser Ghetto," *Prager Tagblatt,* April 23, 1925, 3.

14. On this, see Jack Wertheimer, *Unwelcome Strangers: East European Jews in Imperial Germany* (New York: Oxford University Press, 1987).

15. J. Thon, "Berliner Brief," *Die Welt,* June 10, 1904, 2–3.

16. Michael Brenner, *The Renaissance of Jewish Culture in Weimar Germany* (New Haven: Yale University Press, 1996), 186.

17. Klara Eschenbacher, "Die ostjüdische Einwanderungsbevölkerung der Stadt Berlin," *Zeitschrift für Demographie und Statistik der Juden* 16 (1920), 11, 13.

18. Roth, *The Wandering Jew,* 68–79.

19. On Zangwill's biography, see, most recently, Meri-Jane Rochelson, *A Jew in the Public Arena: The Career of Israel Zangwill* (Detroit: Wayne State University Press, 2008).

20. Todd Endelman, *The Jews of Britain, 1656 to 2000* (Berkeley: University of California Press, 2002), 129.

21. Lloyd Gartner, *The Jewish Immigrant in England, 1870–1914* (London: George Allen and Unwin, 1960), 16–17, 147.

22. Israel Zangwill, *Children of the Ghetto: A Study of a Particular People,* ed. Meri-Jane Rochelson (Detroit: Wayne State University Press, 1998), 61–62.

23. Petticoat Lane was the main hub of the Jewish East End, while the "Great *Shool*" is a reference to the flagship Ashkenazi synagogue in the area, founded in 1690 and known as the Great Synagogue. See Endelman, *The Jews of Britain,* 51.

24. Zangwill, *Children of the Ghetto,* 67–68, 61.

25. Zangwill, *Children of the Ghetto,* 284–285, 95–96.

26. Zangwill, *Children of the Ghetto,* 323.

27. Zangwill, *Children of the Ghetto,* 502.

28. Gartner, *The Jewish Immigrant in England,* 35.

29. "Our 'Judenstrasse,'" *The Jewish Messenger,* April 25, 1862, 121.

30. On Isaacs, see Howard B. Rock, *Haven of Liberty: New York Jews in the New World, 1654–1865* (New York: NYU Press, 2012), 220–224.

31. Hasia Diner, *A Time for Gathering: The Second Migration, 1820–1880* (Baltimore: Johns Hopkins University Press, 1992); Tyler Anbinder, *Five Points: The 19th-Century Neighborhood That Invented Tap Dance, Stole Elections, and Became the World's Most Notorious Slum* (New York: Free Press, 2001); Adam D. Mendelsohn, *The Rag Race: How Jews Sewed Their Way to Success in American and the British Empire* (New York: NYU Press, 2015), 37–47. For an earlier controversy in the American Jewish press stemming from a German Jewish immigrant's comparison of Chatham Street to a "European ghetto" in 1854, see Annie Polland and Daniel Soyer, *Emerging Metropolis: New York Jews in the Age of Immigration, 1840–1920* (New York: NYU Press, 2012), 38–39.

32. Stanley Nadel, *Little Germany: Ethnicity, Religion, and Class in New York City, 1845–1880* (Urbana: University of Illinois Press, 1990).

33. In 1903, the frontispiece for a book titled *The Tenement House Problem,* edited by Robert W. DeForest and Laurence Veiller, was a photograph of a street on the Lower East Side captioned "The Most Densely Populated Spot in the World—the Lower East Side of New York." See Christopher Mele, *Selling the Lower East Side: Culture, Real Estate, and Resistance in New York City* (Minneapolis: University of Minnesota Press, 2000), 46.

34. M. L. Marks, "In a Jewish Bookstore," *Harper's New Monthly Magazine* 57 (October 1878): 765.

35. "New Year in the Ghetto," *New York Herald,* September 29, 1878, 6.

36. Milton Reigenstein, "Pictures of the Ghetto," *New York Times,* November 14, 1897, 1.

37. "Desk Studies for Girls: New Words," *Philadelphia Inquirer,* October 18, 1899, 9.

38. Jonathan B. Sarna, *JPS: The Americanization of Jewish Culture, 1888–1988* (Philadelphia: Jewish Publication Society, 1989), 39–42

39. Dr. Maurice H. Harris, "Extracts from a Lecture on the Children of the Ghetto," *The American Hebrew,* March 17, 1893, 648.

40. F. de Sola Mendes, "The Children of the Ghetto," *The American Hebrew,* January 6, 1893, 325.

41. Cyrus L. Sulzberger, "'The Children of the Ghetto' Again," *The American Hebrew,* December 30, 1892, 296.

42. Sarna, *JPS: The Americanization of Jewish Culture,* 40.

43. Zangwill, *Children of the Ghetto,* 476–477.

44. Israel Zangwill, *Dreamers of the Ghetto* (Philadelphia: Jewish Publication Society of America, 1898), iii.

45. Zangwill, *Dreamers of the Ghetto,* 531.

46. Abraham Cahan, *Yekl and the Imported Bridegroom and Other Stories of Yiddish New York,* ed. Bernard G. Richards (New York: Dover Books, 1970), 13–14.

47. Jacob A. Riis, *How the Other Half Lives: Studies among the Tenements of New York* [1890] (New York: Hill and Wang, 1967), 76–99.

48. Jacob Riis, "The Jews of New York," *Review of Reviews* 13 (1896): 58–62.

49. Henry Cabot Lodge, "The Restriction of Immigration," *North American Review* 152, no. 410 (January 1891): 27–36.

50. For the classic study of the history of immigration restrictionist sentiment from the mid-nineteenth century to the 1920s, see John Higham, *Strangers in the Land: Patterns of American Nativism, 1860–1925* (New Brunswick, NJ: Rutgers University Press, 1955).

51. Edward A. Ross, *The Old World in the New: The Significance of Past and Present Immigration to the American People* (New York: The Century, 1914), 145.

52. Edward A. Ross and S. A. Cudmore, "Significance of Emigration—Discussion," *American Economic Review* 2, no. 1 (March 1912), 86.

53. "The New York Ghetto," *The Jewish Messenger,* September 11, 1891, 4.

54. On the effort of institutions like the Industrial Removal Office, underwritten by Baron Maurice de Hirsch's Jewish Colonization Association, to resettle Jewish immigrants beyond New York, see Jack Glazier, *Dispersing the Ghetto: The Relocation of Jewish Immigrants across America* (Ithaca, NY: Cornell University Press, 1998).

55. Bernard C. Richards, "Where Are the Prairies?" *Reform Advocate,* August 9, 1913, 909. On the editor of the *Reform Advocate* Rabbi Emil Hirsch's brand of radical Reform Judaism and his impact on the Chicago Jewish community as the long-time rabbi at Temple Sinai, see Tobias Brinkmann, *Sundays at Sinai: A Jewish Congregation in Chicago* (Chicago: University of Chicago Press, 2012).

56. Kaufmann Kohler, "American Judaism," *Hebrew Union College and Other Addresses* (Cincinnati: Ark Publishing Co., 1916), 199.

57. Michael Gold, *Jews without Money* (New York: Public Affairs, 1996), 10, 14, 309.

58. Abraham Cahan, "The Russian Jew in the United States," in *The Russian Jew in the United States,* ed. Charles S. Bernheimer (Philadelphia: John Winston Co., 1905), 32.

59. Cahan, "The Russian Jew in the United States," 34.

60. "The New Jewish Quarter of Harlem," *The American Israelite,* February 4, 1904. For a more nuanced account of how Harlem became a second settlement for

Jews, see Jeffrey S. Gurock, *When Harlem Was Jewish, 1870–1930* (New York: Columbia University Press, 1979).

61. In Abraham Cahan's classic 1917 immigrant novel, *The Rise of David Levinsky,* about an impoverished Russian immigrant who climbs the ladder of the garment industry to become fabulously wealthy, the hero reflects on his successful pursuit of assimilation and material success mostly with regret. "My present station, power, the amount of worldly happiness at my command, and the rest of it," the protagonist claims, "seem to be devoid of significance." See Cahan, *The Rise of David Levinsky* (New York: Penguin, 1993), 3.

62. Hutchins Hapgood, *The Spirit of the Ghetto: Studies of the Jewish Quarter in New York* (New York: Funk & Wagnalls, 1902), 9.

63. Hapgood, *The Spirit of the Ghetto,* 135, 270.

64. Hutchings Hapgood, "The Picturesque Ghetto," *Century Magazine* (July 1917): 471.

65. I. M. Rubinow, "Concentration or Removal—Which?" *The American Hebrew,* July 17 and 31, 1903; reprinted in *The Menorah* 35, no. 2 (August 1903): 75, 78.

66. "Di geto fun amol un haynt," *Der morgen zhurnal,* November 23, 1909, 5.

67. Ben Amitai, "A toyter plan: di fervalter fun Baron de Hirsch Fund vilen abshafen di Nyu Yorker Geto" (A Dead Plan: The Administrators of the Baron de Hirsch Fund Want to Abolish the New York Ghetto), *Yudishe Gazeten,* December 30, 1898, 1.

68. Mollie Eda Osherman, "The Word 'Ghetto,'" *American Israelite,* January 16, 1908, 4.

69. Qtd. in M. M. Silver, *Louis Marshall and the Rise of Jewish Ethnicity in America* (Syracuse, NY: Syracuse University Press, 2013), 69.

70. Ernest W. Burgess, "The Trend of Population," *Publications of the American Sociological Society* 18 (1925): 85–97.

71. On Park, see Fred Matthews, *Quest for an American Sociology: Robert E. Park and the Chicago School* (Montreal: McGill University Press, 1977).

72. Robert E. Park, "The Concept of Position in Sociology," *Publications of the American Sociological Society* 18 (1925): 7.

73. Louis Wirth, *The Ghetto* (New Brunswick, NJ: Transaction Publishers, 1997). Hasia Diner's lengthy introduction to this edition is the best treatment of Wirth's biography and Jewish identity to date.

74. Wirth, *The Ghetto,* lxv, 6.

75. Wirth, *The Ghetto,* 18, 38.

76. Wirth, *The Ghetto,* 129, 125

77. Maurice Fishberg, *Jews: A Study of Race and Environment* (New York: Scribner's, 1911), 163–164.

78. Wirth, *The Ghetto,* 82.

79. Louis Wirth, "The Ghetto," *American Journal of Sociology* 33 (1927): 68.

80. Wirth, *The Ghetto,* 256, 255, 290, 287, 267.

81. Deborah Dash Moore, *At Home in America: Second Generation New York Jews* (New York: Columbia University Press, 1981), 30.

82. Erich Rosenthal, "This Was North Lawndale: The Transplantation of a Jewish Community," *Jewish Social Studies* 22 (1960): 68.

83. Nathaniel Zalowitz, "The Future of the Ghetto in the United States," *Forverts,* July 4, 1926, 12.

84. Harry Wedeck, "New York's Ghetto: A Picture of the Mixture and Chaos of Tradition, Poverty, Illiteracy, Pedantry, and Novelty," *Jewish Advocate,* July 3, 1931, 3.

85. "New Ghetto," *Jewish Advocate,* April 16, 1935, 4.

4. The Nazi Ghettos of the Holocaust

1. Michał Głowiński, *The Black Seasons,* trans. Marci Shore (Evanston, IL: Northwestern University Press, 2005), 5–7.

2. Miriam Gebhardt, *Das Familiengedächtnis: Erinnerung im deutsch-jüdischen Bürgertum 1890 bis 1932* (Stuttgart: Franz Steiner Verlag, 1999), 91.

3. On countervailing trends in German Jewish culture in the first three decades of the twentieth century, see Shulamit Volkov, "The Dynamics of Dissimilation: *Ostjuden* and German Jews," in *The Jewish Response to German Culture: From the Enlightenment to the Second World War,* ed. Jehuda Reinharz and Walter Schatzberg (Hanover, NH: University Press of New England, 1985), 195–211; Michael Brenner, *The Renaissance of Jewish Culture in Weimar Germany* (New Haven: Yale University Press, 1996).

4. Yitzhak Arad, Yisrael Gutman, and Abraham Margoliot, eds., *Documents on the Holocaust: Selected Sources on the Destruction of the Jews of Germany and Austria, Poland, and the Soviet Union* (Jerusalem: Yad Vashem, 1981), 77–80, 39–42.

5. Jacob Borut, "Struggles for Space: Where Could Jews Spend Free Time in Nazi Germany?" *Leo Baeck Institute Year Book* 56 (2011): 307–350.

6. Avraham Barkai, "In a Ghetto without Walls," in *German-Jewish History in Modern Times, vol. 4: Renewal and Destruction 1918–1945,* ed. Michael A. Meyer and Michael Brenner (New York: Columbia University Press, 1998), 333–359; Saul Friedländer, "The New Ghetto," in *Nazi Germany and the Jews, vol. 1: The Years of Destruction, 1933–1939* (New York: HarperCollins, 1997), 113–144; Michael Brenner, "Historiography in a Cultural Ghetto: Jewish Historians in Nazi Germany," in *Modern Judaism and Historical Consciousness: Identities, Encounters, Perspectives,* ed. Christian Wiese and Andreas Gotzmann (Leiden: Brill, 2007), 356–367; idem., "Jewish Culture in a Modern Ghetto: Theater and Scholarship among the Jews

of Nazi Germany," in *Jewish Life in Nazi Germany: Dilemmas and Responses*, ed. Francis R. Nicosia and David Scrase (New York: Berghahn Books, 2010), 170–184.

7. On the "ghetto" in German Jewish discourse under the Nazis, see Guy Miron, *The Waning of Emancipation: Jewish History, Memory, and the Rise of Fascism in Germany, France, and Hungary* (Detroit: Wayne State University Press, 2011), 21–53; Dan Michman, *The Emergence of Jewish Ghettos during the Holocaust*, trans. Lenn J. Schramm (Cambridge: Cambridge University Press, 2011), 38–39.

8. Heinz Kellermann, "Ende der Emanzipation?" *Der Morgen* 9 (August 1933): 174.

9. Karl Julius Riegner, "Brücken zum Deutschtum," *Der Morgen* 10 (February 1935): 508.

10. Michael A. Meyer, ed., *Joachim Prinz, Rebellious Rabbi. An Autobiography—the German and Early American Years* (Bloomington: Indiana University Press, 2007).

11. Joachim Prinz, *Wir Juden* (Berlin: Erich Reiss, 1934), 26, 111, 147.

12. Joachim Prinz, "Das Leben ohne Nachbarn: Versuch einer erster Analyse. Ghetto 1935," *Jüdische Rundschau*, April 17, 1935, 3.

13. Alina Cała, "The Discourse of 'Ghettoization'—Non-Jews on Jews in 19th- and 20th-Century Poland," *Simon Dubnow Institute Yearbook* 4 (2005): 456.

14. This discussion of Hungary and Romania is based on Ezra Mendelsohn, *The Jews of East Central Europe between the World Wars* (Bloomington: Indiana University Press, 1983), 85–128, 171–211.

15. Michael A. Meyer and Michael Brenner, eds., *German-Jewish History in Modern Times, vol. 4: Renewal and Destruction, 1918–1945* (New York: Columbia University Press, 1996), 216–217.

16. The two novels are translated in Jacob Glatstein, *The Glatstein Chronicles*, ed. Ruth Wisse and trans. Maier Deshell and Norbert Guterman (New Haven: Yale University Press, 2010).

17. "Good Night, World," in *Sing, Stranger: A Century of American Yiddish Poetry: A Historical Anthology*, ed. Benjamin Harshav and trans. Barbara Harshav (Palo Alto, CA: Stanford University Press, 2006), 453.

18. Jacob Glatstein, "Tsvishn eygene: in farteydikung fun der geto," *Inzikh* 8 (May 1938): 120–122.

19. On this "return to the ghetto" debate in the Yiddish public sphere, see Joshua Karlip, *The Tragedy of a Generation: The Rise and Fall of Jewish Nationalism in Eastern Europe* (Cambridge, MA: Harvard University Press, 2013), 186–191; Miron, *The Waning of Emancipation*, 130–143; David H. Weinberg, *A Community on Trial: The Jews of Paris in the 1930s* (Chicago: University of Chicago Press, 1977), 171–197.

20. My summary of the debate over the "return to the ghetto" is indebted to Tcherikower's overview of the controversy in his article "Der yidisher gaystiker krizis

in shayn fun der prese" (The Jewish Spiritual Crisis in the Reflection of the Press), *Oyfn Sheydveg* 1 (April 1939): 201–217.

21. Shmuel Feigin, "Nakhon li-yeme ha-benayim," *Ha-'Olam*, October 6, 1938, 5.

22. "Tsurik in geto?" *Parizer haynt* (Paris Today), December 21, 1938.

23. The series was titled "Fun vanen ken kumen di hilf? (From Whence Can Come the Help?), and it appeared in the New York Yiddish daily *Der Tog* (The Day) from October 23 to November 19, 1938. Qtd. in Tcherikower, "Der krizis," 208.

24. The article appeared in *Yidishe kultur: Hoydesh-shrift fun dem alveltlekhn yidishn kultur-farband* 2 (December 1938): 1–6. Qtd. in Tcherikower, "Der yidisher krizis," 211.

25. Qtd. in Tcherikower, "Der krizis," 208.

26. The two-part article appeared in *Der Tog*. The first part was titled "Kenen mir zikh sheyden mit der velt?" (Can We Separate from the World?) and appeared on October 21, 1938; the second was called "Mir zaynen nit aleyn" (We Are Not Alone) and ran on November 19, 1938. Qtd. in Tcherikower, "Der yidisher krizis," 210.

27. "Tsurik in geto?"

28. Tcherikower, "Der krizis," 213.

29. Qtd. in Friedländer, *Nazi Germany and the Jews, vol. 1*, 143.

30. Qtd. in Michman, *The Emergence of Jewish Ghettos during the Holocaust*, 40.

31. Arad, et al., *Documents of the Holocaust*, 111; qtd. in Michman, *The Emergence of Jewish Ghettos*, 34.

32. On Nazi *Judenforschung* ("Jew research"), see Max Weinreich, *Hitler's Professors: The Part of Scholarship in Germany's Crimes against the Jewish People* [1946], 2nd ed. (New Haven: Yale University Press, 1999); Alan Steinweis, *Studying the Jew: Scholarly Antisemitism in Nazi Germany* (Cambridge, MA: Harvard University Press, 2006).

33. Peter-Heinz Seraphim, *Das Judentum im osteuropäischen Raum* (Essen: Essener Verlagsanstalt, 1938). On Seraphim's book, see Michman, *The Emergence of Jewish Ghettos*, 45–60.

34. Seraphim, *Das Judentum im osteuropäischen Raum*, 355–356; qtd. in Michman, *The Emergence of Jewish Ghettos*, 48–49.

35. Michman concedes that there is no "'smoking gun'—no document or memorandum written by Heydrich himself or one of his close aides—that provides unequivocal evidence that Nazi officials who dealt with Jewish affairs, especially in Heydrich's circle, ever read Seraphim's book." He nonetheless holds that the acquisition of some familiarity with its contents, however indirectly, offers the only convincing explanation for Heydrich's retreat at the November 12 meeting from his earlier support for a metaphorical "ghetto" for German Jews. See Michman, *The Emergence of Jewish Ghettos*, 56.

36. On this new stage in the segregation of German and Austrian Jews, see Konrad Kwiet, "Without Neighbors: Daily Living in *Judenhäuser*," in *Jewish Life in Nazi Germany: Dilemmas and Responses*, 117–148.

37. The literature on these two ghettos is immense. On Łódź, see Isaiah Trunk, *Łódź Ghetto: A History*, ed. and trans. Robert Moses Shapiro (Bloomington: Indiana University Press, 2006); Andrea Löw, *Juden im Getto Litzmannstadt: Lebensbedingungen, Selbstwahrnehmung, Verhalten* (Göttingen: Wallstein Verlag, 2006); Gordon J. Horwitz, *Ghettostadt: Łódź and the Making of a Nazi City* (Cambridge, MA: Harvard University Press, 2008). On Warsaw, see Yisrael Gutman, *The Jews of Warsaw 1939–1943: Ghetto, Underground, Revolt*, trans. Ina Friedman (Bloomington: Indiana University Press, 1982); Barbara Engelking and Jacek Leociak, *The Warsaw Ghetto: A Guide to the Perished City*, trans. Emma Harris (New Haven: Yale University Press, 2009). On changes in the size of the Warsaw Ghetto's population, which as a result of a forced influx of Jews from the region reached a height of 445,000 in March 1941, see Gutman, *The Jews of Warsaw*, 63.

38. Geoffrey Megargee and Martin Dean, eds., *The United States Holocaust Memorial Museum Encyclopedia of Camps and Ghettos, Volume II: Ghettos in German-Occupied Eastern Europe* (Bloomington: Indiana University Press, 2012).

39. For a historical overview of the historiography of ghettos, see Tim Cole, "Ghettoization," in *The Historiography of the Holocaust*, ed. D. Stone (New York: Palgrave Macmillan, 2004), 65–87.

40. Arad et al., *Documents of the Holocaust*, 111.

41. See Dan Michman, "Why Did Heydrich Write the *Schnellbrief*? A Remark on the Reason and on Its Significance," *Yad Vashem Studies* 32 (2004): 433–447.

42. Christopher Browning, *The Origins of the Final Solution: The Evolution of Nazi Jewish Policy, September 1939–March 1942* (Lincoln: University of Nebraska Press, 2004), 111–168.

43. Browning, *The Origins of the Final Solution*, 113.

44. Michman, *The Emergence of Jewish Ghettos*, 74–75.

45. See, for example, Horwitz's *Ghettostadt*, which situates the creation of the Łódź Ghetto in the larger Nazi project of transforming Łódź into a model German city (renamed Litzmannstadt), populated in part by ethnic Germans "repatriated" from the Soviet Union.

46. H. G. Adler, *Theresienstadt 1941–1945: The Face of a Coerced Community*, trans. Belinda Cooper (Cambridge: Cambridge University Press, 2017), 90.

47. Randolph L. Braham, *The Politics of Genocide: The Holocaust in Hungary*, vol. 1 (New York: Columbia University Press, 1981), 538.

48. The best source on the various stages of ghettoization in Budapest—from conception to implementation to revision—is Tim Cole, *Holocaust City: The Making of a Jewish Ghetto* (New York: Routledge, 2003). Cole gives a number of 44,416 for

the population of "unprotected Jews" who lived in just over 240 buildings in the Pest ghetto from when it was sealed on December 10, 1944 (218).

49. Estimates for the number of "protected" Jews range from 15,600 to as many as 35,000. See Cole, *Holocaust City,* 205.

50. Debórah Dwork and Robert Jan van Pelt, *Holocaust: A History* (New York: W. W. Norton, 2002), 217.

51. Chaim Aron Kaplan, *Megilat yesurin: yoman geto Varshah,* ed. Nahman Blumenthal (Tel Aviv: Am Oved, 1966), 95.

52. Yitskhok Rudashevksi, *The Diary of the Vilna Ghetto, June 1941–April 1943,* trans. Percy Matenko (Israel: Ghetto Fighters House, 1972), 29–30.

53. Mark Dworzecki, *Yerushalayim de-lite in kamf un umkum* (Paris: Yidish-natsionaler arbeter farband in amerike un yidisher folksfarband in frankraykh, 1948), 64.

54. The Yiddish is *abi tsvishn yidn.* Dworzecki, *Yerushalayim de-lite in kamf un umkum,* 64.

55. Yeshayahu Spiegel, "Di mishpokhe Lipshits geyt in geto," in *Likht funem abgrunt: geto-novelen* (New York: Futuro Press, 1952), 44. This quotation also appears in the manuscript original of the story, dated to March 1940, which was initially titled in Yiddish, "M'hot gekokht barilkes" (One Cooked Pears). See Yehiel Szeintuch, *Yeshayahu Spiegel—Proza Sipurit mi-geto Lodz* (Jerusalem: Magnes Press, 1995).

56. Kaplan, *Megilat yesurin,* 351.

57. Emanuel Ringelblum, *Kesovim fun geto,* vol. 1 (Warsaw: Yiddish bukh, 1961), 175; *Notes from the Warsaw Ghetto: The Journal of Emanuel Ringelblum,* ed. and trans. Jacob Sloan (New York: McGraw-Hill, 1958), 82.

58. Yosef Kermish, ed., *'Itonut ha-mahteret ha-Yehudit be-Varshah, vol. 1: Mai 1940–Yanuar 1941* (Jerusalem: Yad Vashem, 1979), 44–52, 45–46, 46. Emphasis mine.

59. Kermish, ed., *'Itonut ha-mahteret ha-Yehudit be-Varshah,* 198–202, 198.

60. Kermish, ed., *'Itonut ha-mahteret ha-Yehudit be-Varshah,* 404–405, 404.

61. Yosef Kermish, ed., *'Itonut ha-mahteret ha-Yehudit be-Varshah, vol. 2: Februar–Yuni 1940* (Jerusalem: Yad Vashem, 1979), 234–236.

62. Reinhart Koselleck, "'Space of Experience' and 'Horizon of Expectation': Two Historical Categories," in *Futures Past: On the Semantics of Historical Time,* trans. Keith Tribe (New York: Columbia University Press, 2004), 255–275.

63. Kaplan, *Megilat yesurin,* 400.

64. Ringelblum, *Kesovim fun geto, vol. 1,* 239.

65. Oskar Rosenfeld, *In the Beginning Was the Ghetto: Notes from Łódź,* ed. Hanno Loewy and trans. Brigitte M. Goldstein (Evanston, IL: Northwestern University Press, 2002), 229, 13, 74.

66. On Ringelblum and the Oyneg Shabes group, see Samuel D. Kassow, *Who Will Write Our History? Rediscovering a Secret Archive from the Warsaw Ghetto* (New York: Vintage, 2009).

67. ARG 455 Ring I 428. RG-15.079M. Konspiracyjne archiwum getta Warszawskiego: Archiwum Ringelbluma. United States Holocaust Memorial Museum Archives, Washington, DC. Translated from the Polish by Katarzyna Pietrzak.

68. Josef Zelkowicz, "In Those Nightmarish Days," in *In Those Nightmarish Days: The Ghetto Reportage of Peretz Opoczynski and Josef Zelkowicz*, ed. Samuel D. Kassow and trans. David Suchoff (New Haven: Yale University Press, 2015), 285.

69. Zelkowicz, "In Those Nightmarish Days," 286.

70. Kaplan, *Megilat yesurin,* 506–507.

71. *Megilat yesurin,* 546.

72. Abraham Lewin, *A Cup of Tears: A Diary of the Warsaw Ghetto*, ed. Antony Polonsky and trans. Christopher Hutton (Oxford: Basil Blackwell, 1988), 157.

73. Rosenfeld, *In the Beginning Was the Ghetto,* 105–106.

74. It was by no means universally held that the nature of the Nazi assault on the Jews invalidated the possibility of Kiddush Hashem. Shimon Huberband (1909–1942), the Warsaw rabbi and member of Ringelblum's underground Oyneg Shabes archive, took a more expansive view of Kiddush Hashem and collated numerous testimonies of instances in which a Jew had given his life to save a fellow Jew or group of Jews under the Nazis. See Shimon Huberband, *Kiddush Hashem: Jewish Religious and Culture Life in Poland during the Holocaust*, ed. Jeffrey S. Gurock and Robert S. Hirt and trans. David E. Fishman (New York: Yeshiva University Press, 1987), 247–273.

75. Qtd. in Joshua D. Zimmerman, *The Polish Underground and the Jews, 1939–1945* (Cambridge: Cambridge University Press, 2015), 219.

76. Estimates of the duration of the Warsaw Ghetto Uprising differ widely. Without question, sporadic attacks by Jewish underground units continued in the wake of the SS commander Jürgen Stroop's May 16 declaration of victory and lasted through the end of May. While most of the bunkers were uncovered and destroyed, at least one bunker remained populated until January 1944. See Gutman, *The Jews of Warsaw 1939–1943,* 398–400.

77. Avinoam Patt, "The Jewish Heroes of Warsaw: The Meaning of the Revolt in the First Year after the Uprising," *American Jewish History* 103, no. 2 (2019): 147–175.

78. From Folder "Council of the Rescue of the Jews in Poland," page #508, WRB Files, FDR Library, Marist University, accessed March 19, 2019, http://www .fdrlibrary.marist.edu/_resources/images/wrb/wrb1436.pdf.

79. "The Battle of Ghettograd," *The Sentinel*, April 13, 1944, 6.

80. L. Hodes, "Di Yiddish-Daytshe milkhome," in *Geto in flamen: zamlbukh* (New York: American Federation of the General Jewish Workers' Union in Poland, 1944), 53.

81. See, for example, Box F20, File 11. RG-67.013M. Warsaw Ghetto Uprising, 8th anniversary, reports, 1951. The World Jewish Congress New York Office records. Series F. The United States Holocaust Memorial Museum Archives, Washington, DC.

82. Philip Friedman, *The Bibliography of the Warsaw Ghetto (On the Tenth Anniversary of the Uprising to the Warsaw Ghetto)* (New York: Jewish Book Council of America, 1953), 1.

83. Isaac I. Schwarzbart, *The Story of the Warsaw Ghetto Uprising: Its Meanings and Message* (New York: World Jewish Congress Organization Department, 1953), 22–23.

84. Schwarzbart, *The Story of the Warsaw Ghetto Uprising*, 23.

85. Hasia Diner, *We Remember with Reverence and Love: American Jews and the Myth of Silence after the Holocaust* (New York: NYU Press, 2010), 74; Samantha Baskind, *The Warsaw Ghetto in American Art and Culture* (State College, PA: Pennsylvania State Press, 2018). According to Baskind, "the Warsaw Ghetto narrative has been more prominent in American culture than any other account from the Holocaust but the story of Anne Frank" (13).

86. Box F20, File 11. RG-67.013M. Warsaw Ghetto Uprising, 8th anniversary, reports, 1951. The World Jewish Congress New York Office records. Series F. The United States Holocaust Memorial Museum Archives, Washington, DC. Emphasis mine.

87. Zelig Hirsh Kalmanovitch, "Der gayst in geto," *Yivo Bleter* XXX, no. 2 (Winter 1947), 170.

88. Kalmanovitch, "Der gayst in geto," 172.

5. The Ghetto in Postwar America

1. Louis Wirth, *The Ghetto* [1928] (New Brunswick: Transaction Publishers, 1998), 6, lxv.

2. *Report of the National Advisory Commission on Civil Disorders* (Washington, DC: U.S. Government Printing Office, 1968), 1.

3. Previous research on the Jewish-to-black transformation of the ghetto in the postwar era has generally focused on the change in the demographics and character of specific neighborhoods. For a book that, like my own, explores not just the socioeconomic but also the semantic implications of the "effective transfer of the concept of the ghetto from Jewish to black," albeit with a greater focus on the reverberations of this "transfer" in fiction and literature, see Eric Sundquist, *Strangers in the Land: Blacks, Jews, Post-Holocaust America* (Cambridge, MA: Harvard University Press, 2005).

4. "'Ghettos' in U.S.—or Propaganda?" *U.S. News & World Report,* August 21, 1967, 63.

5. See, for example, "Guilt by Verbal Association," *Wall Street Journal,* May 13, 1968, 16, which states, "Far from fencing in anybody in a ghetto, American society has tried hard to provide equal opportunities for Negroes as well as all other citizens."

6. Stanley Sanders, "I'll Never Escape the Ghetto," *Ebony* XXII, no. 10 (August 1967): 32.

7. Evelyn E. Smith, "Calliope and Gherkin and the Yankee Doodle Thing," in *The Best from Fantasy and Science Fiction: Nineteenth Series* (New York: Doubleday, 1971), 125.

8. On this effort to "Jim-Crow the neighborhoods," see Carl Nightingale, *Segregation: A Global History of Divided Cities* (Chicago: University of Chicago Press, 2013), 300–307.

9. "Our Own Battles. An Appeal to the People—Committee of One Hundred Points the Way," *Washington Bee,* November 22, 1913, 8.

10. "No Compromise!" *The Appeal,* March 3, 1917, 2.

11. W. E. B. Du Bois, *The Philadelphia Negro: A Social Study* (Philadelphia: University of Pennsylvania Press, 1899).

12. "The Ghetto," *The Crisis: A Record of the Darker Races* 1, no. 2 (December 1910): 20–21. On Du Bois's editorship of *The Crisis,* see David Levering Lewis, *W. E. B. Du Bois: Biography of a Race, 1868–1919* (New York: Henry Holt, 1993), 466–500.

13. The case was unanimous, though the court found the municipal ordinance unconstitutional on the grounds of its interference with "the right of the individual to acquire, enjoy, and dispose of his property" as he saw fit while leaving the infamous 1896 *Plessy v. Ferguson* case's "separate but equal" justification for segregation untouched. On this, see Roger L. Rice, "Residential Segregation by Law, 1910–1917," *Journal of Southern History* 34, no. 2 (1968): 179–199.

14. On the spread of restrictive covenants in particular, see Michael Jones-Correa, "The Origins and Diffusion of Racial Restrictive Covenants," *Political Science Quarterly* 115, no. 4 (Winter 2000–2001): 541–568.

15. For one example, see A. T. Clarke, "Ghetto: A Voice from Within," *The Crisis* 44, no. 2 (February 1937): 44–45, 59, which makes repeated reference to "the ghetto of Jim Crow."

16. St. Clair Drake, "The 'Internal Colony': Mere Analogy or Scientific Concept?" n.d. [c. 1974], typescript, 1–2, folder 8, St. Clair Drake Papers, Schomberg Center for Research in Black Culture, New York Public Library.

17. St. Clair Drake and Horace R. Cayton, *Black Metropolis: A Study of Negro Life in a Northern City* (Chicago: University of Chicago Press, 2015), 174–213, 379–397.

18. Charles Abrams, "Homes for Aryans Only: The Restrictive Covenant Spreads Legal Racism in America," *Commentary* 3, no. 5 (May 1947): 421.

19. National Committee on Segregation in the Nation's Capital, *Segregation in Washington* (Chicago, 1948), 21.

20. Robert C. Weaver, *The Negro Ghetto* (New York: Harcourt, Brace, & Co., 1948).

21. Consolidated Brief for the American Jewish Committee, B'nai B'rith (Anti-Defamation League), Jewish War Veterans of the United States of America, Jewish Labor Committee as Amicus Curiae, p. 5, *Shelley v. Kraemer* 334 U.S. 1 (1948). On the various covenant cases adjudicated in the Supreme Court from the 1920s to the 1950s, see Clement E. Vose, *Caucasians Only: The Supreme Court, the NAACP, and the Restrictive Covenant Cases* (Berkeley: University of California Press, 1959), and, more recently, Jeffrey D. Gonda, *Unjust Deeds: The Restrictive Covenant Cases and the Making of the Civil Rights Movement* (Chapel Hill: University of North Carolina Press, 2015).

22. Drake and Cayton, *Black Metropolis,* 432.

23. Jeffrey S. Gurock, *The Jews of Harlem: The Rise, Decline and Revival of a Jewish Community* (New York: NYU Press, 2016), 71.

24. Gilbert Osofsky, *Harlem: The Making of a Negro Ghetto, 1890–1930,* 2nd ed. (New York: Harper & Row, 1971), 130.

25. James Baldwin, "The Harlem Ghetto: Winter 1948," *Commentary* 3, no. 2 (February 1948): 169, 170.

26. On the role of New Deal housing agencies like the Home Owners Loan Corporation (HOLC) and the Federal Housing Administration (FHA) in embracing an appraisal and homeowners insurance system that systematically discriminated against neighborhoods with any black residents and consequently discouraged private banking institutions from granting mortgages to blacks seeking to escape "Black Belts" to buy homes in "white" suburban areas—in other words, redlining—see Kenneth T. Jackson, *Crabgrass Frontier: The Suburbanization of the United States* (New York: Oxford University Press, 1985), 190–218.

27. Arthur Hertzberg, *The Jews in America: Four Centuries of an Uneasy Encounter: A History* (New York: Columbia University Press, 1989), 309.

28. Qtd. in Edward S. Shapiro, *A Time For Healing: American Jewry since World War II* (Baltimore: Johns Hopkins University Press, 1995), 144.

29. Harry Gersh, "The New Suburbanites of the 50's," *Commentary* 17 (March 1954): 211, 215. For an insightful analysis of the respatializing of Jewish life with the move to suburbia and the ambivalence it engendered, see Riv-Ellen Prell, "Community and the Discourse of Elegy: The Postwar Suburban Debate," in *Imagining the American Jewish Community,* ed. Jack Wertheimer (Waltham, MA: Brandeis University Press, 2007), 67–90.

30. Shapiro, *A Time For Healing,* 147.

31. Simon Glustrom, "Some Aspects of a Suburban Jewish Community," *Conservative Judaism* (Winter 1957): 27–8. Qtd. in Prell, "Community and the Discourse of Elegy," 74.

32. Amitai Etzioni, "The Ghetto—A Re-Evaluation," *Social Forces* 37, no. 3 (March 1959): 257.

33. Jo Sinclair, *The Changelings* (New York: McGraw Hill, 1955). Sinclair was the pen name of Ruth Seid.

34. For pioneering studies of Jews in suburbia that underscored the resiliency of Jewish "in-group" ties, see Herbert J. Gans, "Park Forest: Birth of a Jewish Community," *Commentary* 11 (April 1951): 330–339; and Marshall Sklare and Joseph Greenbaum, *Jewish Identity on the Suburban Frontier: A Study of Group Survival in the Open Society* (Chicago: University of Chicago Press, 1967).

35. Albert I. Gordon, *Jews in Suburbia* (Westport, CT: Greenwood Press, 1959), 140.

36. Eugene Lipman and Albert Vorspan, *A Tale of Ten Cities: The Triple Ghetto in American Religious Life* (New York: Union of American Hebrew Congregations, 1962), 338–339. The concept of a "triple melting pot" was coined in 1944 by sociologist Ruby Jo Reeves Kennedy to refer to the growing prevalence of assimilation within the ranks of Catholics, Protestants, and Jews, which remained as separate religious blocs. See R. J. R. Kennedy, "Single or Triple Melting Pot? Intermarriage Trends in New Haven, 1870–1940," *American Journal of Sociology* 49, no. 4 (January 1944): 331–339.

37. Lipman and Vorspan, *A Tale of Ten Cities*, 341.

38. Philip Roth, *Operation Shylock* (New York: Simon & Schuster, 1993), 132.

39. Bruno Bettelheim, "Freedom from Ghetto Thinking," *Midstream* 8 (Spring 1962): 16–25.

40. "Judaism Urged to End 'Spirit of the Ghetto,'" *Chicago Sun Times*, February 7, 1963.

41. Judith R. Kramer and Seymour Leventman, *Children of the Gilded Ghetto: Conflict Resolutions of Three Generations of American Jews* (New Haven, CT: Yale University Press, 1961).

42. Simon Glustrom, *Living with Your Teenager: A Guide for Jewish Parents* (New York: Bloch, 1961), 84.

43. Richard J. Fein, "Jewishness: The Felt Ambiguity," *Judaism* 16 (1967): 134.

44. Mark Zborowski and Elizabeth Herzog, *Life Is With People: The Jewish Little-Town of Eastern Europe* (New York: International Universities Press, 1952). On the emergence of *shtetl* as a "keyword," see Jeffrey Shandler, *Shtetl: A Vernacular Intellectual History* (New Brunswick, NJ: Rutgers University Press, 2014).

45. Jewish Group Minutes, Box G50, Folder 4, Margaret Mead Papers, Collections of the Manuscript Division, Library of Congress.

46. Jewish Group Minutes, Box G50, Folder 3, Margaret Mead Papers, Collections of the Manuscript Division, Library of Congress.

47. Shapiro, *A Time For Healing,* 151.

48. On the phenomenon of nostalgia for the largest of the Jewish immigrant enclaves, see Hasia Diner, *Lower East Side Memories: A Jewish Place in America* (Princeton: Princeton University Press, 2000).

49. Richard F. Shepard, "Jewish Museum Depicts a Ghetto," *New York Times,* September 21, 1966, 44.

50. Allon Schoener, ed., *Portal to America: The Lower East Side, 1870–1925* (New York: Holt, Rinehart, and Winston, 1967).

51. From Alfred Kazin, "The Writer and the City," *Harper's* (December 1968), qtd. in Marshall Sklare, *Observing America's Jews* (Hanover, NH: University Press of New England, 1993), 140–141.

52. On the "new, more pessimistic Jewish response to city life" in the postwar era, see Eli Lederhendler, *New York Jews and the Decline of Urban Ethnicity, 1950–1970* (Syracuse, NY: Syracuse University Press, 2001), 12.

53. William J. Raspberry, "Rabbi Calls on Jews to Join Rights Fight," *Washington Post,* September 9, 1963, A4.

54. Irving Kristol, "The Negro Today Is Like the Immigrant Yesterday," *New York Times,* September 11, 1966, 51, 124–142.

55. Oscar Handlin, *The Uprooted,* 2nd ed. (Philadelphia: University of Pennsylvania Press, 2002). Chapter 6 of the book is titled "The Ghettos."

56. Handlin, *The Uprooted,* 129–130.

57. Oscar Handlin, *Fire-Bell in the Night* (Boston: Atlantic-Little, Brown, 1964), 97.

58. Oscar Handlin, *The Newcomers* (Cambridge, MA: MIT Press, 1959), 118.

59. The title of August Meier's and Elliott Rudwick's 1966 book is illustrative in this respect: *From Plantation to Ghetto* (New York: Hill and Wang, 1966).

60. Drake and Cayton, *Black Metropolis,* 204, 386.

61. Arnold Hirsch, *Making the Second Ghetto: Race and Housing in Chicago, 1940–1960* (Chicago: University of Chicago Press, 1998), 9, 17.

62. Michael Harrington, *The Other America: Poverty in the United States* (New York: Scribner, 2012), 143.

63. Charles E. Silberman, *Crisis in Black and White* (New York: Vintage, 1964), 39–40, 43.

64. On Clark and *Dark Ghetto,* see Daniel Matlin, *On the Corner: African American Intellectuals and the Urban Crisis* (Cambridge, MA: Harvard University Press, 2013), 36–122; Mitchell Duneier, *Ghetto: The Invention of a Place, the History of an Idea* (New York: Farrar, Straus and Giroux, 2017), 85–138.

65. Kenneth B. Clark, *Dark Ghetto: Dilemmas of Social Power,* 2nd ed. (Middletown, CT: Wesleyan University Press, 1989), 11.

66. Clark, *Dark Ghetto,* 81.

67. Clark, *Dark Ghetto,* 11, 12, 56, 63.

68. Gilbert Osofsky, "The Hebrew Emigrant Aid Society to the United States (1881–1883)," *Publications of the American Jewish Historical Society* 49 (March 1960): 173–187.

69. Gilbert Osofsky, "The Enduring Ghetto," *Journal of American History* 55, no. 2 (September 1968): 243.

70. Allan Spear, *Black Chicago: The Making of a Negro Ghetto, 1890–1920* (Chicago: University of Chicago Press, 1967), 226–227.

71. On PAT, see, most recently, Matthew F. Delmont, *Why Busing Failed: Race, Media, and the National Resistance to School Desegregation* (Berkeley: University of California Press, 2016), 23–53.

72. Bayard Rustin, "The Civil Rights Struggle," *Jewish Social Studies* 27, no. 1 (January 1965): 33–34.

73. *The Negro Family: The Case for National Action* (Office of Policy Planning and Research, United States Department of Labor, 1965), 48; reprinted in Lee Rainwater and Willian L. Yancey, *The Moynihan Report and the Politics of Controversy* (Cambridge, MA: MIT Press, 1967), 94.

74. William Ryan, "Savage Discovery: The Moynihan Report," *The Nation*, November 22, 1965; reprinted in Rainwater and Yancey, *The Moynihan Report and the Politics of Controversy*, 458. For a recent study of the Moynihan Report controversy and its reverberations, see Daniel Geary, *Beyond Civil Rights: The Moynihan Report and Its Legacy* (Philadelphia: University of Pennsylvania Press, 2015).

75. For a history and critique of the use of "damage imagery" in social-scientific literature on black Americans, see Daryl Michael Scott, *Contempt and Pity: Social Policy and the Image of the Damaged Black Psyche, 1880–1996* (Chapel Hill: University of North Carolina Press, 1997). On the tension between notions of "ghetto" and "neighborhood" in mid-twentieth-century social-scientific parlance, and the history of the on-again, off-again analogy between African American residential areas and ethnic communities, see Benjamin Looker, *A Nation of Neighborhoods: Imagining Cities, Communities, and Democracy* (Chicago: University of Chicago Press, 2015), 135–164.

76. Maryemma Graham and Amritjit Singh, eds., *Conversations with Ralph Ellison* (Jackson: University of Mississippi Press, 1995), 92.

77. Ralph Ellison, "A Very Stern Discipline," in *The Collected Essays of Ralph Ellison*, ed. John F. Callahan (New York: Modern Library, 1995), 726.

78. Graham and Singh, *Conversations with Ralph Ellison*, 93.

79. Albert Murray, *The Omni-Americans: New Perspectives on Black Experience and American Culture* (New York: Avon Books, 1970), 18, 65, 66–67, 70, 113, 111–112, 113. On Ellison's and Murray's rejection of the application of the word *ghetto* to black residential areas, see Matlin, *On the Corner*, 23–24.

80. W. E. B. Du Bois, "The Negro and the Warsaw Ghetto," in *Du Bois on Religion,* ed. Phil Zuckerman (Lanham, MD: Rowman & Littlefield, 2000), 199, 200.

81. For a close reading of Du Bois's "The Negro and the Warsaw Ghetto" that portrays the article as a "multidimensional performance" that conjoins without conflating Nazi antisemitism with antiblack racism, see Michael Rothberg, *Multidimensional Memory: Remembering the Holocaust in the Age of Decolonization* (Palo Alto, CA: Stanford University Press, 2009), 111–134.

82. On Syrkin, see Carole S. Kessner, *The Other New York Jewish Intellectuals* (New York: NYU Press, 1994), 51–70.

83. Marie Syrkin, *Blessed Is the Match: The Story of Jewish Resistance* (Philadelphia: Jewish Publication Society, 1947).

84. Marie Syrkin, "Can Minorities Oppose 'De Facto' Segregation?" *Jewish Frontier* 31, no. 8 (September 1964): 6.

85. "'De Facto' Segregation: A Discussion," *Jewish Frontier* 31, no. 10 (November 1964): 5.

86. "'De Facto' Segregation," 10. The argument over Syrkin's article is discussed in Michael E. Staub, *Torn at the Roots: The Crisis of Jewish Liberalism* (New York: Columbia University Press, 2002), 106–110.

87. Bertram R. Gold, "The Urban Crisis and Its Effect upon Jewish Communal Services," *Journal of Jewish Communal Service* 44 (1968): 32. Malcolm Muggeridge's letter, titled "Negro Quarters Not 'Ghetto,'" appeared in the May 5, 1968, edition of the *New York Times.*

88. On this attack, see David Halberstam, "2 Ghetto Worlds Meet in Brooklyn," *New York Times,* April 23, 1964, 41, 77.

89. Rustin, "The Civil Rights Struggle," 35.

90. James Baldwin, "Negroes Are Anti-Semitic because They Are Anti-White," *New York Times,* April 9, 1967.

91. Albert Maltz, "The Word Ghetto Has Changed Its Meaning," *Jewish Currents* 23, no. 7 (July 1969): 21.

92. Judith Coburn, "Passover in the Ghetto: This Year in Washington," *Village Voice,* April 10, 1969, 59.

93. Arthur I. Waskow, *The Freedom Seder: A New Haggadah for Passover* (Washington, DC: Micah Press, 1969), 17–20. On Jews for Urban Justice and the Freedom Seder, see Staub, *Torn at the Roots,* 163–169.

94. Richard Rothstein, *The Color of Law: A Forgotten History of How Our Government Segregated America* (New York: Liveright, 2017).

95. Melvin Jules Bukiet, "The Museum vs. Memory: The Taming of the Holocaust," *Washington Post,* April 18, 1993.

96. Cahan, *The Education of Abraham Cahan,* 355.

Conclusion

1. Susan H. Lees, "Jewish Space in Suburbia: Interpreting the Eruv Conflict in Tenafly, New Jersey," *Contemporary Jewry* 27, no. 1 (October 2007): 57.

2. Qtd. in Lees, "Jewish Space in Suburbia," 55.

3. William Julius Wilson, *The Truly Disadvantaged: The Inner City, the Underclass, and Public Policy* (Chicago: University of Chicago Press, 1987); William Julius Wilson, *When Work Disappears: The World of the New Urban Poor* (New York: Vintage, 1996).

4. Camilo José Vergara, *The New American Ghetto* (New Brunswick, NJ: Rutgers University Press, 1995).

5. On the seminal importance of images of space and place in hip-hop, see Murray Forman, *The 'Hood Comes First: Race, Space, and Place in Rap and Hip Hop* (Middletown, CT: Wesleyan University Press, 2002).

6. The list of rap songs that paint the "inner city" as a bleak, perilous place could fill a book, but here are the lyrics from Grandmaster Flash and the Furious Five's pioneering anthem, "The Message" (1982): "You'll grow in the ghetto livin' second-rate/And your eyes will sing a song called deep hate/The places you play and where you stay/Looks like one great big alleyway/You'll admire all the number-book takers/Thugs, pimps and pushers and the big money-makers/Drivin' big cars, spendin' twenties and tens/And you'll wanna grow up to be just like them, huh. . . . Don't push me 'cause I'm close to the edge/I'm trying not to lose my head/It's like a jungle sometimes/It makes me wonder how I keep from goin' under." From "The Message," E. Fletcher, M. Glover, S. Robinson, & J. Chase, performed by Grand Master Flash & The Furious Five, SugarHill SH 787, 1982, 45 rpm/7 in., © 1982 Sugar Hill Records, Ltd.

7. This is very much the tone of the lyrics for Lauryn Hill's 1998 single, "Every Ghetto, Every City," which reminisces on her upbringing in South Orange, New Jersey: "I was just a little girl/Skinny legs, a press and a curl/My mother always thought I'd be a star/But way before my record deal,/The streets that nurtured Lauryn Hill/Made sure that I'd never go too far/Every ghetto, every city and suburban place I've been/Make me recall my days in the New Jerusalem." From "Every Ghetto, Every City," Lauryn Hill, The Miseducation of Lauryn Hill, Ruffhouse CK 69035, 1998, CD, © ℗ 1998 Ruffhouse Records, LP.

8. J. E. Lighter, ed., *The Random House Historical Dictionary of American Slang, Volume 1, A–G* (New York: Random House, 1994), s.v. "ghetto-blaster," 886.

9. *Green's Dictionary of Slang*, s.v. "ghetto," https://greensdictofslang.com/search/basic?q=ghetto.

10. Roger Cohen, "What Will Israel Become?" *New York Times*, December 20, 2014, https://www.nytimes.com/2014/12/21/opinion/sunday/roger-cohen-what-will-israel-become.html.

11. Carolina Landsmann, "A Ghetto with Nuclear Bombs," *Ha'aretz,* September 8, 2017, https://www.haaretz.com/opinion/.premium-a-ghetto-with-nuclear-bombs-1 .5449259.

12. Giulio Meotti, "Israel's Ghetto Mentality," *Arutz Sheva. Israel National News,* December 20, 2013, http://www.israelnationalnews.com/Articles/Article.aspx/14265.

13. Daniel Greenfield, "The Ghetto Jew and Israel," *Arutz Sheva. Israel National News,* August 17, 2015, http://www.israelnationalnews.com/Articles/Article.aspx /17405.

14. See the film *Gaza Ghetto: Portrait of a Family, 1948–1984,* directed by Per-Åke Holmquist (1985; Stockholm: Konstnärsnämden; in Hebrew).

15. Melvin Goodman, "Gaza and the Warsaw Ghetto," *Counterpunch,* July 23, 2014 https://www.counterpunch.org/2014/07/23/gaza-and-the-warsaw-ghetto/. During Operation Cast Lead in 2009, the United Nations rapporteur on human rights Richard Falk claimed that Israel's treatment of the people of Gaza "evokes the worst kind of international memories of the Warsaw Ghetto." See "UN Human Rights Official: Gaza Evokes Memories of the Warsaw Ghetto," *Ha'aretz,* January 23, 2009 https://www.haaretz.com/1.5066744. Such comparisons have been vociferously countered: see Tamar May, "No, Gaza Is Not the Warsaw Ghetto," *Times of Israel,* August 10, 2014 http://blogs.timesofisrael.com/no-gaza-is-not-the-warsaw-ghetto/.

16. Odeh Bisharat, "Congratulations, Another Arab Ghetto in Israel is Born," *Ha'aretz,* November 20, 2017 https://www.haaretz.com/opinion/.premium -congratulations-another-arab-ghetto-in-israel-is-born-1.5466829.

17. Elias Khoury, *Les Enfants du Ghetto: Je m'appelle Adam,* trans. Rania Samara (Arles: Actes Sud, 2018), 108.

18. Donatella Calabi, *Venice, the Jews, and Europe, 1516–2016* (Venice: Marsilio, 2016).

ACKNOWLEDGMENTS

I began research on this book in earnest as a Kluge Fellow at the Library of Congress in the spring semester of 2013. My gratitude to the John W. Kluge Fellowship Program for endorsing my ambition to write a sweeping history of the word *ghetto* when the project was still at an embryonic stage is enormous. Over the course of this fellowship, I was able to carry out much of the research for what became Chapter 3 (on the migration of the word *ghetto* to America) while also drawing up a chapter plan for the book as a whole. Special thanks must go to the former head administrator of the fellowship program, Mary Lou Reker, as well as to the then-chief librarian of the Hebraica Division, Peggy Pearlstein, for their support of this project while I was in residence at the Kluge Center. I was honored to be invited back to the Library of Congress in the spring of 2015 to participate in Scholarfest, a celebration of the first fifteen years of the Kluge Center, where I participated in a public "lightning conversation" about my work in progress.

In the years since my Kluge Fellowship, I have benefited from several opportunities to workshop chapters and sharpen my overall argument in conferences, colloquia, and public lectures. I want to especially thank the Jewish studies colloquia at Brandeis and Yale and now at George Washington University (GW) for inviting me to present precirculated papers; the feedback I received at these meetings was highly fruitful. I was also fortunate to be asked to give talks at the University of Pittsburgh in the fall of 2015, where I spoke on the Jewish-to-black migration of the ghetto concept, and at two events held to mark the five hundredth anniversary of the

Venice Ghetto in 2016—one at the University of Pennsylvania, the other at a two-day conference at the Center for Jewish History in New York titled "The Ghetto and Beyond: The Jews in the Age of the Medici." All these presentations, including others given at the American Jewish Historical Society's biennial conference in 2014 and at a number of Association of Jewish Studies annual meetings, helped move this project forward.

For eight months in 2018, I held the Sosland Fellowship at the Jack, Joseph, and Morton Mandel Center for Advanced Holocaust Studies at the United States Holocaust Memorial Museum. This provided me with the time and resources to research and write my chapter on the Nazi ghettos of the Holocaust. I am grateful to the outstanding staff historians and librarians of the museum, as well as to the other fellows whose time in residence overlapped with my own, for their interest in my work. I am equally grateful to my former student, Katarzyna Pietrzak, who served as my research assistant during my fellowship and helped translate materials from Polish to English for me. Many thanks as well to the University Facilitating Fund of George Washington University, which financially supported my research in its latter phases.

There are a few individuals I would like to single out for mention. While I was still working on my previous book, at a time this project was merely a vague idea, Menachem Butler, as is his wont, sent me attachments of myriad articles on the subject of the ghetto. Ben Ravid, who knows more about the history of the Venice Ghetto than anyone, was a gracious supporter of this endeavor from the outset. His classic essay on the historical odyssey of the word *ghetto* "from geographical realia to historiographical symbol" sketched the contours of this project and was an early inspiration. Moreover, his reading of Chapter 1 of the manuscript was discerning and perceptive. I came to know Ken Stow (who knows more about the history of the Rome Ghetto than anyone) as a result of our mutual participation in the aforementioned 2016 conference at the Center for Jewish History. His lengthy, substantive responses to my many email queries while I was researching and writing Chapter 1 were invaluable, as were his comments on another essay I wrote on the ghetto for a forthcoming volume on key concepts in the study of antisemitism. I was delighted to host him to give a public talk and visit my seminar at GW in February 2017. Others who provided incisive readings of parts or all of the manuscript include Tyler Anbinder, David Biale, Eliyahu Stern,

James Loeffler, and Arie Dubnov. This leaves out the many who read portions of what became my manuscript in various seminars and colloquia; my thanks to them all. I would also like to commend the GW undergraduates who took my course on the history of the ghetto the two times I offered it while working on this project. Their probing questions and thoughtful insights helped make this a better book.

I am indebted to my editor at Harvard University Press, Joyce Seltzer, for helping me conceive an organization for the book at an early meeting at the Library of Congress in May 2013 and for commenting so trenchantly on my manuscript when it was finally complete. Her edits led directly to a tighter, leaner book. I am only sorry that, with her retirement, I will not have an opportunity to work with her again. The two anonymous readers for the press engaged closely with my manuscript and offered many useful suggestions. I was fortunate to be matched up with an editor as experienced and accomplished as Ian Malcolm upon Joyce's retirement; he expertly oversaw the transformation of the work from manuscript to book. Additional thanks to Kathi Drummy and Olivia Woods for responding promptly to all my questions and for helping shepherd the manuscript through the editorial process.

Any research project will have its share of lulls and dead ends, and rare is the author who is not affected at these times by spasms of worry and self-doubt. My wife, Alisa, who in the years since I began this study has built a flourishing private practice in clinical psychology, could always be counted on to help me through these moments and even extended periods with a ready ear and boundless patience. For that and so much else, I am beyond grateful. In my six years of work on this project, our son, Max, has grown into a handsome, studious runner, fascinated by history and politics, who takes everything in stride and brightens everyone's day; our daughter Sophie has blossomed from a curly-haired five-year-old into a striking, straight-haired eleven-year-old with exquisite artistic skill and baking prowess and a precocious understanding of real estate; and our youngest, Maddie, has gone from an infant to become a beautiful, blue-eyed kindergartener with a passion for learning and friendship. They make our lives full and rich. This book is dedicated to them.

ILLUSTRATION CREDITS

p. 18   Private collection/Bridgeman Images.

p. 23   Private collection/Bridgeman Images.

p. 30   Reproduced from Cecil Roth, *Venice* (Philadelphia: Jewish
               Publication Society, 1930).

p. 33   From Emmanuel Rodocanachi, *Le Saint-Siège et les Juifs. Le ghetto
               à Rome* (Paris, 1891). Bibliothèque Nationale de France.

p. 64   Lebrecht Music & Arts/Alamy Stock Photo.

p. 69   Bildarchiv der Österreichischen Nationalbibliothek, Vienna.

p. 77   Bildagentur-online/UIG/Bridgeman Images.

p. 92   Lebrecht Authors/Bridgeman Images.

p. 100   Reproduced from Charles S. Bernheimer, ed., *The Russian Jew in the
               United States* (Philadelphia: John C. Winston, 1905).

p. 104   Private collection/Bridgeman Images.

p. 114   Reproduced from Robert E. Park, Ernest W. Burgess, and Roderick
               D. Mackenzie, *The City* (Chicago: University of Chicago Press,
               1925), 55.

p. 116   Special Collections Research Center, University of Chicago Library.

p. 119   Reproduced from Maurice Fishberg, *The Jews: A Study of Race and
               Environment* (London: Walter Scott Publishing Co.;
               New York: Charles Scribner's Sons, 1911), 164.

p. 123   Author's collection.

p. 124   David Rumsey Historical Map Collection.

p. 138   United States Holocaust Memorial Museum, courtesy of
               Stephen Glick.

p. 141   United States Holocaust Memorial Museum, courtesy of
   (*top*)   Frank Morgens.

p. 141   United States Holocaust Memorial Museum, courtesy of
 (*bottom*)   Leopold Page Photographic Collection.
p. 160   Courtesy of the Jacob Rader Marcus Center of the American
              Jewish Archives, Cincinnati, Ohio, at americanjewisharchives.org.
pp. 164,165   Source: Google Books Ngram Viewer, http//books.google.com/
              ngrams.

INDEX

About, Edmond, 62, 63

Abrams, Charles, 169

Accademia della Crusca, 35

Addams, Jane, 101

African American culture, 186

African American experience: ghetto as keyword in, 7–8; "ghetto" identified with, 196; vs. immigrant experience, 183

African Americans: black–Jewish relations, 7–8, 167; in Chicago, 179; ghetto associated with, 2; males, 185, 186; migration from South, 179, 184; *Moynihan Report*, 185–186; pathologizing rhetoric applied to, 185; school segregation and, 185. *See also* America; Civil rights; Ghetto, black; Press, African American

Against Flaccus (Philo), 13–14

Age of the ghetto, 5–6. *See also* Judaism, premodern/pre-emancipation

Alexandria, 11

Alienation, in literature, 93

Allgemeine Zeitung des Judenthums (Philippson), 63

Ambivalence toward ghetto, 72–74

America: acculturation/assimilation in, 98, 105–106, 107, 114–115; connotations of ghetto in, 97; efforts to break up ghetto in, 106–107; immigration restriction in, 120; Jewish neighborhoods in, 86–87, 120–122; lack of knowledge of ghetto concept in, 86; religious liberty in, 110. *See also* African Americans; Chicago; Ghetto, American; Ghetto, black; Immigrants, to America; Jews, American; New York City

American Hebrew, The (periodical), 97, 101, 110–111

American Israelite (periodical), 108, 112

Americanization, 107, 115. *See also* Assimilation/acculturation

"Among One's Own: In Defense of the Ghetto" (Glatstein), 134

Amsterdam, 68, 74

Anachronism, association of ghetto with, 74

Ancient Map of the Noble City of Venice (Temanza), 24

Ancona, Italy, 33

Anglicization, 95–96

Anonymity, 129

Anschluss, 132, 133, 137

Antisemitism, 81, 170–172

Appeal, The (periodical), 167

Arrow Cross, 145–146

Arutz Sheva (news outlet), 198

Assimilation/acculturation: in America, 98, 105–106 (*see also* Americanization); coerced, 111; in England, 93, 95–96; in ghetto, 104; ghetto as counter-concept to, 85; hostility to, 189, 190; of immigrants, 114–115; incentives offered for, 112; negatives of, 135; pressure for, 89–90; study of, 114; viability of, 83

Assimilationism, 81

At the Crossroads (periodical), 135

Audeber, Nicolas, 38

Auerbach, Berthold, 67–68

Austria, 50, 132. *See also Individual cities*

Badge, identifying, 26, 34, 41, 61, 139, 147, 153. *See also* Clothing, identifying

Baldwin, James, 171–172, 191

Bane, Mary Jo, 3

Bankers, 27

Baptisms, 59–60. *See also* Conversions

Bari, Italy, 20

Barkai, Avraham, 128

Baron, Salo W., 12, 13

Baron de Hirsch Fund, 112

Bassi, Shaul, 10

"Bastille and Ghetto" (article), 79

Before the Ghetto (Katzman), 183

Begin, Menachem, 198

Ben Amitai, 112

Benvenuto, Immanuel, 41

Berlin, 89–90

Berliner, Abraham, 64

Bettelheim, Bruno, 174–175

"Between the Ghetto Walls," 150–151

Bingham, Theodore, 111

Bisharat, Odeh, 199

Black Americans. *See* African Americans; Ghetto, black; Segregation, African American

Black Chicago (Spear), 183

Black Metropolis (Drake and Cayton), 169, 170, 179

Blessed Is the Match (Syrkin), 189

Bohemia, 68–69, 70, 144

Bonini, Filippo Maria, 38–39

Book of the Vale of Tears (Ha-Kohen), 41

Boundaries, 46. *See also* Enclosures; Segregation

Brenner, Michael, 128

Breslau (Wrocław), enclosures in, 15–16

Brockhaus Conversation Lexicon, 67

Brockhaus Encyclopedia, 66

Bronzeville (Chicago), 169, 170, 179. *See also* Chicago; Ghetto, black

Browning, Christopher, 142, 143

Brown v. Board of Education, 181

Buchanan v. Warley, 168

Budapest, 145

Bukiet, Melvin Jules, 192–193

Bund (organization), 158

Burckhardt, Jakob, 62

Burgess, Ernest W., 113–114

Busing, 184

Cadorna, Raffaele, 64

Cahan, Abraham, 86, 101, 103–104, 107, 109, 112, 113, 194

Calabi, Donatella, 37

Calendar and Yearbook for Israelites in the Year (1847) 5607, 63

Campo Formio, Treaty of, 50

Cantarini, Isaac, 42

Careers: merchants, 30, 31; money-lenders, 27, 37, 59; restrictions on, 76–77 (*see also* Restrictions on Jews); trades associated with Jews, 90, 92

Carrying, on Sabbath, 45–46

Cayton, Horace, 169, 170, 171, 179, 186

Cesena, Italy, 20

Chain of Tradition (ibn Yahya), 41

Chakrabarty, Dipesh, 6

Changelings, The (Sinclair), 173

Chełmno, 154

Chicago: black population of, 179; concentric zones model of, 113–114; Jewish population in, 99, 101, 118, 120, 121; racial segregation in, 168–170

Chicago Defender (newspaper), 167

Chicago School, 113–120, 173, 178, 184

Children of the Ghetto (Zangwill), 91–97, 101–102, 200

Children of the Ghetto: My Name Is Adam (Khoury), 199–200

Children of the Gilded Ghetto (Kramer and Leventman), 175

Chmielnicki, Bohdan, 155

Chortkiv (Czortków), Galicia, 75

Christians: descriptions of ghettos by, 37–39; Judaism as threat to, 19–20, 52, 80 (*see also* Judaizing); segregation from Jews, 15–16, 17. *See also* Church, medieval; Popes; *Individual popes*

Chronicle of the Łódź Ghetto, 154

Church, medieval: anti-Jewish measures, 35; origins of ghettoization and, 15–21. *See also* Christians; Papal states; Popes; *Individual popes*

Civil rights, 177, 178, 185, 189. *See also* African Americans

Clark, Kenneth, 181–183, 185, 186, 187

Cleaver, Eldridge, 192

Clothing, identifying, 41, 55; under Nazis, 139; in papal states, 32; in Rome, 61; in Venice, 26. *See also* Badge, identifying; Restrictions on Jews; Rights, legal; Status, legal

Cohen, Roger, 198

Cologne, 12–13

Color line, 168, 179. *See also* Discrimination, housing; Segregation, African American

Commentary (magazine), 171, 172

Communists, 106–107

Concentric zones model, 113–114

Condotta, 29

Consciousness, Jewish. *See* Jewish consciousness/experience

Conversions: career and, 76; coerced, 59–60; in Spain, 18–19, 20. *See also* Baptisms; Restrictions on Jews

Coryat, Thomas, 38, 39

Council of Ten, 27

Covenants, restrictive. *See* Housing discrimination

Crime, blamed on Jews, 111

Crisis (periodical), 167

Crisis in Black and White (Silberman), 180

Cultural estrangement, 187, 188

Cultural ghetto, 128

Culture, American, 186–188

Culture of poverty, 180

Cum nimis absurdum (papal bull), 16, 31–33, 35, 41, 42

Curfew: in Holocaust ghetto, 154; in Rome, 59; in Venetian Ghetto, 29. *See also* Restrictions on Jews

Czortków (Chortkiv), Galicia, 75

D'Arco, Giovanni Battista Gherardo, 54–57

Dark Ghetto (Clark), 181–183, 185, 187

D'Azeglio, Massimo, 62, 63

Defamiliarization, 126

Defense against the Attacks on the Jewish People in a Book Entitled on the Influence of the Ghetto on the State (Frizzi), 56–57

Definitions, importance of, 4

Definitions of ghetto, 2–5, 35, 36–37, 56, 65–66; Auerbach's, 67–68; broadening of, 67–79; changes in, 193–194; malleability of term and, 135; in slang dictionaries, 197; Villanuova's, 39; Zangwill's, 93

Del Monte, Anna, 59

Deportations, 140, 144–145, 152, 154, 155–158, 159–160. *See also* Ghetto, Holocaust

Descriptions of ghettos, by Christians, 37–39

Desegregation of Jews. *See* Emancipation/liberation

"Desk Studies for Girls" (newspaper column), 101

Dictionaries: *Dictionnaire de la langue française*, 65; etymology of ghetto in, 42; *Fremdwörterbuch*, 70, 71; ghetto in, 35, 56, 65–66; *Grand dictionnaire du XIXe siècle*, 66; Italian, 35, 39; *Oxford English Dictionary*, 66

Dictionnaire de la langue française, 65

Discourse on the Situation of the Hebrews and in Particular Those Dwelling in the Illustrious City of Venice (Luzzatto), 47–48

Discrimination, 188

Discrimination, housing. *See* Color line; Housing discrimination; Redlining; Segregation, African American

Discrimination, racial, 185–186. *See also* Civil rights; Housing discrimination; Racism; Segregation, mandatory/legal

Disorientation, 147

Divorce, 66, 94–95. See also *Get*

Dmowski, Roman, 131

Dohm, Christian Wilhelm von, 52–53, 54, 55

Dolfin, Zacaria, 28, 29

Drake, St. Clair, 168–169, 170, 171, 179, 186

Dreamers of the Ghetto (Zangwill), 102–103

Dror (movement), 149

Du Bois, W. E. B., 167–168, 188–189

Dudum a felicis (papal bull), 34

Duneier, Mitchell, 3, 7

Dupaty, Charles-Marguerite-Jean-Baptiste Mercier, 59–60

Dwork, Debórah, 146

Dworzecki, Mark, 148

Early history of ghettos: establishment of Venetian Ghetto, 28–31; in European Middle Ages, 14–15, 20–21; fear of Jewish contagion and, 15–21; Jewish quarters and, 10–13; Judengasse (Frankfurt), 16–17; medieval church and, 15–21; objectives of ghetto and, 34–35; in papal states, 31–35; in Second Temple times, 13;

Spain and, 18–20; spread of concept, 34; spread of ghettos in Italy, 35–36; violence against Alexandrian Jews, 13–14

Eastern European Jews. *See* Ghetto, American; Ghetto, Holocaust; Immigrants, East European; Immigrants, to America; Jews, Bohemian; Jews, East European; Jews, Galician; Jews, Hungarian; Jews, Polish; Jews, Russian; Warsaw Ghetto

Ebony (periodical), 166

Economy: of ghetto, 59; Holocaust ghetto and, 152; impact of Jews on, 55–57; merchants, 30, 31; money-lenders, 27, 37, 59; trades associated with Jews, 90, 92

Edicts of Tolerance, 55

Education: of Jews, 118; school segregation, 181, 184

Efroykin, Israel, 135

Einsatzgruppen, 146

Ellison, Ralph, 186, 188

Emancipation/liberation, 5–6; ambivalence toward, 83–84; desirability of, 79–82; in Eastern Europe, 87; by French army, 49–51; ghetto as counter-concept to, 85; in Jewish identity, 126; loss of faith in, 135 (*see also* Return to ghetto); modern Judaism associated with, 5–6; skepticism of narrative of, 127, 129; temporalization of concepts and, 74–75; in Verona, 44; viability of, 83. *See also* Homeland, Jewish; Israel; Zionism

Embassy to Gaius (Philo), 13–14

Emigration: of Eastern European Jews, 87–92; in Nazi era, 132, 138. *See also* Immigrants

Enclaves, immigrant/ethnic. *See* Ghetto, American; Immigrant enclaves/ghettos; Immigrants; New York City

Enclosures, 10; carrying on Sabbath and, 45–46; *Fondaco dei Tedeschi*, 31; in Frankfurt, 17; Jewish Question and, 10; of Roman Ghetto, 32, 33; in Spain, 18; in Speyer, 14–15; of Venetian Ghetto, 29; in Wrocław (Breslau), 15–16

Encyclopedia of Camps and Ghettos (United States Holocaust Memorial Museum), 3

Encyclopedia of the Ghetto (Singer), 152

Endelman, Todd, 92

"Enduring Ghetto, The" (Osofsky), 184

England, 102; assimilation in, 95–96; expulsion from, 20, 91; immigrants in, 90–97; lack of segregation in, 46–47; as waypoint for Eastern European Jews, 96–97, 102

Enlightenment, Jewish, 56

Epstein, Jacob, 109

Eruv, 45, 195

Escape from ghetto. *See* Emancipation/liberation

Essay on the Physical, Moral and Political Reformation of the Jews (Grégoire), 53–54

Ethnic "succession," 178

Etymology of ghetto, 1, 42–43, 66

Etzioni, Amitai, 173

Eugenicists, Jewish "physical type" and, 117

Europe: extent of ghettoization in, 47; "ghetto" as marker of, 97. *See also* Middle Ages, European; *Individual cities*; *Individual countries*

Europe, Eastern, 87, 139. *See also* Jews, East European; *Individual countries*

Évian Conference, 134

Exit from ghetto. *See* Emancipation/
liberation; Identity, Jewish; Judaism,
modern; Modernity

Expulsion, 17, 21, 33; compared to
Nazi actions, 156; from England, 91;
in Frankfurt, 20–21; vs. ghetto, 31; in
Nazi era, 132; from Spain, 20, 25

Eynhorn, Dovid, 136

Fagiuoli, Giovanni Battista, 39

Familiants Laws, 70

"Family Lipschitz Goes Into the Ghetto,
The" (Spiegel), 148

Fear of Isaac (Cantarini), 42

Feigin, Shmuel, 135

Fein, Richard, 175

Ferdinand II of Aragon, 19

Ferrari, Ottavio, 42

Ferrer, Vincent, 19

Fiction, Jewish, 67–78. *See also*
Literature

Fiddler on the Roof (musical), 176

Final Solution, 142, 144. *See also*
Deportations; Ghetto, Holocaust

Fishberg, Maurice, 117

Flaccus, 13–14

Florence, 35, 36

Fondaco dei Tedeschi, 31

Foreign merchant district, 15. *See also*
Jewish quarters

Forward (periodical), 86, 121

Foundry, 22

Fourth Lateran Council, 15, 34

France: expulsion from, 20; Jewish
enclaves in, 89; Jewish Question in,
54; lack of segregation in, 47; liberation of Italian ghettos and, 49–51;
mandatory segregation in, 16. *See also*
Napoleon

Frankfurt, 20–21; *Judengasse*, 16–17,
39, 51, 53; possibility of expulsion in,
20–21; resistance to segregation in, 40

Franzos, Karl E., 75–78

"Freedom from Ghetto Thinking"
(Bettelheim), 174

Freedom Seder, 192

Fremdwörterbuch, 70, 71

French army, 49–51, 60–61

French Revolution, 60, 79. *See also*
French army

Friedländer, Saul, 128

Friedman, Philip, 159

Friedrich III (Holy Roman Emperor), 17

Frizzi, Benedetto, 56–57

From the Ghetto: Stories (Kompert),
68–69

Frumkin, A., 89

Galician Jews, 109. *See also* Jews,
East European

Gates. *See* Enclosures

Gaza, 199

Gebhardt, Miriam, 126

Genealogy, 5

Genoa, 25

Genocide, 142

Geographic concentration, 10–13.
See also Segregation

German (language): *Fremdwörterbuch*,
70, 71; "ghetto" in, 66–67; *Ghettoliteratur*, 67–78

German cities: expulsion from, 20.
See also German empire; Germany;
Individual cities

German empire: lack of segregation in,
47; segregation in, 14–15. *See also*
Individual cities

Germany: Eastern European immigrants
in, 89–90; Jewish Question in, 54.

See also Ghetto, Holocaust; Holocaust; Nazis

Gersh, Harry, 172

Get, 41–43, 66, 94–95

Geto, 10

Geto Nuovo, 23

Ghetto, 36, 104; as adjective, 2; ambivalence toward, 83–84; attributes of, 3–4, 13, 65; beginning of, 11–48 (*see also* Early history of ghettos; Venetian Ghetto); changes in meanings / implications of, 2, 65, 67–79; as concept, 85; current use of, 7, 197; debate over meaning of, 57 (*see also* Definitions of ghetto); definitions of (*see* Definitions of ghetto); dismantling of, 87; etymology of, 1; identified with experience of black Americans, 175, 186–188, 196; interpretation of, 178; in Italian dictionaries, 35; Jewish attitudes toward, 40–48; justification of, 52; vs. labor camp, 4; as marker of Europe, 97; as metonym for Jewish people, 56; migration into other languages, 65; as multicultural phenomenon, 163; multiple meanings of, 161–162; mutation of concept of, 34; objections to use of term, 112–113, 186–187; objectives of, 34–35; origin of term, 10–11, 21–26; ownership of term, 7–8, 189–194; periodization of, 5–6; pronunciation of, 24, 25; razing of, 51, 64; as signifier of Jewish past, 175; as signifier of Jewish segregation, 54; spread of concept of, 34; as state of mind, 79; synonymous with traditional Jewish society, 87; temporality of, 178; transference of concept of, 172, 178–188 (*see also* Ghetto, black); universalization of, 6, 7, 202; use of

term, 36; weakening of Italian referent for, 78

Ghetto, American: anxiety about creation of in suburbs, 195–196; decline of, 172–177; defenses of, 107–112; depopulation of, 196; efforts to break up, 106–107; "gilded ghetto," 174–175; nostalgia for, 176–177; objection to use of "ghetto" label for, 112–113; overlapping of race and class and, 196; as place name, 122; sketches of, 109; social deterioration of, 196; transition to black ghetto, 170–172; as way station, 107–109, 114; Wirth on, 115–120. *See also* America; Ghetto, black; Ghetto, immigrant; Immigrants, to America; Jews, American; New York City

Ghetto, black: compared to Jewish ghetto, 188–193; involuntary nature of, 181–185; Jews in, 170–172; in music, 196–197; pathologizing rhetoric applied to, 185; as permanent, 179–181; racism and, 180–181; references to, 166–168; relation with immigrant ghetto, 179–188; rise in references to, 165–166; skepticism about, 166; studies of emergence of, 183–184; uprisings / violence in, 164, 191; white majority's complicity in existence of, 182. *See also* African Americans; America; Discrimination, housing; Ghetto, American; Segregation, African American

Ghetto, Holocaust, 151; chronicles of, 152–157; compared to black ghettos, 191; conditions in, 126, 152, 159–160; creation of ghettos proper, 140, 142; diversity of, 143; goal of, 152; Holocaust Memorial Museum's

Ghetto, Holocaust (*continued*)
definition of, 3; in Hungary, 145;
Jewish attitudes toward, 148; in
Jewish historical consciousness,
149–150; Jewish houses, 140, 145;
official names of, 146; popular
understandings of Nazi ghettoization
policy, 142; vs. premodern ghetto,
151; relevance to black experience,
188–189; as return to Middle Ages,
150, 153–157 (*see also* Return to
ghetto); shift in essential nature of,
143–144; time in, 154; unprecedented
nature of, 151–152, 155–156, 160.
See also Deportations; Final Solution;
Jews, Polish; Return to ghetto; Warsaw
Ghetto; *Individual ghettos*
Ghetto, immigrant, 90–97, 102, 163, 179
Ghetto, new, 85
"Ghetto, The" (column), 167–168
Ghetto, The (Wirth), 11, 79, 113,
115–120, 163, 173
Ghetto, voluntary: first ghettos as,
116–117; as literary conceit, 113.
See also Ghetto, immigrant; Immigrant
enclaves/ghettos; Segregation,
voluntary
"Ghetto and Emancipation" (Baron), 12
"Ghetto and Its Poets, The" (Gold-
baum), 78
Ghetto and the Jews of Rome, The
(Gregorovius), 43, 62
Ghetto benches, 131, 136
Ghetto bend, 117–118
Ghettograd, Battle of, 158–159. *See also*
Warsaw Ghetto Uprising
Ghetto in Flames (publication), 159
Ghettoization, under Nazis, 138–140
Ghettoliteratur, 67–78. *See also*
Literature

Ghetto Nuovo, 10. *See also* Venetian
Ghetto
"Ghetto of Yesterday and Today, The"
(*Morning Journal*), 111
Ghetto Takes Shape, A (Kusmer), 183
"Ghetto thinking," 175
Ghetto tourism, 37
"Gilded ghetto," 174–175
Ginsburg, Ruth Bader, 201
Glatstein, Jacob, 132–133
Glustrom, Simon, 173, 175
Gnignati, Paolo, 201
Gold, Bertram H., 190–191
Gold, Michael, 106–107
Goldbaum, Wilhelm, 78
Golden Sr., Mrs. Bernard, 195
Goldstein, Israel, 161
Goodbye, Columbus (Roth), 174
"Good Night, World" (Glatstein),
132–133
Gorani, Joseph (Giuseppe), 60
Gordon, Albert I., 173–174
Göring, Hermann, 139
Głowiński, Michał 125
Graceful Wreath (Benvenuto), 41
Graetz, Heinrich, 63
Grand dictionnaire du XIXe siècle, 66
Great Britain: immigrants in, 92.
See also England; London
Great Deportation of Warsaw Jewry,
155–157
Great Migration, 179, 184
Green's Dictionary of Slang, 197
Grégoire, Henri Baptiste, 53–54, 55
Gregorovius, Ferdinand, 43, 62, 63
Guido (papal legate), 15

Ha'aretz (periodical), 198
Habsburg Empire, restrictions on Jews
in, 70

HaKohen, David ben Hayim, 25
Ha-Kohen, Joseph, 41
Halakhah, segregation and, 45–46
Halévy, Fromental, 57–58, 61, 65
Halpern, Ben, 190
Handlin, Oscar, 178, 180
Hapgood, Hutchins, 109–110
Harlem, 171–172, 186, 187.
    See also Ghetto, American; Ghetto,
    black
Harlem (Osofsky), 183
"Harlem Ghetto, The: Winter 1948"
    (Baldwin), 171
Harlem Youth Opportunities Unlimited
    (HARYOU), 181
Harper's (periodical), 99, 177
Harrington, Michael, 180
Ha-Shomer ha-Tsa'ir (The Young
    Guard), 150–151
Haskalah, Italian, 56
Hat, identifying, 41. See also Clothing,
    identifying
Hawthorne, Nathaniel, 62
Hebrew Emigrant Aid Society, 184
Hellenistic Diaspora, 11. See also Jews,
    Alexandrian
Herzl, Theodor, 81–83, 85, 95
Herzog, Elizabeth, 175–176
Heydrich, Reinhard, 137–138, 139–140,
    142
Hip-hop, 196–197
Hirsch, Arnold, 179–180
History, Jewish: debate over transfer-
    ence of ghetto concept and, 176–177;
    "ghetto" as signifier for, 175; relevance
    of, 160. See also Jewish consciousness/
    experience
History of the Jews from Antiquity to
    the Present (Graetz), 63
Holland, lack of segregation in, 47

Holocaust: ghetto vs. labor camp in,
    4; resistance during, 189 (see also
    Warsaw Ghetto Uprising); skepticism
    about, 155–156. See also Deporta-
    tions; Ghetto, Holocaust; Holocaust
    Memorial Museum, U.S.; Nazis
Holocaust ghetto. See Ghetto, Holocaust
Holocaust Memorial Museum, U.S., 3,
    193–194
Homeland, Jewish, 83. See also Emanci-
    pation/liberation; Israel; Zionism
"Horizon of expectation," 151
Horthy, Miklos, 131, 145
House of Conversions (Casa dei
    Catecumeni), 59, 60
Housing discrimination, 169, 170,
    171, 172, 179; ghetto concept used
    to justify, 187; against Jews, 173;
    outlawing of, 196. See also Color
    line; Redlining; Segregation, African
    American
How the Other Half Lives (Riis),
    104–105
Hull House Maps and Papers (Addams),
    101
Hungary, 131–132, 145
Huozmann, Rüdiger, 14
Hyman, Paula, 89

Ibn Yahya, Gedalyah, 41
Identification, physical, 147. See also
    Badge, identifying; Clothing,
    identifying
Identity, Jewish: emancipation in, 126;
    "ghetto" and, 165; in suburbs, 173.
    See also Jewish experience/conscious-
    ness; Judaism, modern; Judaism,
    premodern/pre-emancipation
"I'll Never Escape the Ghetto"
    (Sanders), 166

Immigrant enclaves/ghettos, 13, 88–97. *See also* Ghetto, American; Ghetto, immigrant

Immigrant fiction, 86

Immigrants, East European, 107; enclaves, 13, 88–92; in Germany, 89–90; in Great Britain, 90–97; in Vienna, 88. *See also* Immigrants, to America

Immigrants, Puerto Rican, 178, 181

Immigrants, Russian, 107

Immigrants, to America, 86; assimilation of, 114–115; defense of ghetto by, 107; England as waypoint for, 96–97, 102; ethnic "succession" and, 178; experience of, 178, 183; German Jewish, 105; ghetto as way station for, 114; in literature, 101–104; Puerto Rican, 178, 181. *See also* Ghetto, American; Immigrants, East European; Jews, American

Immigration restriction, 105, 120

Influence of the Ghetto on the State, The (D'Arco), 54–57

Innocent XI (pope), 59

Inquisition, 19

Integration, cultural: of immigrants, 115; Jewish, 54. *See also* Assimilation/acculturation

Introspection (periodical), 133–134

Iron Guard, 132

Isaacs, Samuel, 97

Isabella I of Castile, 19

Isolation: ghetto as metaphor for, 126; Wirth on, 115–120. *See also* Segregation; Separatism

Israel, 197–200

Italian (language), 35, 42

Italian Jews, 6. *See also* Italy; Papal states; Roman Ghetto; Venetian Ghetto

Italy: Jewish Question in, 54–57; segregation in, 16, 20; spread of ghettos in, 35–36. *See also* Papal states; Roman Ghetto; Rome; Venetian Ghetto; Venice

Jargowsky, Paul, 3

Jetty, 25

"Jew," use of term, 8

Jewish Advocate (periodical), 121–122

Jewish consciousness/experience. *See* Jewish experience/consciousness

Jewish Currents (periodical), 192

Jewish Daily Forward (periodical), 89

Jewish Enlightenment, 56

Jewish experience/consciousness: decline of "ghetto" as signifier for, 175–176; ghetto as structuring metaphor of, 67–78; ghetto in, 5–7, 51–52, 130; Holocaust ghetto in, 149–150; shtetl and, 175–176; social separatism and, 96. *See also* Identity, Jewish; Judaism, modern; Judaism, premodern/pre-emancipation

Jewish Fighting Organization (ŻOB), 157, 158. *See also* Warsaw Ghetto Uprising

Jewish Frontier (periodical), 189

Jewish Gazette (periodical), 112

Jewish houses, 140, 145

Jewish Labor Underground, 158

Jewish Life (periodical), 188

Jewish Messenger (periodical), 97–98, 106

Jewish Middle Ages, 12

Jewish Museum of New York, 176

Jewish Publication Society of America, 93, 101–102

Jewish quarters: in American cities, 86; in Berlin, 89; vs. ghetto, 13; institution of, 10–13; *Judengasse* (Frankfurt), 16–17, 20, 39, 51, 53; *Judenstadt* (Prague), 51; *Judenstrasse*, 97–98; Juiveries, 54; in Spain, 18. *See also* Segregation

Jewish Question, 54; enclosure and, 10; Nazi plans for, 139, 143; new understanding of, 52. *See also* Rights, legal; Status, legal

Jewish society, traditional, 68, 87. *See also* Judaism, premodern/pre-emancipation

Jewish Stories (Sacher-Masoch), 78–79

Jewry in the Territory of Eastern Europe (Seraphim), 139

Jews, Alexandrian, 11, 13–14

Jews, American: "ghetto" as keyword for, 196; move to suburbs, 172–176. *See also* Ghetto, American; Immigrants, to America

Jews, Bohemian, 70

Jews, East European, 98, 126; association of ghetto with, 75; defense of ghetto by, 107; England as waypoint for, 96–97; shtetl/shtetlakh and, 75, 83, 175–176; universality of ghetto and, 6. *See also* Ghetto, American; Ghetto, Holocaust; Immigrants, East European; Immigrants, to America; Jews, Bohemian; Jews, Galician; Jews, Hungarian; Jews, Polish; Jews, Russian; Warsaw Ghetto

Jews, Galician, 109. *See also* Jews, East European

Jews, German: construction of life stories, 126; German identity of, 128–129; immigrants to America, 105; in Nazi period, 127–130. *See also* Ghetto, American; Ghetto, Holocaust; Holocaust; Immigrants, to America

Jews, Hungarian, 131–132, 145–146. *See also* Jews, East European

Jews, Italian, 6. *See also* Italy; Papal states; Roman Ghetto; Rome; Venetian Ghetto; Venice

Jews, Orthodox, 195

Jews, Polish, 88–92, 130–131, 132–133. *See also* Ghetto, Holocaust; Jews, East European; Poland; *Individual ghettos*

Jews, Russian, 88–92. *See also* Jews, East European; Russia

Jews, Sephardic, 26

Jews: A Study of Race and Environment (Fishberg), 117

Jews for Urban Justice, 192

Jews in Suburbia (Gordon), 174

Jews of Barnow, The (Franzos), 76–78

Jews without Money (Gold), 106–107

Jim Crow, 167, 185

Joseph II (Habsburg emperor), 55

Juan II (monarch of Spain), 19

Judaism (periodical), 175

Judaism, modern, 5–6. *See also* Emancipation/liberation; Identity, Jewish; Jewish experience/consciousness; Modernity

Judaism, premodern/pre-emancipation, 5–6, 84–85. *See also* Identity, Jewish; Jewish experience/consciousness

Judaism, Reform, 106

Judaizing, 19–20

Judengasse: in Frankfurt, 16–17, 39, 51, 53; references to term, 54. *See also* Jewish quarters; Segregation

Judenstadt (Prague), 51. *See also* Jewish quarters; Segregation

Judenstrasse, 97–98. *See also* Jewish quarters; Segregation

"Judith the Second" (Kompert), 70

Juiveries, 54

Kalmanovich, Zelig Hirsch, 148, 162
Kaplan, Chaim Aron, 147, 148,
   151–152, 156
Katz, Jacob, 5
Katzman, David, 183
Kazin, Alfred, 177
Kellermann, Heinz, 128
Kerner, Otto, 163
Kerner Commission, 163–164
Keyword: concept of, 4–5; ghetto as,
   4, 6, 51, 196; ghetto as, in African
   American experience, 7–8; shtetl as,
   175–176
Khoury, Elias, 199–200
Kimhi, Raphael Israel, 45–46
Kohler, Kaufmann, 106
Kompert, Leopold, 68–75
Koselleck, Reinhart, 74, 151
Kramer, Judith R., 175
Kristallnacht, 138–139
Kristol, Irving, 178
Kulturbund (Cultural Federation), 127
Kusmer, Kenneth, 183

Labels, 9, 112–113
Labor camp, vs. ghetto, 4
La Juive (Halévy), 58
Landsmann, Carolina, 198
Law, Jewish, 94–95
Laws of Valladolid, 19
League of Cambrai, 26, 27
Legal rights. *See* Restrictions on Jews;
   Rights, legal; Status, legal
Legal status. *See* Restrictions on Jews;
   Rights, legal; Status, legal
Leopoldstadt, Vienna, 88
Letters on Italy (Dupaty), 59
"Let Us Be Ready for the Middle Ages"
   (Feigin), 135

Levantine Jewish merchants, 30
Leventman, Seymour, 175
Lewin, Abraham, 156
Leyvik, H., 136
Liberation. *See* Emancipation/liberation;
   Homeland, Jewish; Israel; Zionism
Life in the Ghetto (Prinz), 11
Life Is with People (Zborowski and
   Herzog), 175–176
"Life without Neighbors" (Prinz),
   129–130
Lipman, Eugene, 174
Literature, 87; alienation in, 93;
   ambivalence toward ghetto in, 72–74;
   ghetto as literary conceit, 113;
   Ghettoliteratur, 67–78; Goldbaum on,
   78; immigrants in, 86, 101–104;
   Jewish Publication Society of America,
   93, 101–102; nostalgia in, 93–94;
   references to ghetto in, 99, 101–104;
   "return to Middle Ages" motif in,
   153–157; Yiddish, 134. *See also*
   Individual authors; Individual works
*Living with Your Teenager: A Guide for
   Jewish Parents* (Glustrom), 175
Livorno, 36
Loan-banking, 27, 37, 59
Łódź, 147
Łódź Ghetto, 140–142, 143, 148, 152,
   154–155, 157
London, 90–97, 102
Lower East Side, 99. *See also* Enclaves,
   immigrant/ethnic; Ghetto, American;
   Immigrants, to America; Jews,
   American; New York City
"Lower East Side, The" (exhibition),
   176
Lublin Reservation, 143
Luzzatto, Simone, 47–48

Madagascar Plan, 143

Mahler, Gustav, 201

Maltz, Albert, 192

March on Washington, 177

Marshall, Louis, 113

Martyrdom, 157, 161

May Laws, 80

Mead, Margaret, 176

Media. See Literature; Press; Individual
    publications

Ménage, Gilles, 42

Mendelssohn, Moses, 53

Meng, Michael, 4

Merchant of Venice, The (Shakespeare),
    201

Merchants, 30, 31

Méry, Joseph, 62

Metaphor, ghetto, 85, 122, 197–200

Michman, Dan, 143

Middle Ages: European, 14–15; Jewish,
    12; Jews in Spain during, 18–20;
    return to, 153–157; voluntary
    segregation in, 11–13

Minucci, Paolo, 42–43

Modena, Leon, 37, 47

Modernity: definition of, and ghetto, 6;
    designation of, 6; experience in, 151;
    horizon of expectation in, 151; nu-
    anced view of, 6; relation with ghetto,
    52, 83; Roman Ghetto compared to,
    62, 63; secession from, 133–137;
    temporalization of concepts and,
    74–75. See also Judaism, modern;
    Return to ghetto

Modernization story, 126–127. See also
    Emancipation/liberation

Moneylenders, 27, 37, 59

Moravia, 144

Morning, The (periodical), 128

Morning Journal (periodical), 111

"Moses Goldfarb's House" (Sacher-
    Masoch), 78–79

Moynihan, Daniel Patrick, 185

Moynihan Report, 185–186

Muggeridge, Malcolm, 190

Munich Agreement, 134

Murray, Albert, 187, 188

"Museum vs. Memory, The" (Bukiet),
    193–194

NAACP (National Association for the
    Advancement of Colored People),
    167

Names, 9. See also Labels; Place names;
    Words

Napoleon Bonaparte, 61. See also
    France; French army

Napoleonic Wars, 60–61. See also
    French army

Nation, The (periodical), 185

National Advisory Commission on
    Civil Disorders, 163–164

National Association for the Advance-
    ment of Colored People (NAACP),
    167

National Committee on Segregation in
    the Nation's Capital, 169

Nationalism, Jewish, 83. See also
    Homeland, Jewish; Israel; Zionism

Nativists, 105

Nazi Germany and the Jews, Volume 1:
    The Years of Persecution (Friedländer),
    128

Nazi ghettos. See Ghetto, Holocaust

Nazis: Anschluss, 132, 133, 137;
    ghettoization policy, 142–143; mass
    shootings by, 146–147; opposition to
    ghettoization and, 139–140;

Nazis (*continued*)
persecution of Jews by, 146–147; restrictions on Jews and, 127–130; segregation before Anschluss and, 137. *See also* Deportations; Final Solution; Ghetto, Holocaust; Holocaust
"Negro and the Warsaw Ghetto, The" (Du Bois)," 188–189
"Negroes Are Anti-Semitic Because They Are Anti-White" (Baldwin), 191
Negro Family, The (Moynihan Report), 185–186
Negro Ghetto, The (Weaver), 170
Neighborhoods, Jewish, 120–122. *See also* Jewish quarters
Netanyahu, Benjamin, 198
Neue Freie Presse (newspaper), 77
New Egypt, 17
New Ghetto, The (Herzl), 81–83, 95
"New Jewish Quarter of Harlem, The" (*American Israelite*), 108
New Stories from the Ghetto (Kompert), 71
New York City: ghettos in, 121; Jewish community in, 98, 103–104, 120–122; Lower East Side, 99; poverty in, 106–107; "uptown Jews" in, 105. *See also* America; Ghetto, American; Ghetto, black; Immigrants, to America
New York Herald (newspaper), 99
New York Times (newspaper), 113, 176, 178, 190, 191; "Pictures of the Ghetto," 101
Nietzsche, Friedrich, 2, 5
Niger, Shmuel, 136
Nightingale, Carl, 15
Nirenberg, David, 19
Nisko Plan, 143
Noise, and Jews, 17, 39–40, 56
Nordau, Max, 83
North American Review (periodical), 111
Nostalgia: for ghetto, 74; in hip-hop music, 196–197; in literature, 93–94
Notes from the Warsaw Ghetto (Ringelblum), 192
Nuremberg Laws, 127, 138. *See also* Nazis; Restrictions on Jews

Ochs, Adolph, 113
Old European Jewries (Philipson), 79–81, 83, 87
Old World, "ghetto" as marker of, 97
On the Civil Improvement of the Jews (Dohm), 52–53
On the Genealogy of Morals (Nietzsche), 2
Opatoshu, Joseph, 136
Operation Shylock (Roth), 174
Opposition to ghettoization, 40. *See also* Resistance
Origines linguae italicae (Ferrari), 42
Orthodox Jewish families, 195
Osherman, Mollie Eda, 112
Osofsky, Gilbert, 183, 184
Ostjude. *See* Jews, East European
Other America, The (Harrington), 180
Out of the Ghetto (Katz), 5
Oxford English Dictionary, 66
Oyneg Shabes group, 153
Oz, Amos, 198

Pacifici, Antonio, 61
Paduan ghetto, 42
Pale of Settlement, 80, 87. *See also* Russia
Palestinians, 199–200

Papal bulls, 61; *Cum nimis absurdum*, 16, 31–33, 35, 41, 42; *Dudum a felicis*, 34

Papal states, 31–35; ghettos in, 16 (*see also* Roman Ghetto; Rome); during Napoleonic Wars, 61; restrictions on Jews in, 32. *See also* Popes; *Individual popes*

Parents and Taxpayers (PAT), 184

Paris, 89. *See also* France

Park, Robert E., 113, 114, 115, 163, 173

Particularism, Jewish, 52–54, 56. *See also* Assimilation/acculturation; Separatism

"Passover in the Ghetto," 192

Pathologizing rhetoric, 182, 185

Paul IV (pope), 16, 31–35, 41, 42, 43–44

"Peddler, The" (Kompert), 72–74

Periodization, of ghetto, 5–6. *See also* Age of the ghetto; Emancipation/liberation

Persecution of Jews, 146, 188; during Nazi period, 146–147; skepticism about, 155–156. *See also* Holocaust; Pogroms; Restrictions on Jews; Rights, legal; Status, legal; Violence

Philadelphia Negro, The (Du Bois), 167

Philippson, Ludwig, 63

Philipson, David, 79–81, 83, 87

Philo, 13–14

Philpott, Thomas, 183

"Physical type," Jewish, 117–118

"Picture of Christ, The" (Franzos), 76

"Pictures of the Ghetto" (*New York Times*), 101

Pisa, 36

Piłsudski, Józef, 131

Pius V (pope), 33, 34

Pius VI (pope), 59, 61

Pius VII (pope), 61

Pius IX (pope), 40

Place names, 13; ghetto as, 122; reflecting Jewish quarters, 12, 16–17; survival of, 50

Pletzl, Paris, 89

Poale Zion Left, 150

Poale Zion Right, 150

Poet and Merchant (Auerbach), 67

Pogroms: 14, 17, 89; Kristallnacht, 138–139. *See also* Persecution of Jews; Violence

Poland: pogroms in, 89. *See also* Europe, Eastern; Ghetto, Holocaust; Jews, East European; Jews, Polish; Łódź Ghetto; Warsaw Ghetto; Warsaw Ghetto Uprising; *Individual cities*

Polish Jews. *See* Jews, East European; Jews, Polish

Polish-Lithuanian Commonwealth: lack of segregation in, 47; small towns in, 75 (*see also* Shtetl/shtetlakh);

Popes: anti-Jewish measures, 35; motivations of, 52. *See also* Christians; Papal bulls; Papal states; *Individual popes*

Posture, Jewish, 117–118

Poverty: African American, 180; culture of, 180; in ghetto, 94; in New York, 105, 106–107; in Roman Ghetto, 60

Prague Daily Paper (periodical), 89

Premodern: use of term, 6. *See also* Judaism, premodern/pre-emancipation

Press, African American, 167–168. *See also Individual publications*

Press, Jewish, 106; defenses of ghetto in, 111; ghetto in, 97–98, 101; role in

Press, Jewish (*continued*)
Americanization, 108; Roman Ghetto in, 63; underground, 150; view of Jewish neighborhoods in, 121–122. *See also Individual publications*
Prinz, Joachim, 11, 129–130, 177
Puerto Rican immigrants, 178, 181

Race riots, 163
Racism, 183, 185–186; black ghetto and, 180–181; compared to legal segregation, 190; ghetto concept used to justify, 187; Jewish "physical type" and, 117. *See also* Discrimination, racial; Housing discrimination
"Randar's Children, The" (Kompert), 70
Random House Historical Dictionary of American Slang, 197
Rap music, 196–197
Ravid, Benjamin, 3, 11, 13
Realism, 109
Redlining, 168. *See also* Discrimination, housing
Refamiliarization, 126
Refuge, ghetto as, 84
Refugees, Jewish, 134. *See also* Ghetto, Holocaust; Holocaust
Religious liberty, in America, 110
Relocation. *See* Deportations; Refugees, Jewish; Segregation, mandatory/legal
Resistance, 40, 161, 162. *See also* Opposition to ghettoization; Warsaw Ghetto Uprising
Restrictions on Jews: careers and, 76–77; before emancipation, 126; Familiants Laws, 70; liberalization of, 70; under Nazis, 127–130, 131–132, 138; in papal states, 32; precedents for, 34; in Rome, 59, 60–61; in Venice, 50.

See also Clothing, identifying; Curfew; Rights, legal; Segregation; Status, legal
Return to ghetto: call for, 133–137; Holocaust ghetto as, 150; opposition to, 136; as secession from Jewish modernity, 133–137; support for, 135–136. *See also* Ghetto, Holocaust
Riegner, Karl Julius, 128
Rights, legal: discourse on, 52–57; Edicts of Tolerance, 55; under French in Italy, 60–61; loss of after Napoleon's retreat, 51; reforms, 54–55. *See also* Clothing, identifying; Restrictions on Jews; Status, legal
Riis, Jacob, 104–105
Ringelblum, Emanuel, 149, 152, 153, 156, 192
Roman Ghetto, 33–35, 57–61, 63; conditions in, 60, 62, 63; in dictionaries, 65; dismantling of, 40, 51, 64, 80, 87; enclosures of, 32, 33; endurance of, 62; Halévy on, 57–58; Jewish attitudes toward, 42, 43–44; liberation of, 51, 60–61, 64; objectives of, 34–35; reinstatement of, 61–62; response to, 40–41; writings about, 62–63
Romania, 87, 105, 132
Roman Republic, 61
Rome: conquest of, by Cadorna, 64; Halévy in, 57–58; Jewish legal status in, 59
Rosenfeld, Morris, 101
Rosenfeld, Oskar, 152, 154, 157
Ross, Edward A., 105
Roth, Cecil, 44
Roth, Philip, 174
Różycki, Stanisław, 153
Rubinow, Isaac Max, 110
Rudashevski, Yitskhok, 147

Rue des Rosiers, Paris, 89

Rumkowski, Mordechai Chaim, 152

Russia, 87, 105; ghetto system in, 80; May Laws of 1882, 80; Pale of Settlement, 80, 87; pogroms in, 89. *See also* Europe, Eastern; Jews, Russian

"Russian Jew in the United States, The" (Cahan), 107

Russian Jews. *See* Jews, East European; Jews, Russian; Russia

Rustin, Bayard, 184–185, 191

Ryan, William, 185

Sabbath, carrying on, 45–46

Sacher-Masoch, Leopold, 78–79

Sanders, Stanley, 166

Sansovino, Francesco, 24, 36

Sanuto, Marino, 28

Schama, Simon, 201

Scheunenviertel, Berlin, 90

Schoener, Allon, 176–177

Schwarzbart, Ignacy, 159, 160–161

Second Temple times, 13

Secret Memoirs and Criticisms of the Courts, Governments, and Customs of the Main Italian States (Gorani), 60

Segregation: arguments against, 52–54; effects of, 93, 117, 118, 181, 183, 187, 188; foreign merchant districts, 15; ghetto as general signifier of, 54; historic connection with "ghetto," 29; Jewish attitudes toward, 46–48; motivation for, 52; precedent for, 31, 34; role in anti-Jewish violence, 13–14; in suburbs, 173–175; terms for, 65; in Vienna, 88–89. *See also* Isolation

Segregation, African American, 166, 167, 168–169, 181–185. *See also* Color line; Ghetto, black; Housing discrimination

Segregation, de facto, 189

Segregation, mandatory/legal, 4, 189; at apartment level, 145; black ghetto as, 181–185; demise of, 40 (*see also* Emancipation/liberation); in Frankfurt, 16–17; ghetto benches, 131, 136; ghetto concept used to justify, 187; in Italy, 20; Jewish houses, 140, 145; of merchants, 30, 31; methods of establishing, 21; racism compared to, 190; in Spain, 19; use of "ghetto" and, 13. *See also* Relocation; Restrictions on Jews; Rights, legal; Status, legal; *Individual ghettos*

Segregation, school, 184

Segregation, under Nazis, 137–139. *See also* Ghetto, Holocaust; Holocaust

Segregation, voluntary, 4, 174; in America, 87, 106–107; defense of, 110; in European Middle Ages, 11–13, 14–15; in London, 91; opposition to, 106–107; in Speyer, 14–15. *See also* Ghetto, American; Ghetto, immigrant; Jewish quarters; Return to ghetto; Separatism

Segregation in Washington (National Committee on Segregation in the Nation's Capital), 169

Self-segregation. *See* Segregation, voluntary

Sentinel, The (periodical), 158

Separatism, 78, 96. *See also* Isolation; Particularism, Jewish; Return to ghetto; Segregation, voluntary

Seraphim, Peter-Heinz, 139, 143

Sermoneta, Joseph, 25–26

Shakespeare, William, 201

Shapiro, Edward, 173

Shelley v. Kraeme, 170

Shtetl/shtetlakh, 75, 83, 175–176

Shylock (fictional character), 201

"Shylock of Barnow, The" (Franzos), 78

Silberman, Charles E., 180, 181

Sinclair, Jo, 173

Singer, Oskar, 152

Sixtus V (pope), 42

Slavery, 185

Slum and the Ghetto, The (Philpott), 183

Slums, 105

Small, Mario, 3

Smells, of Jewish quarter, 38, 89

Society, Jewish traditional, 68, 87. *See also* Judaism, premodern/pre-emancipation

Sociology/sociologists: analyses of African American life, 186; Chicago School, 113–120, 173, 178, 184; definitions of ghetto, 3; on immigrant ghetto, 163. *See also Individual sociologists*

Solidarity, Jewish, 54

Songs of the Ghetto (Rosenfeld), 101

Soul on Ice (Cleaver), 192

Sounds of ghetto, 39. *See also* Noise

Soviet Union. *See* Europe, Eastern; Russia

"Space of experience," 151

Spain, 16, 18–20, 25

Spatial confinement, 10

Spear, Allan, 183

Speyer (German city), 14–15

Spiegel, Isaiah, 148

Spingarn, Joel, 167

Spinoza (Auerbach), 67–68

Spinoza, Baruch, 74

"Spirit in the Ghetto, The" (Kalmanovitch), 162

Spirit of the Ghetto, The (Hapgood), 109–110

Star, yellow, 147. *See also* Badge, identifying; Clothing, identifying

Star of David, 147. *See also* Badge, identifying; Clothing, identifying

State-building, 36

State of mind, ghetto as, 79

Status, legal: arguments for amelioration of, 52–54 (*see also* Emancipation/liberation); liberalization of, 48; in Rome, 59. *See also* Clothing, identifying; Restrictions on Jews; Rights, legal

Stendhal, 62

Stereotypes, 81

Stories of a [Jewish] Street (Kompert), 71

Story, William Wettmore, 62

Story of the Warsaw Ghetto Uprising, The (Schwarzbart), 159

Suburbs: anxiety about creation of Jewish "ghetto" in, 195–196; Jewish identity in, 173; move of Jews to, 172–176

Suffering and Heroism in the Jewish Past in the Light of the Present (Dror), 149

Sulzberger, Mayer, 102

Sun (New York), 86

Synagogues: limits on, 34; memberships in, 173; noise of, 39–40

Syrkin, Marie, 189–190

Szálasi, Ferenc, 131

Tcherikower, Elias, 135, 136

Teller, Judd, 190

Temanza, Tomasso, 24

Tenafly, New Jersey, 195–196

Tenement system, 105. *See also* Slums

Teza, Emilio, 24

Theodosian Code, 34

Theresienstadt (Terezin), 144–145

Third Lateran Council, 15, 34

Thon, Jacob, 90

Time, in Holocaust ghetto, 154

Tourism, ghetto, 37

Towns, small, 75. *See also* Shtetl/shtetlakh

Trades, associated with Jews, 90, 92. *See also* Careers

Travel accounts, 37–39

Ukraine, 89, 155. *See also* Jews, East European

United States. *See* African Americans; America; Ghetto, American; Ghetto, black; Immigrants, to America; Jews, American

Universal Critical-Encyclopedical Dictionary of the Italian Language (Villanuova), 39

Uprooted, The (Handlin), 178

Urban renewal projects, 51, 64

U.S. News and World Report (periodical), 166

Van Pelt, Robert Jan, 146

Venetian Ghetto: commemoration of, 200–201; enclosure of, 29; endurance of, 29–30; establishment of, 1, 21, 28–31; liberation of by French army, 49–50; name of, 21–23; objectives of, 34; and origin of "ghetto," 10; survival of name of, 50. *See also* Early history of ghettos

Venice: controlled by Austrians, 50; creation of official Jewish community in, 31; Jewish presence in before ghetto, 26–28, 29; segregation of merchants in, 30, 31. *See also* Venetian Ghetto

Venice, the Most Noble and Unique City (Sansovino), 24

Vergara, Camilo José, 196–197

Verona, 44

Vienna: antisemitism in, 81; Jewish population in, 88–89

Village Voice (periodical), 192

Villanuova, Francesco Alberti di, 39, 56

Vilna Ghetto, 147, 148, 162

Violence, 155; in Alexandria, 13–14; in black ghettos, 164, 191; massacres in Spain, 18; mass shootings of Jews, 146–147. *See also* Pogroms

Vocabolario della lingua italiana (dictionary), 35

Vorspan, Albert, 174

Wacquant, Loïc, 3

Walls. *See* Enclosures

Warsaw Ghetto, 142, 143, 191, 200; chronicles of, 149, 156; compared to black ghettos, 191; conditions in, 152; deportations from, 155–157; Głowiński on, 125; liquidation of, 157–158 (*see also* Deportations); relevance to black experience, 188–189. *See also* Ghetto, Holocaust; Holocaust; Jews, Polish

Warsaw Ghetto Uprising, 157–161, 188–189; commemoration of, 158; compared to violence in black ghettos, 191; as paradigm of resistance, 158–159

Washington Bee (newspaper), 167
Washington Post (newspaper), 193
Waskow, Arthur, 192
Weaver, Robert, 170
We Jews (Prinz), 129
"What Is Jewishness?" (Opatoshu), 136
Williams, Raymond, 4, 51
Wilson, William Julius, 3, 196
Wirth, Louis, 7, 11, 13, 79, 113, 115–120, 163, 173, 176
Words, significance of, 9
World, as ghetto, 130
World, The (periodical), 135
World Jewish Congress, 159
World War II. *See* Deportations; Final Solution; Ghetto, Holocaust; Holocaust; Nazis
Worten, Helen, 122
Wrocław (Breslau), 15–16

Yekl (Cahan), 101, 103–104
Yellow-star houses, 146
Yiddish, use of, 89, 92

Zalowitz, Nathaniel, 121
Zangwill, Israel, 7, 91–97, 101, 102–103, 112, 113, 117, 200
Zborowski, Mark, 175–176
Zelkowic, Josef, 154–155
Zeublin, Charles, 99, 101
Zionism, 129, 135, 148, 150, 198; ambivalence toward ghetto in, 83–84; assimilation and, 190; Dror, 149; First Zionist Congress, 84; Ha-Shomer ha-Tsa'ir (The Young Guard), 150–151; political, 83; skepticism of emancipation narrative in, 126–127. *See also* Homeland, Jewish; Israel
Zionist parties, 158
ŻOB (Jewish Fighting Organization), 157